The Singing Milkmaids:

Life in
Post-Restoration Huntingdonshire
c.1660-c.1750

The Singing Milkmaids:

Life in
Post-Restoration Huntingdonshire
c.1660-c.1750

Edited by
Evelyn Lord

With a Foreword by
David Cozens MBE

EAH Press — Cambridge

EAH Press
7 Thornton Court
Thornton Road
Girton
Cambridge CB3 ONS

First published in Great Britain in 2019

Cover design by
Blue Ocean Publishing, Cambridge

Printed in Great Britain by
Biddles, Kings Lynn

ISBN 0-978-09576147-3-4

TABLE OF CONTENTS

ACKNOWLEDGEMENTS

Many people have aided our research. We are grateful to:

Clive Coward and Tate Britain for the cover photograph:
    George Morland Cowherd and Milkmaid 1792

Map illustrations by Alumina studios

Paul Johnson and National Archives for reproduction of Hearth Tax

Roger Merritt for reading the manuscript

Ken Sneath for layout, preparing the text for publication and producing the index.

Camilla Ford for layout assistance.

Publication of this volume has been made possible by a grant from the Huntingdonshire Local History Society Goodliff Fund.

FOREWORD

The Singing Milkmaids, the recipient of a Goodliff award, assembles in nine chapters the scholarship of six authors giving an insight into Huntingdonshire life between 1660 and 1750.

The Goodliff Fund was established in 1996 to promote the study and dissemination of the local history of Huntingdonshire. At that time I was the Chairman of the Huntingdonshire Local History Society and over the last 22 years the Society has made just over 200 awards.

The objectives of the Goodliff Fund are admirably achieved by this publication, edited by Evelyn Lord, which reminds us of the multifaceted nature of history at whatever level it is studied. The highly detailed information provided by the authors makes this book a valuable source for any one researching the history of Huntingdonshire.

David Cozens M.B.E.

February 2019

LIST OF MAPS

LIST OF FIGURES

LIST OF TABLES

ABBREVIATIONS

Ag.HEW	The Agrarian History of England and Wales
Agr. Hist. Rev.	Agricultural History Review
CUP	Cambridge University Press
EHR	English Historical Review
Ec.HR	Economic History Review
HA	Huntingdonshire Archives
J. Econ. Hist.	Journal of Economic History
OUP	Oxford University Press
PCAS	Proceedings of the Cambridge Antiquarian Society
P & P	Past and Present
TNA	The National Archives
VCH	Victoria History of the Counties of England

NOTES ON CONTRIBUTORS

Evelyn Lord (editor)
Prior to retirement Evelyn Lord was Course Director for the University of Cambridge Masters in Local History, and staff tutor in local history for the Institute of Continuing Education. Before returning to full-time education she worked at the British Museum, and spent several years residing in The Netherlands. Her Ph.D. was awarded by the University of Leicester, and was followed by a post-graduate research post at the Deansgate John Rylands Library of the University of Manchester, and as a lecturer in local history at the University of Derby.

Simon Clemmow
Simon Clemmow is a retired adman whose thirty-year career working in, founding and running a series of London and international advertising agencies was spent developing campaigns for many clients including Nike, Samsung, Toyota and Virgin. Simon is a published writer on brand planning and marketing communications and was listed in *Who's Who* in 2009. Since retirement he has transferred his skills in research and interpretation to the pursuit of history as an academic discipline and has been studying with the Institute of Continuing Education at the University of Cambridge. He has been awarded a diploma and an advanced diploma in local history, and the date of publication of this book sees him undertaking a Master of Studies degree in British local and regional history, supervised by Dr Ken Sneath.

Liz Ford
Following her degree in Economic and Social History from Birmingham University, Liz Ford gained a PGCE from Bristol University and taught history for several years. Although currently employed in the insurance industry she is a volunteer transcriber at Huntingdonshire Archives, has studied Local and Regional History for many years and recently gained a Master of Studies degree in English Local History from the University of Cambridge. Her research is concentrated upon the seventeenth and early eighteenth centuries and she has recently contributed to the forthcoming British Record Society volume on the Huntingdonshire Hearth Tax.

William Franklin
After retiring following a thirty-four-year career as a mental health nurse and health service manager, William Franklin has devoted much of his time to researching local history and the history of the landscape and agriculture

of Cambridgeshire, Huntingdonshire and Northamptonshire. His publications include *Burwell: The History of a Fen-edge Village* (1995), *Rothwell with Orton: A History of a Midland Market town* (2013), *By Mere and Fen: A History of Soham* (2014), *Open Fields to Enclosure: The Parliamentary Enclosure of Burwell* (2016), *An Agricultural History of Ely* (2017) and has written articles for a number of journals including, *Agricultural History Review, Northamptonshire Past and Present* and the *Proceedings of the Cambridge Antiquarian Society.* He holds a degree Health Sciences BSc., from the University of Leicester, and Masters Degree in Business Administration (MBA) from Anglia Ruskin University and an MPhil (Nursing) from the University of Essex.

Tony Kirby

Until his retirement, Tony Kirby was Co-ordinator of Strategic & Curriculum Planning at Anglia Ruskin University, having previously been Principal Lecturer in History. He is a past President of the Cambridge Antiquarian Society and Chair of the Cambridgeshire Records Society, and is currently Secretary of the Cambridgeshire Association for Local History and the County Advisory Group on Archives and Local Studies. Until last year, he was editor of *Nieuwsbrief,* the quarterly journal of the Benelux Railways Society. Apart from transport (he remains an unrepentant 'platform ender', armed with notebook and camera) his historical interests lie in market towns, seaside and inland resorts and the social history of religion since the Reformation. With Susan Oosthuizen he edited *An Atlas of Cambridgeshire and Huntingdonshire History* (2000) and is the author of *Anglia Ruskin University, 1858 – 2008: A Celebratory History* (2008). He contributed a chapter on 'Railways and Towns' to *How Railways Changed Britain* (ed David St John Thomas) (2015). He has also written several commentaries on early 20th century 25" Ordnance Survey maps for Alan Godfrey Editions, most recently Braintree (2017), Brentwood and Halstead (2018).

Ken Sneath

Following retirement, Dr Ken Sneath embarked on academic study in history, achieving a first-class honours degree, a Master of Studies degree in English Local History, an MPhil and a PhD in Economic and Social History at the University of Cambridge. His doctoral thesis examined the origins of the consumer revolution in the 18th century. Publications include *Godmanchester: a celebration of 800 years* (2011) and various articles on consumption in early modern England, the hearth tax and funerals in the 17th and 18th centuries. He is a lecturer in 17th- and 18th-century history at the Institute of Continuing Education, University of Cambridge and until recently was Assistant Director of Studies for Economic History at Peterhouse College, University of Cambridge.

Huntingdonshire Parishes

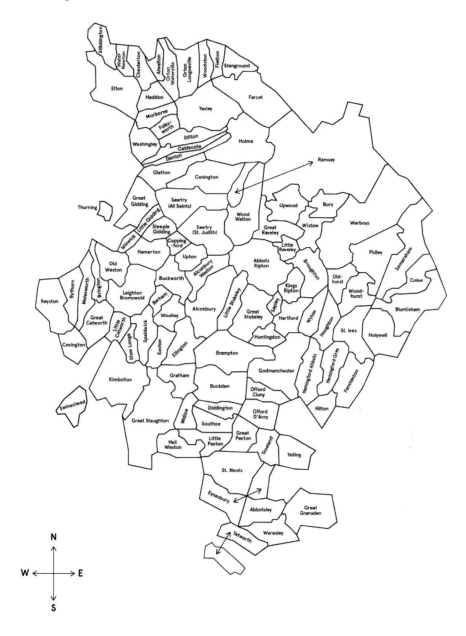

INTRODUCTION

The title of this book comes from a description in Samuel Pepys diary for 1662 '… took a melancholy walk with my father to Portholme, seeing the country maids milking their Cowes (they now being at grass) and to see with what mirth they come home together in pomp with their milk, and sometimes music going before them….'[1] Pepys was one of the narrators of life in post-Restoration Huntingdonshire, describing nutting in Brampton woods, frolics at Goody Gorhams's and details about the rebuilding of Hinchingbrooke House. He had spent part of his boyhood with his uncle Robert in Brampton, attended Huntingdon Grammar School, and hoped to inherit Robert's estate.

At the Restoration, his mentor and employer Edward Montagu seamlessly changed sides from Parliament to Royalist and became the Earl of Sandwich. Pepys, himself, who had attended the execution of Charles I, was worried that might be held against him as he was known at school as being a 'great roundhead' who said on the day of the King's execution the 'memory of the wicked shall rot' and he was 'afeared' that these words would be remembered.[2] The other Huntingdonshire Montagu, the Earl of Manchester of Kimbolton Castle, also speedily inveigled himself into royal favour and retained his title and his possessions. But Huntingdonshire was the birth place of Oliver Cromwell and the residence of at least one other regicide Valentine Wharton. Like Pepys, the shire viewed the restoration of the monarchy with some apprehension, and rather than restoration reconstruction was the order of the day; reconstruction of the loyalty of the shire to the crown, reconstruction of war damage, such done at the 'Sack of Huntingdon' at the behest of Charles I, the return and reconstruction of parishes as ministers ejected by the Earl of Manchester in the 1640s returned, and the reconstruction of local

---

[1] R. Latham & W. Matthews eds., *The Diary of Samuel Pepys*, Vol. III, 1662, Harper Collins, 1995, p. 221; A similar scene in Bedfordshire was described by Dorothy Osborne in a letter to William Temple in 1653'I walked out into the common where a great many wenches keep sheep and cows, and sit in the shade singing ballads.' E.A. Parry ed., *Letters from Dorothy Osborne to Sir William Temple 1652-1664*, revised ed., 1903, pp., 86,87; in the 16th century Bartholomew Dowe, whose mother was chief dairymaid at Sibton Abbey in Suffolk described how some cows like milkmaids to sing to them' quoted in J. Thirsk, *Food in Early Modern England,* Hambledon Continuum, 2006, pp. 39, 40.

[2] R. Latham & W. Matthews eds. *The Diary of Samuel Pepys*, Vol. I, 1660, Harper Collins, 1995, pp. 265, 280.

administration and its hierarchy of Lord Lieutenant, Sheriff, Recorder and Justices of the Peace into a group of loyalists.[3]

Nationally, the Restoration of the monarchy created economic problems. The Commonwealth's debts had to be settled, and an income provided for the King which was sufficient to prevent him levying un-parliamentary taxes as his father had done. Feudal dues and court of wards fees were abolished, and instead the King was granted the income from the excise of beer and brewing. By 1662 it was clear this was not enough. Another, more embracing tax was needed, that included all potential taxpayers. The result was the Hearth Tax of 2s a year levied on every hearth in England and Wales.

The impetus for this book comes from the work of the editorial team on the forthcoming volume of the volume of the Huntingdonshire Hearth Taxes of 1662 and 1674.[4] During research on this volume many aspects of life in post-Restoration Huntingdonshire were studied, but could not be included in that volume, and so appear here, with research by other local historians relevant to life in post-Restoration Huntingdonshire. The aim is to broaden the scope of the hearth tax volume and enhance the life and landscape of the post-Restoration shire, and to include the wider historical context and historical debates about the period. Throughout, Samuel Pepys is a guide to the world of Huntingdonshire in the late seventeenth and early eighteenth centuries.

Pepys of course lived in London, and was no country gentleman, but as an adult he made frequent journeys to and within Huntingdonshire; residing at Brampton with his parents, or visiting friends and relatives in the shire. His sister lived in Ellington and he had cousins in Yelling, drinking companions in Huntingdon and the overseer of his estates in the shire was John Turner vicar of Eynesbury.[5] The routes that Pepys took travelling to and fro between London and Huntingdonshire are described in Tony Kirby's essay on the post-Restoration road and water networks in the county.[6] This shows that by the late seventeenth-century Huntingdonshire was a communications hub with two main roads from London crossing it, as well as two important east-

---

[3] Any accounts of plunder and torture by Royalists or Parliamentarians have to be examined carefully for bias and exaggeration, especially in the pamphlets and news sheets of both sides.

[4] E. Lord, L. Ford & K Sneath eds., *The Huntingdonshire Hearth Tax, 1662 and 1674*, The British Record Society, and the Cambridgeshire Records Society, forthcoming.

[5] R.C. Latham & W. Matthews eds., *The Diary of Samuel Pepys*, Vol. X, Companion to the Diary, Bell & Hayman, 1983, p.6.

[6] For example, Latham & Matthews, Diary Vol. II, p.225.

west routes, and it was linked by the rivers Nene and Ouse to the coast and its international trade possibilities. Despite being a small inland county Kirby's paper shows that it was not isolated but played an important part in the country's economy.

While staying in Brampton Pepys had a wide range of acquaintances from the Earl of Sandwich and his lady, to ale wives, and the carrier who carried Pepys wife and mother from London to Huntingdon.[7] Ken Sneath's paper on the social structure of post-Restoration Huntingdonshire discusses how social structure can be categorised, and uses probate inventories to chart the distribution across the county and across time of society from gentlemen to labourers. The Politics of the Parish by Evelyn Lord is also concerned with the social structure, in this case of a particular parish, Great Gransden. It takes as its starting point an agreement made between parishioners about grazing during a drought in 1684, and examines this in the context of Keith Wrightson's discussion on the duality in a parish of the included and the excluded.

The estate that Pepys and his father inherited not only included the property in Brampton but also cottages held on life leases, and both freehold and cop-yhold land. Entries in the diary describe both the problem in untangling the inheritance and also the dealing necessary to establish claim to lands in the Brampton manorial court.[8] This theme is continued in Bill Franklin's essay on The Fields of Huntingdonshire c1660-c1750, which describes and dis-cusses pre-enclosure fields and land usage pre and post-enclosure, and the imparkment at Kimbolton Castle. Sneath's work on probate inventories is further utilised to analyse the distribution of arable and pastoral farming within the context of the 'Agricultural Revolution'. Marriage patterns in six parishes are listed to examine the relationship of the farming year and vital events, while the ownership of livestock and crops listed in inventories is divided between gentlemen, yeoman, husbandmen and labourers, with the general conclusion that many of those who were engaged in agriculture also had by-employments in other trades.

---

[7] Latham & Matthews, Diary Companion, p.160; R.G. Latham & W. Matthews, *The Diary of Samuel Pepys*, Vol. IV, Harper Collins, 1996, p.313. Pepys relation-ship with the Earl of Sandwich and his family can be followed through every vol-ume of his diary. His comments on the rebuilding of Hinchingbrooke House are in Volumes I, II, III.

[8] See for example Latham & Matthews *Diary Companion*, p.6, *Diary* Vol. II p.172, Latham & Matthews eds., *The Diary of Samuel Pepys,* Vol. IV, Harper Collings 1996, p.30.

Pepys complained in his diary about chimney men being able to inspect private houses, and when the tax was abolished in 1689 purchased a broadside ballad celebrating this.[9] Pepys house at Brampton appears in the 1662 tax return with 11 hearths, but by 1665 this had been reduced to 9 hearths, having entered two too many. The hearth tax shows that by 1674 it was leased out, and in 1683 occupied by Pepys brother-in-law Bathasar de Mt Michel.[10] Can't Pay, Won't Pay is directly related to the hearth tax. It uses the lists of tax-payers in arrears to examine the extent of non-payments and the reason for this. It asks if the arrears were due to poverty, or to a reluctance to pay the tax, and identifies serial refusers in the shire. Many who could not pay the tax were indeed receiving poor relief. In order to regularise who was eligible to receive relief from the parish the 1662 Act for the Better Relief of the Poor, commonly known as the Settlement Act, codified the means by which legal settlement and entitlement for poor relief could be acquired in a parish. This created a large amount of bureaucracy and paper-work. Liz Ford's paper on the impact of the laws of settlement on Huntingdonshire c1660-c1780 uses the documents surrounding Settlement Act to explore the treatment of individuals and families seeking relief.

Like all post-Restoration gentlemen Samuel Pepys was required to attend church every Sunday.[11] His diary shows that he recorded the topic of the sermon and made value judgements on its delivery, preferring some clergymen to others. Liz Ford's essay on post-Restoration clergymen in Huntingdonshire takes the hearth tax as its starting point and the number of hearths in the parsonage as a guide. It then looks at their lives, careers and financial arrangements of the clergy in post-Restoration Huntingdonshire. One aspect of post-Restoration Huntingdonshire which cannot be ascertained in the hearth tax is the extent of those who were Dissenters and did not take communion in the Anglican Church. This can be recovered in the contemporary Compton Census which lists the numbers of Anglican Communicants, Dissenters and Papists, and which supplies a comparison for the numbers of householders in the hearth tax.[12] Simon Clemmow uses the Compton Census to map the extent and location of dissent in the county, and within the context of national administration how far the dissent listed in the seventeenth century Compton Census survived into the eighteenth century and beyond.

[9] R. G. Latham & W. Matthews, *Diary vol. II*, p.153; Magdalen College, Cambridge Pepys Collection of Broadside Ballads.
[10] Lord, Ford & Sneath, *Huntingdonshire Hearth Tax*, forthcoming; College of Arms, *Visitation of Huntingdonshire King's copy of the Hearth Tax 5+ houses from the Michaelmas 1683 return.*
[11] For example, Diary Vol. 1, p. 233.
[12] A. Whiteman ed., *The Compton Census of 1676*, Oxford: OUP, 1986.

There are other areas of post-Restoration life that are missing from this volume, and still to be studied, for example the political rivalry between Sandwich and the Barnards, recorders of Huntingdon, and the eventual Montagu monopoly of the borough and county Parliamentary seats, or the cultural life of the shire. The neo classical Walden House, was built c1665-c1670[13] and Huntingdon's Town Hall and Assembly Rooms by 1745. By 1750 Huntingdonshire was reconstructed and part of polite society, with a burgeoning middling sort of attorneys, physicians and wealthy merchants, and a healthy spread of tradesmen and retailers in its towns.

---

[13] CPMG Architects Claim Walden house was built c 1670. *Hunts Post* 4 July 2007 dated it c1664-c1674. 1674 Hearth Tax assessment for 16 hearths. Lord, Ford & Sneath *Huntingdonshire Hearth Tax* forthcoming.

1

ON THE MOVE: ROAD AND WATER TRAFFIC IN POST-RESTORATION HUNTINGDONSHIRE

Tony Kirby

A definitive account of transport in post-Restoration Huntingdonshire is impossible. For both roads and rivers, there is an absence of basic source materials, both from those responsible for maintenance (Quarter Sessions, Surveyors of the Highways and the like) and those who used them. Some evidence comes from depositions in court cases, which provide much incidental information, but sadly the deponents were unaware of what economic historians three centuries later would like to know. So this is essentially an impressionistic account, whose finding will hopefully be modified by future researchers.

Huntingdonshire's road network in 1660 was the product of centuries of largely organic growth, responding to both local and national needs. Rather surprisingly, roads are rarely shown on early maps of the county, although their existence can be inferred from other sources and archaeological evidence. The quickening tempo of commercial life in post-Restoration Britain meant that there was a ready potential market for maps showing at least the main roads, and this was first met with the publication of John Ogilby's two volumes of 'strip' maps of principal routes in 1675.[1] The first volume covered main roads radiating from London, with pride of place, so far as Huntingdonshire is concerned, going to the road from London to 'Barwick' via Royston, Huntingdon and Stilton. At Stilton this threw off a branch to Boston, via Yaxley and Peterborough, which was duplicated as far as Peterborough by the road to Flamborough Head via Lincoln and Barton-on-Humber, which Ogilby shows starting at Tempsford.[2] London to Tempsford was the subject of a separate map, which would guide the traveller on via St Neots and Great Staughton to Oakham.

---

[1] J. Ogilby, *An Actual Survey of all the Principal Roads of England and Wales. ...,* London M. Senex, 1675.
[2] This perhaps rather unlikely journey, at least from end-to-end, involved a ferry crossing of the Humber to Hull.

Map 1.1 The Roads (1768)

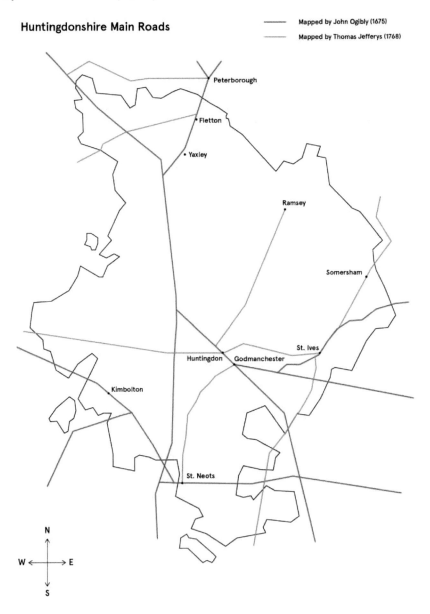

Volume 2 included two 'cross roads' through Huntingdonshire, from Cambridge via Huntingdon and Northampton to Coventry, and from Huntingdon

to Ipswich. To modern eyes, this was a curious route, leading from Huntingdon to St Ives via the Hemingfords, then across the Fens to Ely and through Soham to join the Cambridge – Ipswich road at Kentford.

The rather fragmented coverage of what is today's A1 would suggest that in the late 17th century the eastern branch of the Great North Road (Royston – Huntingdon – Alconbury, today's 'Old North Road') was the more important, although it is notable that Samuel Pepys, on his travels to and from Brampton, used the former, albeit often with some difficulty even in the summer: on 6 August 1661 the road was 'very bad' and his journey seemingly slower than expected: he was forced to stay the night at 'Baldwick' [Baldock] where he had 'a good supper' (and, being Pepys, noted that 'the landlady [was] a pretty woman, but I durst not take notice of her, her husband being there').[3] In September 1663, he rode south to 'Bigglesworth' [Biggleswade] but needed the help of two locals that led us through the very long and dangerous waters, because of the ditches on either side, as it begun to get very dark.[4]

A few years later, the intrepid Celia Fiennes observed that the road from Cambridge to Huntingdon was 'a very pleasant country to travel in the Summer, but after raines its in some places deep' [5] and that further north, between Stilton and Peterborough, was a stretch of '5 long miles, the ways deep and full of sloughs'.[6] In the Fens, matters were even worse. On her journey from Cambridge to St Ives, Celia came to Earith:

There was [a] bridge over a deep place in the river under where the boats and barges went, and this bridge was in the water so one must pass thro' water to it, and so beyond a good way, and the road was so full of holes and quick sands I durst not venture, the water covering them over, and a stranger thus cannot easily escape the danger, tho' I see the Carryers went that way to save the expense of the ferry.[7]

Unsurprisingly, those whose business took them into the Fens tended, post-drainage, to use the new river embankments as roads as far as possible. Built largely of peat, and thus inherently unstable, the banks suffered and so did drainage.

---

[3] Pepys, Samuel, *Diary,* www.pepysdiary.com (last accessed 16 August 2018).
[4] Pepys, Diary 20th September 1663.
[5] C. Fiennes, *The Journeys of Celia Fiennes,* London: Futura, 1983, p.88.
[6] Fiennes, p.189.
[7] Fiennes, p.189.

There seems little doubt that by the later 17th century, traffic was outstripping the capacity of the road network to carry it, a trend possibly exacerbated and/or made more obvious by the shift from packhorses as the main means of carriage to wheeled vehicles.[8] Responsibility for maintenance lay with individual parishes, which under the terms of the 1555 Highways Act were to elect two Surveyors of the Highways annually, with all parishioners expected to perform four (six from 1562) days' labour on the roads ('statute labour'), or furnish men, money or materials in lieu. The drawbacks of this system are well known: surveyors were untrained in road-mending, parishioners were unwilling to turn out (or treated the statute labour days as a holiday) and even where maintenance was carried out, it was on the roads the locals used most (e.g. to the nearest market town) rather than those which might be more important regionally or nationally. From the few accounts that have survived, it seems that roads were well down the list of parochial priorities: at Fenstanton, for example, the Surveyors spent only £3.13.6d on the roads in 1723, whilst £53.9.4d went on poor relief,[9] and these proportions changed little over the following decades, with expenditure on the roads never reaching double figures except in 1738 when for no apparent reason it leapt to £68.14.2d. The next year it was back to £2.15.6d. The only exception to parish maintenance was in the case of bridges, which were generally the responsibility of the county justices; a few were private property (and valuable for their toll revenue): the best-known Huntingdonshire example is St Ives, which belonged to the Earl of Manchester, who had acquired it from the Crown (in whose possession it had been since the Dissolution of Ramsey Abbey) in 1628.[10]

Central government was well aware of the deficiencies of the roads, but lacked the resources to do anything about them, other than the expedient of legislation attempting to limit the damage caused by increasingly heavy vehicles: in 1662, for example, vehicles drawn by more than seven horses or fitted with wheels less than four inches in width were banned.[11] The solution eventually achieved was (to modern eyes) blindingly obvious: road users should pay for upkeep.

---

[8] S. Porter, 'Farm Transport in Huntingdonshire, 1610–1749', *Journal of Transport History,* 3 Ser, Vol III, 1 (1982), p.39.
[9] HA HP27/8/3/1.
[10] B. Burn-Murdoch, *St Ives Bridge and Chapel: A History and Guide.* St Ives: Friends of the Norris Museum, 2 ed, 2001, p.17. The bridge was taken over by Huntingdonshire County Council in 1921 and made toll-free.
[11] H.J. Dyos, and D.H. Aldcroft, *British Transport: an economic survey from the seventeenth century to the twentieth,* Leicester: Leicester University Press, 1969, p.33.

Huntingdonshire plays an important role here: it saw the country's first turn-pike road, when in 1663 the county justices, together with those of Cam-bridgeshire and Hertfordshire, obtained powers to erect tollbars on the Old North Road and charge travellers a toll. That it was this road, rather than the western branch that was selected for treatment suggests that it was the more important: it was certainly carrying an increasing amount of heavy traffic, especially malting barley from Huntingdonshire and West Cambridgeshire to the maltings at Ware, whence it was transported by barge down the River Lea to London. Tollbars ('turnpikes') were to be erected at Wadesmill (Herts), Caxton and Stilton, but it seems that only the first-named ever came into operation. That no other Turnpike Acts were passed until 1697 suggests that the experiment was not a success, and it was only in the 18th century that turnpiking really took off, with the crucial difference that administrative re-sponsibility now rested with local gentlemen as Trustees rather than the JPs. These new powers were applied to the Old North Road in a second Act of 1710, evidently not wholly successfully: as the preamble to a further Act in 1727 stated, the Trustees had

> applied all, or the greater part of the money collected by the Tolls and Duties at Cunnington Lane and Godmanchester towards the re-pairs of so much of the Great Road as lies next the Town of Hun-tingdon and done little or nothing towards repairing of such part of the said Great Road, as lies between a place called the White Post upon Alconbury Hill and Wandsford Bridge... which said Road is at least Fourteen Miles and much worse than it was.. although the said Tolls have been duly collected and paid, to the great Damage of such Travellers as pass and repass the same... The money col-lected hath been laid out in repairing the Roads at the North and South sides of Huntingdon...

The solution adopted was to divide the road into three Divisions, North (Wansford – Alconbury), Middle (Alconbury – the county boundary with Cambridgeshire) and South (to Royston), each with its own body of Trus-tees. Gradually the condition of the road improved, although the Middle Di-vision always suffered from the lack of suitable road-mending materials lo-cally.

Turnpiking slowly gathered pace, with Chatteris Ferry to Somersham fol-lowing in 1728. The preamble to the Act graphically explained why:

> by reason of the many heavy Carriages and droves of Dren and other Cattle frequently passing through, and the Floods and Inundations of the Waters often overflowing the said Road, [it] is become very

ruinous and bad, and many parts, in the Winter Season, so deep, that Passengers cannot pass and repass without danger.[12]

The much more important road from Godmanchester to Newmarket Heath followed in 1745, followed by a flurry of Acts in the 1750s: Market Harborough – Brampton in 1752, Oundle – Alconbury in 1753, and Ramsey – Huntingdon, Great Staughton - Wellingborough and Bury – Stratton all in 1755; by the 1820s virtually every road that was in the 20th century to receive an A or B classification had been turnpiked.

Additionally, of course, there was a complex network of local roads in the upland parts of the county, first mapped fully by Jefferys later in the 18th century.[13] Many of these were to be swept away by Parliamentary Enclosure and perhaps simply because there were now fewer roads to maintain their condition had improved by the early 19th century:

> Both the high and cross roads in Huntingdonshire are in general pretty good. Formerly the cross roads were scarce passable in winter, but since the enclosures have been made, a great and manifest improvement for the better has taken place.[14]

One ostensibly 'local' road that had a wider significance, however, largely survives to this day: the 'Bullock Road', running largely to the west of the Great North Road and which can be traced from Newark south to King's Ripton. This was a route of great antiquity (parish boundaries follow much of its length) and its purpose can be deduced from its name: it was the great cattle-droving route from Scotland and the north of England to St Ives market and the rich meadows of the Ouse valley which so impressed Defoe in the 1720s:

> to see them in the Summer season, cover'd with such innumerable stocks of cattle and sheep, is one of the most agreeable sights of its kind in the world.[15]

This continued in use after turnpiking, and indeed probably gained in importance as drovers sought to avoid tolls and also to take advantage of the

---

[12] I Geo II c.4, 1728 (copy in the Norris Museum Library, St Ives). Diligent research has failed to uncover what exactly 'dren' were.

[13] T. Jefferys, *The County of Huntingdon Surveyed,* London: T. Jefferys, 1768 (HA reprint).

[14] R. Carruthers, *History of Huntingdon,* Huntingdon: A.P Wood, 1824, p.33.

[15] D. Defoe, *Tour through the Whole Island of England and Wales,* London: Everyman Edition, n.d., p.110.

pastures *en route* for resting and grazing their animals, something increasingly difficult as Enclosure restricted such opportunities.

Map 1.2 Huntingdonshire Navigable Waterways c.1750

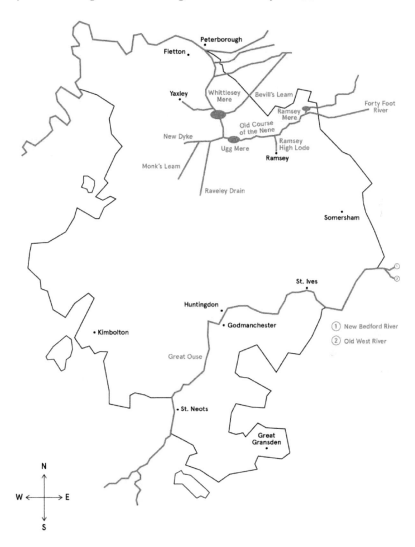

The backbone of the county's waterway system was the Great Ouse. How far upstream this was navigable before the 17th century is uncertain, although the so-called Danish 'docks' at Willington (Beds), which may have been where their longboats were overhauled and serviced, suggest that in the Dark

Ages this was easier than in later centuries.[16] The Danes had sailed or rowed up a river following a very different course to today's, flowing north below Earith along 'West Water' and eventually into the Wash below Wisbech; in the 13th century the course of the lower river was diverted – whether by natural or man-made means is unclear – along the 'Old West River' via Ely and Littleport to Kings Lynn. In the 16th century it was tidal as far upstream as St Neots, but to all intents and purposes the head of navigation for all but the smallest vessels was St Ives, which benefitted greatly from its entrepot position and whose watermen continued to dominate the river trade until the coming of the railways.

Navigation above St Ives was hampered by natural obstacles – gravels and shallows – and man-made, in the shape of mill dams: the 17th century history of the river is dominated by attempts to circumvent these and make the river navigable to Bedford. These started with a Crown grant of Letters Patent to Thomas Girton, a Westminster vintner, and Arnold Spencer, member of a minor gentry family from Cople (Beds) to improve the river upstream from St Ives. Spencer took the leading role, building sluices (to bypass mills) at Hemingford, Houghton, Godmanchester, Offord and St Neots in the 1620s: by the late 1630s, navigation was possible to Great Barford, which thus acquired a sudden importance as an inland port, with yards and wharves along the river and a substantial trade in coal, salt, iron, fish, corn, hempseed and timber.[17] Extension to Bedford was halted by the Civil War and the river, especially above St Neots, deteriorated through lack of maintenance. Spencer resumed his work in the late 1640s, but died in 1655, deeply in debt as 'his being concerned in the navigation did much waste his estate'.[18] The creditors obtained an Act to improve the river in 1665, but no work seems to have been undertaken until 1674, when Henry Ashley, a St Neots tanner, acquired Spencer's former rights for £160 p.a. He wasted no time in rectifying the neglect of the previous 25 years, restoring the existing sluices and adding a new one below St Ives and others at Eaton mills and Roxton and staunches at Tempsford, Roxton and Great Barford: as a result it was able to take larger vessels than hitherto (12 chaldrons, rather than 7/8) Finally, in 1689, he succeeded in making the river navigable to Bedford. He was also involved in a dispute with John Jemmatt, one of Spencer's creditors, over the ownership of the stretch between St Ives and Great Barford: a long and

---

[16] D. Summers, *The Great Ouse: The History of a River Navigation*, Newton Abbot: David & Charles, 1973. p.25.

[17] T.S. Willan, *The Navigation of the Great Ouse between St Ives and Bedford in the Seventeenth Century.* Bedford: Bedfordshire Historical Records Society, XXIV, pp 43-44.

[18] Willan, p.62.

bitter court case was eventually settled in 1699 in a compromise which none-theless gave the Ashley family the leading role in managing the navigation.[19] Ashley's work meant a dramatic improvement in the profitablility of the river: over the whole period 1661 -74 the profits were only £39.8.8d,[20] by 1683 they were averaging 'near £100 a year' [21] and in 1689-90 £800 was col-lected.[22]

But the problems of the river were still far from over. In an era of a more extreme climate than today, traders suffered from the river freezing in winter and summer droughts and the effects of flooding after heavy rainfall. A per-petual bone of contention was the fact that Godmanchester Corporation con-trolled the sluices there and at Houghton and Hemingford [23] and had powers to open them when there was any threat of flooding. And at dry times of year, millers and navigation interests competed for water: in 1702, the Ash-leys came to an agreement with the Earl of Manchester regarding their re-spective rights at Hemingford mill, but this was an exception.[24]

Huntingdonshire's other major river, the Nene, formed the northern county boundary from Elton to Stanground, and was beset by similar problems. It was naturally navigable for sea-going vessels as far upstream as Castor (where stone from the Barnack quarries had been loaded in medieval times). Beyond this smaller craft could reach the upper river only by means of por-tages around mill dams and other obstructions: it was claimed in 1648 that 16 portages were needed between Peterborough and Higham Ferrers.[25] Alt-hough several surveys of the river were carried out in the 17th century on behalf of Northamptonshire landowners, it was not until 1713 that an Act to improve the river was passed. This had the curious stipulation that unless nine of the Commissioners (from the lengthy list in the Act) could agree with 'some person or persons' to improve all the river up to Northampton, noth-ing could be done.[26] Inevitably, nothing happened. In 1724 a second Act em-powered the Commissioners to make any part of the river navigable and in 1726 Robert Wright and John Spence contracted for the Alwalton – Oundle stretch, which was completed in 1730. Navigation was extended to Thrapston

[19] Summers, pp54-55.
[20] Willan, p.68.
[21] Willan, p.77.
[22] Willan, p.111.
[23] Willan, p.65.
[24] Willan, p.125.
[25] H.J.K. Jenkins, *Along the Nene,* Wheaton: Cambridgeshire Books, 1991, p.21.
[26] J. Boyes, John and R. Russell, *The Canals of Eastern England*, Newton Abbot: David & Charles, 1977, p.198.

in 1736, Wellingborough in 1759 and Northampton in 1761, by which time the river was under the control of the Squire family (Peterborough brewers), who retained it until 1794 when it reverted to Commissioners. The Squires had not been careful custodians: in 1794 it was claimed that the river

> is in many Places grown up and decreased in depth, so that Boats and Lighters navigating thereon, for want of a proper and sufficient Depth of Water, are frequently stopped.[27]

The final piece in this particular jigsaw was put in place in 1815, when the river was linked to the Grand Junction Canal at Blisworth, thus becoming the only East Anglian waterway to be joined to the national canal system.[28]

The history of the lower courses of both rivers is inextricably linked with fen drainage. Traders had to contend with uncertain and shallow channels across the undrained fens: the Old West River in 1618 was

> generally fowle and overgrown with weeds, stopped with weare [weirs] and against Ely made shallow by gravel and fordes.[29]

although this had a hidden advantage, inasmuch as the 'Ely Hards' acted as a sort of dam and helped maintain water levels in the summer.

Improvement of the lower Nene started very early. Throughout the late Middle Ages, the route from Peterborough to the sea was by what is still marked on Ordnance Survey maps as 'River Nene (Old Course)', via Whittlesey Mere, March and the Well Creek to join the Ouse at Salter's Lode.[30] This was bypassed c.1470 by Morton's Leam, from Peterborough to Guyhirne, thus allowing access to Wisbech. Forty feet wide and four feet deep, this was much easier to navigate, but was itself bypassed in 1728 by Smith's Leam (the present-day main course of the river).

It was only after the Civil War that the Ouse received a similar fillip, as a result of Vermuyden's Fen drainage works: the New Bedford River (the 'Hundred Foot') cut off the great loop of the river round by Ely and provided

---

[27] Boyes, p.202.

[28] As a result of this, some commercial traffic continued on the upper river downstream to Wellingborough, until 1969.

[29] Summers, p.41.

[30] There was an even earlier route via Crowland and the Tydds to the Wash, but this seems to have fallen into disuse in the early medieval period, although its legacy remains the triangular bridge desolately marooned on dry land in the centre of Crowland.

a direct route from Earith to Denver Sluice. Denver was to lead to much controversy almost from the time it was built, allegedly contributing to the silting-up of the Ely Ouse and its tributaries, but the traders and consumers of Huntingdonshire benefitted greatly from a far more direct access to Lynn and a fall in shipping costs from 6/6d a load to 4/-.[31]

Vermuyden's great project also led to the construction of a series of new channels in the Huntingdonshire Fens, whose purpose was mainly drainage but also benefitted navigation, particularly the Sixteen, Twenty and Forty Foot rivers (all 1649-51) and the rather earlier Bevill's Leam (c.1630). In theory at least, these allowed the newly-drained Fens access to Lynn and Wisbech, as well as improving the accessibility of those communities formerly dependent on medieval cuts to the Old Nene: Yaxley, Ramsey and Sawtry, for example.

But there remained a major problem: the condition of the outfalls. The slow flow of the rivers below Wisbech and Lynn, coupled with the lack of tidal scour in the Wash, meant that channels were constantly changing, a major hindrance to coastal and overseas trade and almost certainly restricting the flow of exports and imports from and to Huntingdonshire.[32] These problems were eventually solved by extensive works in the estuaries from the 1820s onwards (and the construction of the Eau Brink Cut just above Lynn in 1821), but these are beyond the scope of this survey.

Traffic, Trade and Towns

Although as a general rule water transport scored over the roads in terms of cost, especially for bulk cargoes such as coal, this may not always have been the case in post-Restoration Huntingdonshire, especially where the all-important and growing London market for its agricultural products was concerned: the metropolis was far closer by road and the delays that often attended river and coastal transport were a further complicating factor. In the absence of hard evidence, however, the relative importance of the two means of transport is impossible to determine.

---

[31] Summers, p.70.
[32] Wisbech in particular suffered badly in the 18th century, being at times almost inaccessible by sea-going vessels. Its magnificent legacy of Georgian architecture is due far more to its role as a prosperous market town than to water-borne trade.

As noted above, road transport was increasingly in wheeled vehicles rather than by packhorse from the 16th century onwards. In the early Stuart period two-wheeled carts were the norm, but after 1660 farmers' inventories suggest that four-wheeled waggons were becoming increasingly common, especially in the highly-commercialised arable NW Huntingdonshire, with its easy access to the Great North Road.[33] Although there is little local evidence in our period, waggoners were emerging as a distinct occupational group, acting as haulage contractors for longer journeys, and cargoes such as the 3,000 brace of wildfowl Defoe said were carried to London from the Fens each week.[34] Smaller consignments were the province of carriers, who had first appeared in and around London in the 14th century. By the 17th century they had become a sophisticated national network: in 1632, carriers from Stamford, Lincoln, Sheffield, Wakefield, Hull, Leeds and York were passing through Huntingdonshire, and there was a weekly London service from Huntingdon itself: the carriers

> doe lodge at the White Hart without Cripplegate, they come up on Thursdaies and gow away on Fridaies.[35]

As well as packages of all sorts, carriers conveyed passengers: in January 1661 Pepys despatched his mother by 'Bird, the carrier' from London to Brampton.[36] By 1715, St Ives had five weekly services to London, Huntingdon and St Neots three each.[37] They brought in an increasingly wide range of consumer goods, such as the thread, paper, tobacco, silk, candles, cotton and sugar noted in the inventory of a St Ives shopkeeper in 1725.[38]

Other freight could, of course, carry itself, such as the cattle droves previously noted. Also self-propelled were those poor and desperate people using the roads to find work or relief. Parish accounts give us occasional glimpses of these unfortunates: in 1661, the Churchwardens of Great Staughton recorded payments to itinerant Irishmen, several families, '2 men that had lost their meanes by sea', 'a man that had great losses by sea' and 'a woman that

---

[33] Porter, p.39.
[34] Defoe, Vol 1, p.79. He was perhaps rather too credulous in accepting the story that many of these, from the Low Countries, had been lured to their fate by decoy ducks.
[35] J. Taylor, *The Carriers Cosmographie,* London, 1632, http://ota.ox.ac.uk/tcp/headers/A13/A13431.html (last accessed 7 July 2018).
[36] *Diary,* 3rd January 1661 www.pepysdiary,com (last accessed 31 August 2018).
[37] M. Carter (ed), *Edmund Pettis' Survey of St Ives, 1728,* Cambridge: Cambridgeshire Records Society, 2002, p.33.
[38] Carter, p.23.

had lost her husband & all their goodes at Sea'.[39] At Hilton, relief was given to '18 lame soljours' in 1709 (the 6d they were given cannot have helped them on their way very much).[40]

Stagecoach services appear to have started on the Great North Road shortly after the Restoration,[41] with three daily services connecting London and York by 1700.[42] Before this, other than by carriers' cart, journeys were made either on horseback or by private carriage. Travellers had to be catered for, and innkeeping became an important occupation on main roads from late medieval times, with a particular concentration in those towns and villages which were to become coaching centres in the 18th century heyday of the coaching trade, particularly St Neots and Huntingdon, where the *Falcon, Fountain* and *George* were all important coaching inns and the new prosperity brought to the town (which had been in economic decline since the Civil War) lead to a wave of rebuilding in the High Street and Market Place from the 1720s onwards. At Buckden the *George* and *Lion* were calling points for coaches, but the most famous of all coaching inns was the *Bell* at Stilton, largely because of its association with Stilton cheese, adroitly publicized by its owner, Cooper Thornhill.[43] Defoe was a devotee of 'our English Parmesan', which was

> brought to table with the mites, or maggots round it, so thick, that they bring a spoon with them for you to eat the mites with, as you do the cheese.[44]

Travellers perhaps needed fortifying before or after braving Sawtry Lane:

> a deep descent between two hills, in which is Stangate Hole, famous for being the most noted robbing place in all this part of the country.[45]

Some idea of the extent of trade on the roads can be gained from the War Office Stabling Returns of 1686, which list the number of beds and amount

---

[39] HA HP82/5/1. It is impossible to escape the impression that word had got round that Great Staughton was a soft touch.

[40] HA HP42/8/3/1.

[41] Pepys saw his aunt and two cousins on to a coach for Brampton on 12 September 1664.

[42] Dyos and Aldcroft, *British Transport,* p.33.

[43] www.thebellstilton.co.uk/bell-inn-history (last accessed 11 August 2018).

[44] Defoe, Vol II, p.110.

[45] Defoe, p.110.

of stabling available in each parish.[46] Most parishes could offer some accommodation, albeit very limited: Grafham, for example, had one bed and
room for four horses. The list is dominated by towns and villages on or near
the Great North Road: Huntingdon had 195 beds and stabling for 498 horses,
Godmanchester 24 and 134 respectively, Buckden 56 and 139, St Neots 92
and 372, Alconbury 23 and 80 and Stilton 63 and 87. The only other places
that came anywhere near these figures were the market towns: Kimbolton
25 beds and stabling for 50 horses and St Ives with 182 and 426 respectively,
surprisingly large figures for a town that was not a major centre of road
transport. Equally surprising, perhaps, is Ramsey, well off any main roads,
with 64 beds and stabling for 174 horses.

Water transport remains tantalizingly vague in its details, due to the paucity
of source materials. It is possible to say with some certainty what was being
carried, but where to and from and in what quantities, is uncertain. Post-
drainage, most traffic was handled by Fen lighters, with a carrying capacity
of about 25 tons and hauled or sailed depending on conditions, some owned
by millers, maltsters and other merchants, others engaged in general carrying: here the watermen of St Ives were dominant on the Ouse.[47] One snap-
shot of the river trade does exist, however, the toll book for Hemingford
Sluice for Lady Day to Midsummer 1710, which records about 3,000 loads
passing, of which 784 (it is not stated of what) were on behalf of the Bedford
merchant Thomas Wilkes, 360 for William Faldo (also of Bedford) and 380
for Mr Douce of Huntingdon; 530 loads were carried for two Tempsford
merchants (16 of these were barley). A few loads were identified: barley,
malt, turves, freestone, wood, bricks and tiles, pots and 'fish trunks'.[48] Notable by its absence is coal, but it would be safe to assume a large proportion
of the unspecified cargoes were of this commodity.

It was the river trade that was the life-blood of the towns and villages of the
Ouse valley, with the curious exception of Huntingdon, which seems effectively to have turned its back on its river. St Ives and Earith still show in
their plans long yards running back from the east-west streets to what were
once riverside wharves, and at St Neots the canalized Hen Brook mimics in
miniature the topography of King's Lynn, with the same pattern of ware-
houses and wharves. There were pubic wharves on the Ouse itself, at the

---

[46] TNA WO 30/48. I am grateful to Dr Max Satchell of the Cambridge Group for
the History of Population and Social Structure for making a digital version of the
Returns available to me.

[47] Summers, p.128. Before drainage, sea-going 'keels' were common; the lighters
were better-adapted for the Fenland waterways.

[48] Willan, pp.127–133.

west end of the Market Place, and at Brookside.[49] St Neots had undoubtedly benefitted from its river: William Barwick, a waterman of St Ives testified in 1672 that

> before the navigation the town of St Neots was an inland town and a place of small trade for such commodities as are brought up by boat. Since the making of the river navigable great quantities of corn, grain, deal boards, fir timber, iron, fish and other commodities have been brought by boat to St Neots.[50]

Apart from mills and maltings, the rivers had little effect on industrial location in the county, with the exception of Joseph Eayre's bell foundry at St Neots, established in 1735 and continuing to function into the late 18th century.[51] The foundry was on the east bank of the Ouse immediately north of St Neots bridge, and had an extensive quay. it manufactured bells for a large number of churches in western East Anglia and the East Midlands, 39 in the Diocese of Ely alone between 1735 and 1770.[52] Some of these would have been carried by road (to Great Gidding in 1756, for example) but wherever possible water transport would have been used, as to Stow Bardolph (1767) and Downham Market (1769), although the logistical problems of supplying Thriplow (1743) and Sawston (1755) must have been immense.

For other people, whether to use water or road transport must depended on costs and convenience. A rare glimpse is provided from the diary of the Revd William Cole, who moved from Bletchley to Landbeach in 1767. He travelled by chaise via Ampthill, Biggleswade (where he slept overnight) and Longstanton (where he dined with Sir Thomas Hatton),

> His heavy goods were taken to Bedford and came by water on two lighters, which started on Saturday and were expected to be at Waterbach on Monday, going on the West River by Earith and Hermitage [Sluice]. Meantime two waggonloads came by road, each drawn by two horses... . The waggons contained his more perishable goods, such as his two servants, Tom and Molly, two cats, a sow,

[49] C.F.Tebbutt, *St Neots,* Chichester: Phillimore, 1978, p.85.
[50] Tebbutt, p.86.
[51] R. Young, *St Neots Past,* Chichester: Phillimore, 1996, p.69.
[52] *National Bell Registry*, www.georgedawson.homestead.com/nbr/html, last accessed 17 August 2018.

two blackbirds, three bantam chickens, etc. Luckily they arrived on a fine day.[53]

The roads and rivers were to continue to play a vital role in Huntingdon-shire's economy until their sudden eclipse by the railways in the 1850s, which at a stroke affected the county profoundly: Huntingdon and St Neots became simply wayside stations on the Great Northern main line and Peter-borough was now the great crossroads for east-west and north south traffic. Stilton, a rather romantic inter-war writer said, was turned by the railways from 'a vast coaching emporium into a corpse of a town'.[54] But the last – wistful – word should perhaps belong to an elderly St Ives waterman, Henry Smith, in his evidence in the court case of Attorney General v Simpson in 1898:

> It was fifty or sixty years ago that I saw fifteen or twenty gangs of lighters lying together in the river. Trade has been falling off since the Great Northern was built… I should think it was five or six years since I saw a cargo of coals come up the river. I am on the bridge a great deal, and should see them if there were any.[55]

Were he to return to the bridge today, he would see the river busy again, although with pleasure rather than commercial traffic; and one imagines he would have some pithy comments to make on the navigational skills of river users.

---

[53] W.M. Palmer, *William Cole of Milton,* Cambridge: Galloway & Porter, 1935, p.44. I am grateful to Dr Philip Saunders for drawing my attention to this refer-ence.

[54] T.W. Outram, *Coaching Days and Coaching Ways,* London: Macmillan, 1931, p.327. The growth of motor traffic on what had by 1931 become the A1 was about to breathe life into the corpse.

[55] HA BLC5/5/1.

2

CHANGING SOCIAL STRUCTURE IN AN

AGRICULTURAL COUNTY

Ken Sneath

This chapter explores the social structure of a small, rural 'lost shire'. Huntingdonshire is just the sort of county that gets overlooked by historians, but it has an excellent collection of records, including hearth tax returns and probate inventories. The county's probate inventories have a wider chronological span than most counties and unusually include large numbers relating to labourers. This chapter together with chapter 4, includes important new research based upon analysis of these records. It begins by considering the varying factors that are the basis for social status and gives a brief evaluation of attempts to establish social structures in the early modern period. The second half of the chapter explores the contribution that an analysis of some of Huntingdonshire's rich collection of records can contribute to the debate.

Defining social structure

Many have attempted to define the structure of early modern society. We begin with Gregory King and Daniel Defoe who were contemporary with our period. King calculated the number of families in 1688 and divided them into those who were increasing the wealth of the kingdom (i.e. those whose incomes exceeded their living expenses) and the substantially more who decreased it. (Table 1)

King's table has attracted great attention from historians and was reworked by Lindert and Williamson in 1982.[1] In 2015, it was revised again by Stephen Broadberry *et al* who concluded that in 1688 three quarters of families had annual incomes of £17 or more and could therefore have been able to purchase a 'respectability basket of consumables'. The remaining quarter consisted of cottagers and paupers (income £6), who survived on the cheaper

---

[1] P.H. Lindert and J.G. Williamson 'Revising England's social tables 1688-1913' *Explorations in Economic History*, 19, 385-408.

'barebones basket' of goods and the small group of vagrants (income £2) who survived as best they could.[2] In Broadberry *et al's* analysis, labourers fall into the higher social grouping whereas in King's, they fall into the lower grouping. The position of labourers in the social hierarchy is discussed towards the end of the chapter.

---

[2] S. Broadberry, B. Campbell, A. Klein, M. Overton and B. van Leeuwen, *British Economic Growth 1270-1870* Cambridge.: CUP, 2015, pp.322-3.

TABLE 1 GREGORY KING's RANKS AND DEGREES

Number of families	Ranks, degrees, titles and qualifications	Heads per family	Number of persons
160	Temporal Lords	40	6,400
26	Spiritual Lords	20	520
800	Baronets	16	12,800
600	Knights	13	7,800
3,000	Esquires	10	30,000
12,000	Gentlemen	8	96,000
5,000	Persons in greater Offices and Places	8	40,000
5,000	Persons in lesser Offices and Places	8	30,000
2,000	Eminent Merchants and Traders by Sea	8	16,000
8,000	Lesser Merchants and Traders by Sea	6	48,000
10,000	Persons in the Law	7	70,000
2,000	Eminent Clergy-men	6	12,000
8,000	Lesser Clergy-men	5	40,000
40,000	Freeholders of the better sort	7	280,000
120,000	Freeholders of the lesser sort	5 1/2	660,000
150,000	Farmers	5	750,000
15,000	Persons in Liberal Arts and Sciences	5	75,000
50,000	Shopkeepers and Tradesmen	4 1/2	225,000
60,000	Artizans and Handicrafts	4	240,000
5,000	Naval Officers	4	20,000
4,000	Military Officers	4	16,000
500,586		5 1/3	2,675,520
50,000	Common Seamen	3	150,000
364,000	Labouring People and Out Servants	3 1/2	1,275,000
400,000	Cottagers and Paupers	3 1/4	1,300,000
35,000	Common Soldiers	2	70,000
849,000		3 1/4	2,795,000
	Vagrants; as Gipsies, Thieves, Beggars, &c.		30,000
	So the general Account is		
500,586	Increasing the Wealth of the Kingdom	5 1/3	2,675,520
849,000	Decreasing the Wealth of the Kingdom	3 1/4	2,825,000
1,349,586	Neat Totals	4 1/13	5,500,520

About twenty years after Gregory King's precise calculations of ranks and degrees, Daniel Defoe suggested the frequently quoted social structure based on wealth and consumption:

- The great who live profusely
- The rich who live plentifully
- The Middle sort who live well
- The working trades who labour hard but feel no want
- The country people, farmers etc who fare indifferently
- The poor who fare hard
- The miserable that really pinch and suffer want.[3]

Defoe's seven categories provide a contemporary insight into society, but they are too vague to be of much use for our present purposes.

Social structure has proved an enduring fascination for social scientists and historians. For Marxist historians, the social structure of communities resulted from production and distribution of wealth. They believed that social groups were inherently in conflict with each other as a result of property division. On the other hand, stratification theory differs from the Marxist approach by emphasising social *co-operation* rather than conflict. Social groups were not so clearly defined and there were several dimensions of stratification including wealth, status and power.[4]

More recently, historians have focussed attention on *terms* used by people in early modern England. Keith Wrightson explored the concepts of estates, degrees and sorts. As the economy expanded, professional groups, tradesmen and yeomen increased their wealth and the medieval language of estates gave way to degrees and 'sorts'. Designation of people into broad groupings such as 'better sort' or 'meaner sort' was based on wealth.[5] Henry French also explored how individuals understood their position in society, how they identified with others and how they generated a sense of belonging together. For example, French found that in the late seventeenth century at village level, terms such as 'better sort' were frequently used by people who were

[3] R. Porter, *English Society in the Eighteenth Century* Harmondsworth: Penguin, 1990, p.53.
[4] H. French, 'Social status, localism and the middle sort of people in England, 1620-1750' *Past and Present*, 166 2000, 66-99.
[5] K. Wrightson, 'Sorts of people in Tudor and Stuart England' in J. Barry and C. Brooks, eds., *The Middling Sort of People*, Basingstoke: Palgrave, 1994, p.50.

not poor but also did not have the status to call themselves gentry.[6] Although individuals were the key to understanding social identity, French argued that historical individuals were born into a 'dense web of social and behavioural constraints'. The autonomy of individuals was heavily circumscribed by pre-existing value systems.[7]

Craig Muldrew endorsed the importance of morality in the way individuals viewed self-identity within society. Virtuous living enhanced a person's reputation on which obtaining credit depended and which could be crucial for survival.[8] Early Modern England was a competitive society where households strove to be successful. The terms 'better sort' and 'meaner sort' were words of judgement for the former were successful whereas the latter were not.[9] The language of sorts reflected contemporary social tensions as society became more polarised.[10] Gwyneth Nair highlighted contemporary use of the terms by an example from the parish register of Highley in 1678. Giles Rawlins the Vicar left money to be 'set forth yearlie by the Churchwardens for the best use of the poor of the Parish at the discretion.........of the best sort of the said parish'.[11] In Highley, churchwardens were among the best sort for they were economically successful.

In his latest study on the topic, Muldrew has explored changing attitudes towards material improvement which occurred in response to economic and religious developments in the sixteenth and seventeenth centuries. A cultural identity of the middling sort emerged in response to the rapid growth of commercialism and the resulting changes in what constituted acceptable behaviour. Honest profit ceased to be a dangerous temptation to self-interest and trade became the route to material improvement. This benefitted wider society for it led to greater employment opportunities for those further down

[6] H. French, 'Social status, localism and the middle sort of people in England, 1620-1750', *Past and Present*, 166 2000, 66-99.
[7] H. French and J. Barry, 'Identity and agency in English Society, 1500-1800-Introduction', in H. French and J. Barry eds. *Identity and agency in England, 1500-1800*, Basingstoke: Palgrave, 2004, pp.22-3.
[8] C. Muldrew, *The economy of obligation: the culture of credit and social relations in early modern England* London: Palgrave, 1998, chapter 5.
[9] C. Muldrew, 'Class and credit: social identity, wealth and the life course in early modern England, in H. French and J. Barry eds., *Identity and agency in England, 1500-1800* Basingstoke: Palgrave, 2004, p.149.
[10] S. Hindle, *The state and social change in early modern England, 1550-1640* Basingstoke: Palgrave, 2002, p.49.
[11] G. Nair, *Highley* Oxford: OUP, 1998, p.129.

the social scale and enabled the poor to be better supported following the enactment of the Elizabethan Poor Laws.[12]

In considering social structure, this chapter focusses largely on the middling sort. Margaret Hunt concluded pessimistically that the composition of the middling sort 'is and must remain somewhat vague'.[13] Our working definition of the middling sort is that they fell between the landed elite and the poor and were broadly synonymous with the inventoried population. Three historians have proposed social structures for the seventeenth and early eighteenth centuries based on probate inventories and hearth tax records as sources.

Lorna Weatherill: Social Hierarchy

Lorna Weatherill criticised Gregory King's approach for mixing occupations and status designations, rather than employing one set of criteria. Weatherill used Brodsky Elliott's study of apprenticeship choices and marriage partners in London and Kent between 1583 and 1640 to construct a social hierarchy in *Consumer behaviour and material culture.*[14] Using occupational descriptors in probate inventories, Weatherill created three groupings of these occupations which she placed in a relationship with agricultural ranks when she analysed probate inventory data in her study. Weatherill suggested that occupations of 'high status' such as clergy, apothecaries and doctors, and occupations she categorised as of 'intermediate status' such as innkeepers, malsters and tanners, should be placed between gentry and yeomen. For Weatherill, trades of 'low status' such as butchers, bakers and cordwainers fell between yeomen and husbandmen.[15]

Weatherill's construct of a social hierarchy was a brave attempt but there are inevitably problems in any system of social classification. Both status and occupational descriptors covered a wide variety of practice, as Weatherill recognised. A tradesman or craftsman could be a substantial employer or a

---

[12] C. Muldrew, 'The Middling Sort: An Emergent Cultural Identity' in K. Wrightson ed., *A Social History of England 1500-1750* Cambridge: CUP, 2017, pp.290-309.

[13] M.R. Hunt, *The Middling Sort: commerce, gender and the family in England 1680-1780* Los Angeles: University of California Press, 1996, p.15.

[14] V. Brodsky Elliott, 'Mobility and marriage in pre-industrial England' unpublished PhD thesis, University of Cambridge, 1978.

[15] L. Weatherill, *Consumer behaviour and material culture,* 2nd edn. London: Routledge, 1996, pp.208-212.

poor employee.[16] Location also impacted on status and occupational designations. For example, Weatherill found that the term 'husbandman' could simply mean farmer, especially in the south of England. In the north, it commonly meant a smallholder whose farming activities fell somewhere between those of yeomen and labourers.[17] One problem that Weatherill faced was how to deal with those simply classified as a farmer. Her solution was to place 'large farmers' (defined as having an inventory valued at over £60) with yeomen and 'small farmers' (having an inventory valued at under £60) with husbandmen.

When Weatherill's results of an analysis of values for 2902 inventories were plotted against her proposed social hierarchy, results for husbandmen were inevitably relatively low. More than three quarters (256) of Weatherill's category of 332 husbandmen were recorded as farmers and not husbandmen in their inventories.

Weatherill's own selected probate inventory mean values largely accord with her proposed hierarchy except for yeomen, whose mean value (£165) was slightly higher than her trades of intermediate status grouping (£157). Weatherill nearly always used mean rather than median values in her analysis. However, the median is a more effective measure of central tendency because the mean can be unduly influenced by extreme values. It is also important to use an additional method, the standard deviation, to describe the amount of dispersion of the data around the mean. A further measure, the coefficient of variation, enables the degree to which variables differ from their respective means to be compared.[18]

A new and much larger set of inventory data from 15 counties throughout England has been assembled.[19] An analysis of nearly 4500 (4474) inventory values for the period 1660-1749 is given in Table 2. The results shed light on Weatherill's construction of a social structure. Median inventory values do not support Weatherill's placement of high and intermediate status occupations above yeomen, nor low status tradesmen above husbandmen.

---

[16] B. Reay, *Popular cultures in England 1550-1750* Harlow, Routledge, 1998, p.187; Weatherill, *Consumer behaviour and material culture*, p.177.

[17] Weatherill, *Consumer Behaviour and Material Culture*, p.174.

[18] R. Floud, *An introduction to quantitative methods for historians* London: Methuen, 1973, pp.75-6 and p.82.

[19] Full results from the data set will be published in the forthcoming *The Origins of the Consumer Revolution in England* by Jo Sear and Ken Sneath.

Weatherill combined widows with spinsters into one status group. Only 7 percent of Weatherill's selected inventories for England related to females and less than one in seven of her female inventories were for spinsters. In Table 2, 15 percent of inventories were for females, but they were still seriously under-represented in the inventory data. Amy Froide maintained that single women in late seventeenth-century England comprised at least a third of all adult women. Factoring in the proportions of widows, only about half of all adult women in early modern England were married at any given point in time.[20] Married women did not leave inventories because the property of married women became the possession of their husband on marriage.[21] There was not a great difference between inventory values of widows (£29) and spinsters (£25), but spinsters (CV=202) and widows (CV=195) had the greatest degree of variation of any group.

---

[20] A.M. Froide, 'Hidden women: rediscovering the singlewomen of early modern England' *Local Population Studies*, 68 2002, pp.26 and 38.

[21] A. Erickson, *Women and property*, London: Routledge, 1993, pp.24 and 237; A. Erickson, 'Coverture and capitalism' *History Workshop Journal*, 59 2005, p.3.

TABLE 2: INVENTORY VALUES BY STATUS AND OCCUPATION IN SELECTED ENGLISH COUNTIES 1660-1749						
	Sample size	Lowest	Median	Highest	Mean	Standard Deviation	Coefficient of Variation
STATUS GROUPS	No.	£	£	£	£	£	
Gentry	142	5	196	3158	396	606	153
Yeomen	764	2	118	3369	190	252	133
High status occupations	188	2	96	5060	250	471	188
Intermediate status trades	394	0	66	1443	140	218	156
Husbandmen	194	3	63	766	102	108	106
Low status tradesmen	805	1	39	3113	83	156	188
Labourers	216	1	18	233	27	32	119
Widows	622	1	29	2509	74	144	195
Spinsters	56	3	25	851	73	148	202
Unknown	1093	1	41	2139	96	160	167
ALL INVENTORIES	4474	0	51	5060	123	235	191
SELECTED OCCUPATIONAL GROUPS							
Apothecaries/ Doctors	17	9	261	894	278	243	87
Shopkeepers etc	86	4	154	5060	374	648	173
Tanners	21	18	138	650	235	207	88
Clergy	31	19	109	552	161	147	91
Innkeepers etc	133	3	80	1163	155	214	138
Bakers	33	9	68	347	106	88	83
Butchers	37	5	39	790	113	178	158
Glovers	25	3	38	394	78	98	126
Blacksmiths	70	1	37	509	61	90	148
Cordwainers/Shoemakers	69	1	37	387	59	70	119
Weavers	38	4	35	531	86	117	136
Carpenters/Joiners	87	4	30	558	64	91	142
Tailors	51	2	24	459	44	67	152
Bricklayers	15	4	21	167	40	46	115

Weatherill considered carpenters (categorised as low status) to be of lower status than joiners (categorised as intermediate status). In Weatherill's own data, her selected carpenters had a higher mean inventory value (£70) than her sample of just four joiners (£48). Of the 87 carpenters and joiners in Table 2, 70 were carpenters with a median value of £29 (mean £66) and 17 were joiners with a median value of £35 (mean £55). Woodward argued there was a 'disputed no-man's land' between the work of carpenters and joiners that proved difficult to police. Woodward cited the case of carpenters employed by the council in Hull in 1671 to make beds and doors which was strictly the work of joiners. Woodward also found a detailed bill of work for Hull Council for the year 1713 relating to 11 master carpenters and two joiners in which both groups were paid the same rate of pay.[22] In the light of this evidence, it is therefore not easy to justify Weatherill's categorisation of joiners and carpenters.

Weatherill distinguished between drapers and mercers (high status) and shopkeepers (intermediate status). Taken together these groups had the second highest median probate inventory value of occupational groups in the period 1660-1749 (£154). Weatherill's data demonstrated that mercers (£341) had the highest mean values followed by drapers (£274), whereas mean inventory values of general shopkeepers (£133), specialized shopkeepers (£92) and chandlers (£95) were much lower.[23] Mui and Mui referred to the many 'mere shopkeepers' whose income and lifestyle placed them among the lower echelons of the middling groups.[24] The present study also found that drapers (£403) and mercers (£350) had high mean values but sample sizes at this level of disaggregation were very small.

High inventory values for shopkeepers were often the result of levels of stock in their shop rather than the value of household goods or other personal assets. These stocks were frequently purchased on borrowed money. The inventory of William Eastwood, a grocer in Wakefield, was valued at £1200 in 1735 of which goods in his shop represented £992. Revealingly, his probate account recorded that he also owed a total of £992 in debts and therefore it would appear that his very substantial shop goods were financed on credit. Whilst a true estimate of a person's moveable assets is net assets after the deceased's borrowings have been deducted, this can usually only be ascertained from probate accounts rather than probate inventories. Not only are

---

[22] D. Woodward, *Men at Work Labourers and Building Craftsmen in the Towns of Northern England, 1450-1750*, Cambridge: CUP, 1995, p.18.

[23] Weatherill, *Consumer behaviour and material culture*, pp.209-211.

[24] L. Mui and H-C Mui, *Shops and shopkeeping*, London: Routledge, 1989, p.6.

probate accounts much rarer than probate inventories, they also appear to be biased sources.[25] Probate accounts tend to represent individuals with above average levels of gross inventoried wealth and people more likely to be in debt than the inventoried population as a whole. However, the ability to borrow particularly large sums like the grocer William Eastwood is itself an asset.

The focus of this book is upon Huntingdonshire and it is therefore important to establish the extent to which the county differs from England as a whole. Results for Huntingdonshire are set out in Table 3. The patterns of these inventory values are broadly similar to those for 15 counties in England in Table 2 but there were some exceptions. Overall, median inventory values in Huntingdonshire were significantly lower (£33) than the median (£51) for England. However, Huntingdonshire yeomen (£157) had higher values than elsewhere in England (£118), as did those with high status occupations (£169 compared to £96). The county's husbandmen (£74) had more than double the inventory values of low status tradesmen (£35) that Weatherill considered to be of higher status.

---

[25] Mortimer, 'Why were probate accounts made?', pp.8-11.

TABLE 3: INVENTORY VALUES BY STATUS AND OCCUPATION HUNTING-DONSHIRE 1660-1749							
	Sample size	Lowest	Median	Highest	Mean	Standard Deviation	Coefficient of Variation
STATUS GROUPS	No.	£	£	£	£	£	
Gentry	28	5	149	1351	317	364	115
High status occupations	28	24	169	1400	288	305	106
Intermediate status trades	68	3	63	1163	153	230	150
Yeomen	120	2	157	1231	185	185	100
Low status tradesmen	184	1	35	790	70	103	147
Husbandmen	38	3	74	689	131	133	102
Labourers	157	2	17	165	24	25	104
Spinsters	8	14	31	59	33	18	55
Widows	138	1	20	405	46	68	148
Unknown	200	2	30	1448	80	141	176
ALL INVENTORIES	969	1	33	1400	97	164	169
SELECTED OCCUPATIONAL GROUPS							
Shopkeepers etc	11	13	280	1400	442	408	92
Apothecaries/ Doctors	6	54	237	562	274	215	78
Tanners	6	74	147	562	261	215	82
Clergy	9	24	99	299	114	83	73
Bakers	15	30	87	322	121	86	71
Innkeepers etc	48	3	63	1163	159	253	159
Glovers	6	8	55	184	71	61	86
Butchers	12	9	53	790	163	239	147
Blacksmiths	13	4	39	509	92	150	163
Cordwainers/Shoemakers	25	1	33	173	47	45	96
Carpenters/Joiners	22	4	27	114	33	25	76
Bricklayers	9	4	21	85	34	30	88
Weavers	11	4	17	67	20	19	95
Tailors	16	2	16	153	29	38	131

Keith Wrightson, David Levine and Social Status

Keith Wrightson and David Levine divided households into four 'status categories' based on numbers of hearths per household when they analysed hearth tax records for Terling, Essex. They suggested that houses with more than six hearths were likely to be occupied by gentry and 'very large farmers', while at the other end of the social scale labourers and poor craftsmen were defined as persons with either only one hearth or exempt from the tax.[26] Yeomen and wealthy craftsmen with three to five hearths fell into Wrightson and Levine's second category and husbandmen and craftsmen (category three) typically had two hearths. This schema was devised for Terling, a rural village in a prosperous part of the country: Essex.

Wrightson and Levine's theory can be tested to an extent. When they compiled hearth tax returns, constables designated gentlemen in certain tax returns and these individuals can be compared to those who occupied properties with six or more hearths. The theory was examined in five market towns and fifteen rural parishes in Huntingdonshire in the hearth tax returns for 1664/1665.[27] In total, Wrightson and Levine's theory appeared to work reasonably well, for 89 persons were designated gentry in the tax returns for the 20 parishes and 83 properties had six or more hearths. (Table 4)

[26] K. Wrightson and D. Levine, *Poverty and piety in an English village* 2nd edn. Oxford: Clarendon, 1995, p.35.
[27] TNA E 179/122/226.

TABLE 4: DESIGNATED GENTRY AND SIZE OF PROPERTIES RECORDED IN HEARTH TAX RETURNS				
Parishes	Designated Gentry or above	Properties six or more hearths	Hearths of designated gentry	
	No.	No.	Mean	Median
Kimbolton	16	6	7.0	4
St Ives	9	17	5.4	5
Godmanchester	22	5	4.7	4
Ramsey	2	5	19.5	19.5
Huntingdon	14	24	11.1	8
Barham	0	0	0	0
Easton	2	0	3.5	3.5
Spaldwick	2	3	9.7	8
Buckden	3	6	14.7	4
Leighton	0	2	0	0
Stow Longa	2	2	11.5	11.5
Woodhurst	3	2	7	7
Great Gidding	0	0	0	0
Botolph Bridge	1	0	4	4
Orton Longueville	4	2	9.8	5.5
Orton Waterville	1	2	10	10
Upwood	1	1	16	16
Great Gransden	5	3	4.4	5
Wyton	0	2	0	0
Upton	2	1	6	6
Totals	89	83	8	5

However, results at parish level, do not stand up. In Godmanchester, 22 in-dividuals were recorded as gentry in the returns whereas only five properties (occupied by four gentlemen and a widow) had six or more hearths. This clearly does not accord with Wrightson and Levine's theory because even without adding any 'very large farmers', there were far more gentry than properties with six or more hearths. A similar situation was found in Kim-bolton where there were 16 people recorded as gentry but only six properties with six or more hearths. The reverse position is found in two more urban parishes: the county town of Huntingdon and St Ives. Gentry gravitated to-wards the county town which was where the Earl of Sandwich resided at

Hinchingbrooke House (44 hearths) Sir Nicholas Pedley (15 hearths) and Sir Lionel Walden at Walden House (6 hearths). But of the eight properties with ten or more hearths, only half were occupied by the gentry or above. As Table 3 demonstrated, innkeepers were by far the largest occupational group amongst inventoried males in the county and many of these inns were in Huntingdon and St Ives. Large properties not occupied by gentry such as Philip Soper, (26 hearths), Henry Bowes (19 hearths) and Thomas Wallwyn (18 hearths) may have been inns. In St Ives, only four of the 17 properties with six or more hearths were occupied by gentry. This means that in St Ives it was more common for gentry to live in properties with less than six hearths.

A further problem concerns systems for heating houses. The open halls of the medieval period had fireplaces which were gradually replaced by enclosed flues. As the number of rooms increased within houses, the number of hearths increased but these changes did not take place across the country at the same pace. It was therefore perfectly possible for gentry to live in grand houses with limited numbers of hearths. The picture is further complicated by inns which could have large numbers of hearths but were not gentry houses. This is relevant to a county like Huntingdonshire which is located on the important road between London and the north of England. How then should gentry and other ranks be defined?

Gentry and social mobility

A person's position in society was not fixed. Mary Carter gave the example of Thomas Houghton, a yeoman from Kimbolton. After marrying Sarah Austin, a widow of St Ives, Houghton moved to the town and built up a property portfolio, by inheritance through his wife and acquisition. Houghton's son became sheriff of the County.[28] It was both possible to join the ranks of the gentry from below but also gentry could fall substantially down the social scale. In Brampton, Giles Chapman, gentleman was recorded as exempt from the hearth tax by reason of poverty. The assumption is that for some reason Chapman had probably fallen on hard times. Gentry were not a legally defined group and wealthy and prominent tradesmen often made claims to gentry status. It is not surprising therefore that Henry French concluded that gentry often elude easy definition in terms of their membership or common attributes.[29]

---

[28] M. Carter, 'Town or Urban Society? St Ives in Huntingdonshire 1630-1740' in C. Phythian-Adams ed. *Societies, Cultures and Kinship 1580-1850* London: Leicester University Press, 1993, p.116

[29] H. French, 'Gentlemen, Remaking the English Ruling Class' in K. Wrightson ed. *A Social History of England 1500-1750* Cambridge: CUP, 2017, p.269.

Although there were certain 'indisputable qualifications' for gentry status such as the sovereign's commission, a call to the bar or a university degree, there was a considerable degree of dispute as to who should be accepted as a gentleman. Felicity Heal and Clive Holmes argued that by the early modern period, flexible definitions of gentility were a necessary feature of the rather mobile society of England with the key determinants being land, lordship and local acknowledgement.[30] This was succinctly encapsulated in the early seventeenth century by Thomas Adams who wrote, 'first riches and then honour for it is lightly found…reputation is measured by the acre'. Land implied income from rents.

Given this imprecise definition, it is not surprising that claims for gentility were often disputed. In his study of Lancashire gentry, Blackwood suggested that the term was often vague and meaningless because it was too readily used for town officials or even men of lower status who did not claim gentility. As a result, some historians have argued that herald's visitation lists held at the College of Arms are the most reliable guides to gentry status.[31] From 1530 to 1688, heraldic visitations operated under the crown as a means of regulating the gentry, and kings of arms were empowered, under their commissions, to deface or remove bogus arms. The 'official badge of gentility' was a coat of arms but Sir Thomas Smith in *De Republica Anglorum* (1583) argued that the reputation of being a gentleman came first, with confirmation by a king of arms following, if necessary, thereafter. Peter Coss warned that possession of a coat of arms was problematic as a test for gentry status, as not all gentry were armigerous and heraldic visitations were intermittent.[32]

John Bedells used heralds' visitation returns to assess numbers of gentry in Huntingdonshire. Two visitations for Huntingdonshire in the seventeenth century were held in 1613 and 1684. The 1613 visitation accepted 60 families living in forty-eight different parishes in Huntingdonshire and 53 gentry families in 1684. These numbers are substantially lower than those recorded as gentry in Hearth Tax records and also suggested that gentry households represented only just over 1 percent of Huntingdonshire households.[33]

---

[30] F. Heal and C. Holmes, *The gentry in England and Wales, 1500-1700* Basingstoke: Palgrave, 1994, pp.7-9.

[31] B.G. Blackwood, *The Lancashire gentry and the Great Rebellion* Manchester: Manchester University Press, 1978 p.11; K. Wrightson, *English society, 1580-1680* London: Routledge, 2003, p.31.

[32] P. Coss, *The origins of the English gentry* Cambridge: CUP, 2003, p.6.

[33] J. Bedells, 'The gentry of Huntingdonshire', in *Local Population Studies*, 44 1990, 35-6.

The next question to address is what distinguished lesser gentry from yeomen? Wrightson argued that possession of gentility was a fundamental dividing line in society.[34] Two contemporaries offer support to this interpretation. For William Harrison, an essential element of gentry status was that gentlemen were those who 'can live without manual labour'.[35] Sir Thomas Overbury described the important difference between yeomen and gentlemen by writing that the yeoman 'even though he be master, says not to his servants go to the field but let *us* go'.[36] Chapter 4 Feeding the People provided an analysis of inventory values of yeomen. It demonstrated that there was often no sharp distinction between lesser gentry and richer yeomen in Huntingdonshire. A quarter of yeomen had inventory values that would place them in the top half of gentry values.

Whilst Wrightson contended that gentlemen occupied a place of special estimation in the social order and stood apart, even the 'lesser gentry' were not a homogenous group. In England, their median moveable wealth was substantially above other ranks but with a coefficient of variation of 153, there was considerable variation within the group. (Table 2) In Huntingdonshire, the much smaller sample of 'lesser gentry' did not stand apart and their median movable wealth (£149) was a little less than Weatherill's 'high status occupations' and yeomen. The contrasting results from hearth tax records and heralds' visitation returns in the county further support the contention that the dividing line between gentry and some other ranks was rather more fluid.

Labourers 'The Meaner sort'

At the opposite end of the scale were Gregory King's 'labourers, cottagers and paupers'. King estimated that 'labourers, cottagers and paupers' and their families comprised 46 percent of the population in 1688.[37] For Wrightson, the most striking feature of King's calculation was the 'yawning gap' between the yearly income of the least well off of the 'middle sort' and those

---

[34] Wrightson, *English society* p.31; French, 'Gentlemen, Remaking the English Ruling Class', p.272.

[35] W. Harrison, *Description of England* Washington: Folger Shakespeare Library, 1968 p.114.

[36] E. Rimbault, ed., The miscellaneous works in prose and verse of Sir Thomas Overbury London: J R Smith, 1856, p.149.

[37] B. Coward, *Social change and continuity*, London: Longman, 1997, p.56.

of labouring people.[38] King estimated the annual income of a farmer's family to be £42 10s, whereas families of labourers and servants had £15 and cottagers and paupers only £6 10s.[39] This might appear to be another fundamental dividing line in society but, like other ranks, labourers represented a wide range of people.

Labourers with probate inventories were more affluent than labourers as a whole. If, as Gregory King suggested, families of labourers, cottagers and paupers represented approaching half the population, then inventoried labourers were not far from the centre of the social structure in England. As chapter 4 of this volume shows, the upper quartile of inventoried labourers (with inventory values exceeding £30) were not purely waged labourers but most owned cows, sheep, pigs and grew crops. Wrightson acknowledged that more fortunate labourers might hold an acre or two or enjoy the benefits of customary common rights.[40] Not all those designated labourers in probate inventories were agricultural labourers although most were. Labourers typically worked for wages and/or goods in kind. Their earnings varied considerably and were subject to many vagaries. Household income came from a range of sources. Wage earning was supplemented by gleaning in the fields and gathering fuel. Wives and children of labourers frequently did paid work and family income could also be supplemented by poor relief payments. Further down the scale were cottagers who got a living where they could, by wringing all that was possible out of the piece of ground which might be attached to their hovel.[41] Thus 'labourers, cottagers and paupers' embraced a wide range of people from more affluent inventoried labourers who held some land to cottagers and paupers at the lowest level of society.

A group who could easily be overlooked is servants. According to Kussmaul, servants constituted around 60 percent of the population aged fifteen to twenty-four in early modern England.[42] The most common form of employment for servants was as household servants or in husbandry. Servants in husbandry were unmarried young men and women hired on an annual contract and who lived in the farmhouse as part of the farmer's family.[43] Jeremy Boulton estimated that in the seventeenth and eighteenth centuries,

---

[38] K. Wrightson, *Earthly necessities*, New Haven: Yale, 2000, p.307.

[39] P. Laslett, *The world we have lost-further explored*, 3rd edn. London: Routledge, 1983, p.32.

[40] Wrightson, *English society*, p.41.

[41] Laslett, *The world we have lost-further explored*, p.45.

[42] A. Kussmaul, *Servants in husbandry in early modern England* Cambridge: CUP, 1981, p.3.

[43] M. Overton, *Agricultural revolution in England*, Cambridge: CUP, 1996, p.41.

between a third and a half of all hired agricultural labour was supplied by 'unmarried servants in husbandry'.[44] They did not appear in hearth tax returns nor in probate inventories because of their stage in the life cycle.

Henry French's 'Middling Sort'

The 'middling sort' can be placed between gentry and labourers and comprised the great majority of the inventoried population.[45] In Huntingdonshire, between 1660 and 1749 a quarter of the inventoried male population whose occupations were recorded were yeomen and husbandmen. The relationship of yeomen to husbandmen is considered in chapter 4. Despite being a largely rural county, professionals and increasing numbers of tradesmen comprised much of the inventoried population in Huntingdonshire. (Table 3) The larger groups supplied accommodation and produced food and drink (innkeepers, bakers and butchers), produced clothing (shoemakers and tailors) or were carpenters and joiners.

As well as experiencing the beginnings of an agricultural revolution during the period under consideration, significant changes were taking place in peoples' homes. The middling sort were at the centre of these changes. Analysis of probate inventories revealed that their homes were being transformed. The gentry had led the way in owning many new goods such as clocks, knives and forks and items associated with the new hot drinks, tea and coffee. However, in the eighteenth century, new consumer goods were rapidly being acquired by the middling sort. These trends can be seen in Huntingdonshire particularly in market towns, although clock ownership was even higher in rural parishes.[46]

Whilst there is some sense in which the 'middling sort' were a social group, in that they largely produced goods and services for the market rather than sold their labour, they represented a wide range of people. They included relatively wealthy yeomen as well as relatively poor tradesmen. In Huntingdonshire, these lowly tradesmen such as weavers, tailors and bricklayers had

---

[44] J. Boulton, 'The Meaner Sort: Labouring People and the Poor' in K. Wrightson ed. *A Social History of England 1500-1750* Cambridge: CUP, 2017, p.311.

[45] H.R. French, *The Middle Sort of People in Provincial England 1600-1750* Oxford: OUP, 2007.

[46] K. Sneath, 'Consumption, wealth, indebtedness and social structure in early modern England', University of Cambridge, 2009 (doctoral thesis). https://doi.org/10.17863/CAM.16041. J. Sear and K. Sneath, *The Origins of The 'Consumer Revolution'* ((forthcoming).

very similar assets to labourers and had more in common with them than yeomen with larger farms.

During the period covered by this volume the structure of English society was changing in several ways. Urbanisation was expanding and new workers of the growing population of the eighteenth century were increasingly employed in the secondary and tertiary sectors in towns and cities rather than villages.[47] These changes were not entirely absent, even in a rural 'lost shire' like Huntingdonshire. The changing social composition of Huntingdonshire inventories is set out in Table 5. The striking column is the last one, the increasing percentage of inventories relating to tradesmen and craftsmen. By the mid-seventeenth century, two fifths of the inventoried population were tradesmen and craftsmen and they were the majority by the second half of the eighteenth century. It is important to remember that this is not the whole population of the county, which had large numbers of labourers, cottagers and paupers without inventories. Changes were afoot even though Huntingdonshire remained a largely agricultural county.

TABLE 5: SOCIAL STRUCTURE FROM HUNTINGDONSHIRE PROBATE INVENTORIES: CHANGE OVER TIME								
	Gentry	Yeomen	Husbandmen	Labs	Spinsters	Widows	Sub Total	Tradesmen
	%	%	%	%	%	%	%	%
1600-49	6.3	11.8	6.9	18.1	1.4	23.6	**68.1**	31.9
1650-99	4.4	16.4	6.3	9.4	1.3	21.7	**59.5**	40.5
1700-49	4.1	18.9	5.4	8.1	1.1	19.2	**56.8**	43.2
1750-1800	2.2	29.0	2.2	0.7	1.4	10.9	**46.4**	53.6

Conclusions

The analysis found in this chapter provides little support for Marxist interpretations of social structure. If wealth is considered an important determinant of social status, then there were many gradations within social groups. Each rank and occupation represented a wide range of people and changing circumstances meant that it was possible to rise and fall within society. Furthermore, structural changes within society were profound and could be detected even within parts of the country which remained largely agricultural.

---

[47] L. Shaw-Taylor 'The occupational structure of England and Wales, 1600-1911' Economic History Society Conference, University of London, 2017, p.377.

Whilst tradesmen and craftsmen were an increasing percentage of the male workforce, it is important to remember that as chapter 4 shows, by-employment was widespread. Most tradesmen and craftsmen did not simply practice their trade but spent a significant proportion of their time engaged in agriculture. In some inventories, engagement by tradesmen with agriculture was so great that it brings into question whether their designated trade was their principal employment. An important factor in moveable wealth was the extent to which agriculture was practised. This was also true for inventoried agricultural labourers who owned cows, pigs and sheep. Animals and crops could represent a substantial part of a person's moveable assets. These agricultural assets were the reason why yeomen and husbandmen inventories exceeded the value of those of emerging groups of craftsmen and tradesmen that Lorna Weatherill considered to be of higher status.

3

POLITICS OF THE PARISH

Evelyn Lord

1684 was the year of the great drought. Following a hard winter, a warm dry spring led onto an extremely hot and dry summer. On 10th August 1684 John Evelyn's diary entry described the weather 'as such a drought no man living had experienced', and on 24th August 1684 'It was most excessively hot: we not having above one or two considerable showers (and those storms) these eight or nine months, so trees have lost their leaves like winter, and many quite died for want of refreshment.'[1]

In the East of England fen blows turned day into night with dust storms which coated the world with black particles, so that trees, houses and people looked as if they were in mourning. The dykes and ditches dried up, leaving a crazy pavement of cracks. Water retreated from the Fen meres, fish died struggling for breath, water fowl from starvation.[2]

At Great Gransden in the south of Huntingdonshire the grass turned yellow, withered and died, and the brooks crossing the parish became trickles and then puddles. There was no grazing for livestock, and no possibility of turning cattle and sheep onto the fallow Lammas land after Lammas Day, (August 1st). Angry voices began to be raised. Some were accused of sneaking their cattle on to pastures which were not theirs. Others threatened litigation.[3]

The harmony of the parish was disrupted and in order to solve the problem a parish meeting was held on 16th September 1684. This resulted in an agreement which was copied into the constables' accounts, the churchwardens' book, and the Overseers of the Poor accounts, and is a prime example of the politics of the parish working towards a negotiated settlement instead of direct or violent action.[4]

---

[1] E.S. De Beer ed. *The Diary of John Evelyn*, Vol. IV 1673-1689, Oxford: Clarendon Press, 2000, pp.379, 384, 385.

[2] Fen blows are still a feature of the fenland landscape in a hot dry summer.

[3] HA HP 36/9/1 Great Gransden Constables' Accounts.

[4] HA HP 36/9/1; HA HP 36/5/1 Great Gransden Churchwardens' Book, HA HP 36/5/1 Great Gransden Overseers of the Poor Accounts.

Great Gransden is a parish of about 3400 acres, 10 miles south of Hunting-don. The soil is clay and lower greensand, and in the seventeenth-century it was farmed as open field arable and pasture. The 1674 hearth tax assessment records 73 householders, so probably a population of about 330 persons. Although there were some enclosed closes, enclosure of the open fields only took place in the nineteenth century. Six brooks crossed the parish, with Home Dole Brook forming the boundary between Little and Great Gransden. In the late-seventeenth century the houses occupied an irregular four sided site, with the church and a new brick vicarage in the north west of the village.[5] The 1664 hearth tax assessment shows that these householders were mostly living in modest dwellings with one or two hearths, and 30 percent of the occupants were exempted from paying the tax.[6] The larger houses in the village were Ripponden Manor purchased by Sir Charles Casear in 1631 and Gransden Hall owned by Simon Mason, a barrister and the principal land owner in the parish. The vicar in 1684 was Barnabus Oley a well known Royalist supporter, ejected from the parish in 1644, but returned after the Restoration. The landscape of the village was completed by two windmills and Baldwin's Manor.

The Politics of the Parish

Since Patrick Collinson's professorial inaugural lecture *De Republica Anglorum,* which aimed to put the politics back into social history, and asked the question 'Did the peasants have politics?' this theme has been explored in depth by social historians.[7] Collinson's definition of politics was not the politics of faction, political parties and national government, but as part of a thick narrative which explored the depths of social life as demonstrated in the self-governing village with local officers responsible for the more mundane functions of government, including the preservation of peace and law enforcement.[8]

Collinson's question was taken up by Keith Wrightson, who saw the need to broaden the definition of politics to include the social distribution of

---

[5] W. Page, G. Proby, & S. Inskipp Ladds eds, *The Victoria History of the Counties of England, Huntingdonshire,* London: Institute of Historical Research, Dawson Reprint, 1974, Volume 2, pp.296-302.

[6] TNA E 179/122/226

[7] P. Collinson, *De Republica Anglorum'* in P. Collinson, *Elizabethan Essays*, Basingstoke: The Hambledon Press, 1994, pp.1-29. Collinson used local examples to illustrate his lecture, but it is doubtful if he would have described himself as a local historian.

[8] Collinson, pp.11,12.

power and its processes. In Wrightson's view the politics of the parish were defined by a process of inclusion and exclusion, dispute and resolution, public presentments and private litigation. A duality of opposites powerful and powerless, and the elite and the plebeian.[9] The latter were the concern of Andy Wood's work on the lead miners of Derbyshire which examined the clash between the elite and the plebeian in the context of the ownership of resources in a world divided by hierarchy. [10]

Many case studies examining the politics of the parish concentrated on enclosure, where disputes could result either in violence and fences torn down, or negotiated agreements. Steve Hindle's work on the Caddington Common enclosure dispute looked at the social profile of the opponents to enclosure, entering into the thick narrative of the dispute. Hindle saw the opposition 'as part of the idiom of popular notions of justice and social responsibility.'[11]

By 2011 M. Clarke re-examined the case studies on enclosure riots and the personnel involved and suggested that focussing on the riots and the personnel involved could be misleading 'as it is based on the generalised conclusion of specific local or regional case studies. No two farming regions are the same.' This paper argued that going to court was not separate from local negotiations over land use, which could bring different sections of the community into alliance.[12]

Negotiation was indeed one of the features of Collinson's lecture. One of his examples was of a town meeting held in Swallowfield, Berkshire in 1596, where it was agreed to hold regular meetings 'to the end that we may better and more quietly live together in good love and unity.[13]

Swallowfield and the Great Gransden agreement were part of the politics of the parish with parishioners working towards the harmony of the community

---

[9] K. Wrightson 'The Politics of the Parish in Early Modern England' in A. Fox & S. Hindle eds., *The Experience of Authority on Early Modern England*, Basingstoke: Macmillan, 1996, pp 11-13, 19, 22,25,31
[10] A. Wood, *The Politics of Social Conflict. The Peak Country 1520-1700*, Cambridge: CUP 1999, p.5; A. Wood 'Plebian, Languages and Defiance in England c. 1520-1640' in T. Harris ed *The Politics of the Excluded*, London: Palgrave, 2001, pp.67-98.
[11] S. Hindle 'Persuasion and Protest in the Caddington Common Enclosure Dispute 1635-1639' *Past and Present* 185, Feb. 1998, pp.37-78.
[12] M. Clark, 'The gentry, the commons and the politics of common right c 1558-1603' *The Historical Journal*, Vol. 54:3, Sept., 2011, pp.609-630.
[13] Collinson, p.23.

and the preservation of the peace for the present and the future. Great Gransden's agreement states 'Therefore we do all of us by a general consent of the whole parish being willing to a certainty to make an End to all controversies and misunderstandings now started amongst us.'[14]

The Agreement

The reason for the parish meeting was made explicit in the preamble to the agreement 'Concerning Commons and the Lammas Meadows. And we are fearful if we do not nip it in the bud, but suffer it to be a Law Suit; it may in all probability breed ill blood in our veins; which might cause future Disturbances and Quarrels between us and our posterity.' This was to be an agreement for the present and future. This is clear from its closing phrases. 'And we do order William Lucas the church clerk to order this Parish Agreement verbatim into those parish books which are usually kept by our Constables, churchwardens and overseers of the poor: that all our children and successors may know of this amicable agreement, in order for the future good of our parish & c.[15]

This means that the agreement as a source is a copy of an original, and the signatures to the agreement is a list of names rather than actual signatures. Who or what is missing can only be checked against the now lost original document. However, the copies in the constables', churchwardens' and overseers' books match, and are true copies of each other if not of the original.[16] We do not know who drafted the agreement, perhaps Charles Caesar, or Barnabus Oley. Neither do we know what happened at the meeting, if the points made in the agreement were discussed, and whether the final version was read out so that all present at the meeting could hear and understand what it contained, or if documentary sources were consulted by the meeting to verify what the agreement contained. The possibility that either a manorial custumal, by-laws or the memory of the older generation in the parish is there in the agreement as it accepts that this is 'altering customs hitherto used.'

'We do Declare that this shall be our custom and usage for the future in our Lammas meadows that we will endeavour to get our grass-mowed & our Hay made and carted away: if the weather permit us before Lammas-day comes which is the first day of August, every year. But if we are Hindered by wet weather, we will not take any advantage to spoil another man's grass

---

[14] HA HP36/9/1
[15] HA HP 36/9/1
[16] HA HP 36/12/1 Overseers of the Poor Accounts, Great Gransden. The agreement is on page 169.

for by Reason that the meadows are not cleared by the ancient Records, writing & custom of this parish: they ought to have been; But we will patiently stay for Our Commons until the Hay is all carried out of the Lammas meadow. And if the Summer proves very dry & Hot as it did this present Summer 1684 That if Burnt & wasted that little grass we had that if forced us to mow before Lammas Day, then in that case we do all promise and agree Like Loving neighbours that every person may feed his own Rowen or Eddish grass until the Twentieth Day of July and no longer: for upon that day yearly henceforward it should be Lawful for the Herdman or his Deputy if the Hay be all gone; or room enough for pasture an keep on the Common a Herd of Cattle:'[17]

The text in the body of the agreement reveals several important features. First, it is pragmatic and covers two eventualities which might hinder hay making and prevent livestock being turned out onto the Lammas land; extremely wet weather or extremely hot weather as being experienced in 1684. Second that the parish meeting had access to ancient records and writings that created the custom of Lammas grazing, and that the word 'Lawful' as applied to the herd man refers to this custom and perhaps a manorial by-law. Third the phrase 'every person may feed his own Rowen or Eddish grass until the Twentieth Day of July' contains two archaic words, 'rowen' is a dialect word for 'after-grass', that left over after hay-making, and eddish comes from the Anglo-Saxon *ediac* enclosure or pasture.[18] The agreement then contains a list of names, who were presumably those who signed the original; the first names are Charles Caesar, Esquire, Barnabus Oley vicar, Charles Griffin gentleman, and John Basse gentleman, followed by another 55 names.

The Lammas lands can be identified as the church ground, which was usually leased out from April to Lammas Day, Hoback Meadow lying beyond the road to St Ives leased out for the same period, Lammas meadow abutting Abbotsley Brook, the Little Baulk abutting Abax meadow, The Huns in Long Meadow, and Hobby Land and Henshall on Moor Common. As well as glebe lands belonging to the vicarage. A terrier of the glebe was pasted into the parish register between the years 1674 and 1676, so was almost contemporary with the agreement. It amounted to 130 acres in Manden, Middle and Moorfields.

---

[17] HA HP 36/9/1

[18] J.O. Halliwell *Dictionary of Archaic Words,* London: Bracken Books 1850, facsimile ed., 1989, p. 695, Halliwell gives Suffolk dialect as his source: H. Sweet, *The Student's Dictionary of Anglo-Saxon*, Oxford: Clarendon Press, 1991, p.49.

The politics of the parish: Inclusive or Exclusive?

There were 59 names on the agreement, but the 1674 hearth tax assessment lists 73 households[19]; so clearly there is a mismatch between the two lists. However, the preamble to the agreement emphasises its inclusivity '…we do *all* of us by the *general consent* of the parish… '(my italics). It is possible that the number of households had decreased in the decade between 1674 and 1684, but another source shows this was not the case. A constable's rate taken in February 1683/4 lists 59 rate-payers, but 24 of these were not on the agreement. This suggests that there were at least 82 households in the parish in 1684 a figure which almost coincides with the figure of 85 families given in a visitation of 1709[20]; 31 percent of rate-payers present in the parish in 1684 were not party to the agreement. Here is an example of Wrightson's definition of parish politics being part of the inclusion and exclusion in the social distribution of power.[21]

Setting the rate itself is another example of parish politics at work. 'A Rate for the Constables made by the *Consent of the Parishioners* of Gransden at six shilling per plow and 1s 6d a cottager…'. The definition of who is to pay the rate confines this to two groups who are landholders. Cottagers probably had 4-5 acres of land, perhaps attached to their dwelling by ancient custom. Plough lands were a variable unit of land measurement, but tilled arable rather than grazing.[22]

The Included

Those who stood to gain most from the agreement were land owners or tenants with Lammas grazing rights. Details of 38 individuals who signed the agreement have been traced; of these ten did not pay cadastral rates so were not in possession of agricultural land as listed in the rate book, but some were listed on the 1674 hearth tax assessment. They included James and Widow Barwick who were exempt from paying the hearth tax and assessed at one hearth each, George Brewer a carpenter and Thomas Ibbitt were also exempted in 1674 with one hearth each, but both paid the rate in 1684. Edmund Easy and Henry Stiles exempt in 1674 signed the agreement but did not pay rates. John Read also exempt in 1674 signed the agreement and paid the rate.

---

[19] TNA E 179/122/226
[20] J. Broad, *Bishop Wake's Summary of Visitation Returns for the Diocese of Lincoln 1706-1715,* London: The British Academy Records of Economic and Social History, New Series 50, 2012, pp.535, 536.
[21] Wrightson pp.11-13.
[22] S. Coleman & J. Wood, *Historic Landscape and Archaeology Glossary of Terms* Bedfordshire County Council, 1988 rev.ed., pp. 19, 47.

Thirteen of those signing and paying the rate paid for plough-lands and a further 13 paid as cottagers. Occupations have been traced for 24 of those who signed the agreement and paid the rates. Eight of these were directly engaged in agriculture; 6 yeomen, 1 husbandman and 1 shepherd. The remainder were craftsmen or tradesmen including 2 shoemakers, 2 carpenters, 2 grocers, and one blacksmith, fuller and parish clerk, 5 labourers as well as 3 gentlemen and Barnabas Oley the vicar.

Many of those who signed the agreement served as parish officers. Between 1670 and 1705 eleven were churchwardens, seven of whom were also constables, plus another eight who were constables during that period. This shows that 19 or 33 percent of those who signed the agreement were actively involved in parish governance.

The Excluded

The details of 15 persons who paid the constables' rate but did not sign the agreement have been traced. Only one was directly involved in agriculture, a husbandman; other occupations of those who paid the rate but did not sign the agreement included a tailor, a collarmaker, a miller and one gentleman. Three of the excluded paid on plough-lands, the rest were cottagers. Only 4 can be identified on the 1674 hearth tax assessment two with 1 hearth (but no exemptions) and 2 with 2 hearths.

The first references in the parish register for others who paid the rate is 1684, and for some it is their marriages which appear from 1684 onwards. There is one exception to this John Gregory who was assessed for one hearth in 1674. In the rate book he is described as Mr Mason's tenant. The combination of the rate book and the agreement suggests a divide between those with Lammas grazing and those without; those without being relative newcomers to the parish living in houses which were not customarily endowed with grazing rights.

It is in the distribution of parish officers that the major difference between the included and the excluded occurs. Between 1670 and 1689 10 of the excluded were constables, but only 2 served as churchwardens, one serving both as constable and churchwarden. Was this because they were relative newcomers to the parish, or is this what Wrightson and Levine refer to as the hierarchy of parish offices, with the most prestigious post being that of the churchwarden which went to the wealthier occupiers of the parish, while the humbler office of the constable went to husbandmen and more modest craftsmen.[23] It is also possible that the position of Overseer of the Poor was

---

[23] Wrightson & Levine, p.104.

also seen as a more prestigious office as between 1670-1689 only 4 who were in the rate book but did not sign the agreement served as Overseers of the Poor, compared to 24 who had signed the agreement and were in the rate book, and two who had signed the agreement but were not in the rate book. The evidence is that those excluded from the agreement were from the more modest section of the parish and that power through parish offices was vested in the wealthier.

Included or Excluded? Family and Kinship Links

Under-pinning the social system of Great Gransden were core families, linked by marriage or blood. David Hey was one of the first local historians to refer to these as core families, but Alan Everett working on Kent described them as 'dynastic families' who helped to produce a sense of loyalty and stability to a parish. More recently Alan Fox working on Leicestershire and Lincolnshire also refers to these families as 'dynastic', and suggests that in Leicestershire dynastic families were likely to be yeomen or graziers, while Anne Mitson working on south west Nottinghamshire shows that the wealthier families were like to form core or dynastic families. [24] The word dynastic implies longevity and a vertical progression of family and kin links over time, and it is likely that farming families with an investment in land are the most stable in a rural community. The relationship links discussed here are those around the time of the 1684 agreement, extended from 1660 to 1720, remembering that those who signed had the right to Lammas grazing in common.[25]

Two family groups contained links by marriage and blood only with those who signed the agreement, so it might be posited that they were of the same status in the parish; these were the Aires and Pedley families, and in turn they were related to a group of four families who all signed the agreement, Gray, Elwood, Kidman and Tomes families. However, the Kidmans were a long-established family who first appear in the parish register in 1541, and with at least eight different branches in Great Gransden during the 1680s.

---

[24] D. Hey, *An English rural community. Myddle under the Tudors and Stuarts,* Leicester: Leicester University Press, 1974; A Everett, *Landscape and Community,* London: Hambledon Press, 1985, pp.8, 320; A. Fox, *A Lost Frontier Revealed,* Hatfield: University of Hertfordshire Press, 2009, pp.138-140; A. Mitson, 'The Significance of Kinship Networks in the Seventeenth Century: South West Nottinghamshire' in C.V. Phythian-Adams ed., *Societies, Culture and kingship 1580-1850,* Leicester: Leicester University Press, 1993, pp.24-76

[25] Source for these relationships is the Great Gransden Parish Register, HA HP 36/1/1.

Their occupations varied from 3 yeomen, 6 weavers, 2 butchers, 3 shoemakers, and 1 each labourer, ale man and ale wife and Hayward. They are what Wrightson and Levine describe as a 'settled generation with at least three generations in the parish'.[26] The Kidman family was firmly embedded in parish life, and the Kidman marriage pattern in the 1680s shows an interesting recurring choice of partners with two marriages with the Tomes family and two with the Grays.

Another long-lived family were the Elwoods, who can be traced from the 1630s onwards. Edward Elwood who signed the agreement was related by marriage to other signees the Mumfords and the Tassells. Timothy Elwood whose relationship to Edward is not known did not sign the agreement but was part of at least two generations in Great Gransden. Timothy the elder died in 1684, Timothy the younger a carpenter married Elizabeth Kettle a member of a family which by 1700 achieved gentry status, and their son Charles married Elizabeth Tassell in 1724 thus taking the link between the Elwoods and the Tassells into another generation and another century.

Thomas Ingrey who did not sign the agreement was related by marriage and blood to the Livett, Graves and Safford families who did. Robert Graves senior was a yeoman described by the eighteenth century as a farmer and grocer. The Graves were a dynastic family with links going back to 1540. The Saffords were husbandmen who appear in the registers from 1618 onwards, but it is with the Livett family where social mobility can be traced from 1684 to the early eighteenth century. Nicholas Livett a yeoman was assessed on 3 hearths in 1674, signed the agreement and paid the rate as a cottager. He was the son of William Livett, yeoman buried in 1679. Nicholas junior married Avery (surname unknown) in 1683/4 and in 1698 is described as a gentleman. Their son Andrew baptised in 1684/5 is also described as a gentleman and a maltster in 1709. Neither Nicholas nor Andrew are included in Gregory King's 1683 extract of the Lady Day hearth tax assessment for Huntingdonshire created with the purpose of identifying potential armigerous gentry, although a Thomas Redman with 5 hearths is included. Redman could be a mistake for Kidman as Thomas Kidman junior was assessed with 5 hearths in 1674.[27]

In Terling, Essex, Wrightson and Levine worked out that of the 122 families in the parish in the 1670s and 80s between 39 and 53 percent were related to other families.[28] In 1684 there were at least 82 families in Great Gransden.

---

[26] Wrightson & Levine, p.82.
[27] College of Arms, Visitation Papers, Huntingdonshire 1683/1684; TNA 179/249/2
[28] Wrightson & Levine p.85.

Fifteen were part of a wider kinship network, 18 percent of the whole. Of this fifteen all but two had signed the agreement, which points towards a parish oligarchy with a shared identity of mutual benefit.

The Politics of the Parish: Centre and Locality

The parish was a unique unit, but it was part of the wider world, and much of what appears to be part of the politics of the parish was imposed on it from central government. For example, the 1555 Statute on Highways decreed that the constables and churchwardens of every parish were required to hold a meeting on the Tuesday or Wednesday of Easter week to elect two honest people as surveyors of the highways. Or the 1601 Poor Law Act stated that the churchwardens of every parish and 2 to 4 substantial householders were to be nominated and called 'overseers of the poor.' The 1662 Act for the Better Relief of the Poor usually known as the Settlement Act set up the legal machinery for relieving those with legal settlement in a parish and removing those who did not, and the 1662/63 Act on Vagrancy set up a rate to be levied on every inhabitant in a parish to raise funds to reimburse constables when payments to vagrants were made. Other statutes set up the local machinery for local assessments and collections of national taxes, such as the Hearth Tax.[29]

What made the 1684 agreement different is that it was not made as part of an obligation to central government, but in response to local conditions. Although the impetus for the meeting on the problem caused by the drought might have been embedded in manorial or parochial custom it shows that one or several parishioners could recognise that discontent over the lack of grazing had the potential for litigation or at the worst violence.

Who might have arranged and organised the meeting? Was it the result of consultation by the first three signatures on the agreement; Charles Caesar Esq., Barnabus Oley the vicar, and John Basse gentlemen? One name stands out, someone whose life-experience would have taught him the mortal danger of dissension and disagreement in the community, Barnabus Oley the vicar of Great Gransden, fellow of Clare College, Cambridge and in the

---

[29] *The Complete Parish Officer*, Devizes: Wiltshire Family History Society, facsimile edition 1999, p. 37; A.E. Bland, P.A. Brown and R.H. Tawney, *English Economic History Select Documents*, London: G. Bell & Sons, 1925, pp.380, 647,648; M. Brayshay, *Land Travel and Communication in Tudor and Stuart England*, Liverpool: Liverpool University Press, 2014, pp. 32; E. Lord, K. Sneath & L. Ford, *The Huntingdonshire Hearth Taxes* : London & Cambridge, British Record Society and Cambridgeshire Records Society, forthcoming.

1640s an ardent Royalist marooned in a Parliamentarian enclave. When civil war seemed imminent Oley collected money and university plate to send to the king. His wagon train was ambushed by Oliver Cromwell and his brother in law Valentine Wharton and the goods seized for Parliament. In April 1644 Oley was ejected from his living and spent the next 18 years wandering around England. In July 1660 he was restored to his fellowship and to the living of Great Gransden, and he became a benefactor to the parish, endowing a school and alms houses, and rebuilding the vicarage. He died in February 1686/7.at the age of 85.[30]

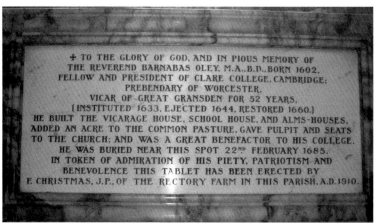

Figure 3.1 Memorial to Barnabas Oley Great Gransden Church

Change in the Parish

The agreement changed local custom and the usage of land for the future; whether it worked or not is not revealed in the sources. By the first decades of the eighteenth century although the population of the parish did not increase, its optimum number recorded as 85 families in 1709[31], the way in which land was allocated did. This is evident from the parish register where the occupation 'farmer' appears from 1714 onwards. The original meaning of the word 'farmer' was someone who collected taxes and revenues paying a fixed sum for a share of the proceeds. Thus in the hearth tax 'farmers' took over the collection of the tax from 1666-1669 and 1674-1689.[32] However, by

---

[30] H.C. Matthew & B. Harrison, *Oxford Dictionary of National Biography,* Oxford OUP, 2004, Vol.41 pp.716-718.

[31] J. Broad, ed., *Bishop Wake's Summary of Visitation Returns for the Diocese of Lincoln, 1706-1715, Part 2,* London: The British Academy, Records of Social and Economic History, New Series 50, 2012, pp. 535,536.

[32] Huntingdonshire Hearth Tax forthcoming.

the late seventeenth century the word 'farmer' in common usage meant someone who rented land and cultivated it, a 'tenant farmer'.[33]

Between 1714 and 1725 ten 'farmers' appear in the parish registers. Two of these had formerly been listed as husbandmen, John Rowning and Humphrey Curtis. One of the remainder shares a surname, Dixey, with a family which had been in the parish since 1548, but no descent line can be traced, and the first mention of in the parish register of this branch is a marriage in 1723, similarly the surname Lane was recorded in the parish register since a marriage in 1627, but again no lineal descent can be traced with John Lane farmer who buried a child in 1725. Mr Philip Chapman farmer first appears in the register in 1719, William Stoughton in 1717, Robert Smith junior in 1722, and Henry Warboise in 1625. James Graves who also appears in 1725 was almost certainly a member of the core family, and Henry Warboise may have been related to Richard Warboys parish constable in 1683.

Conclusion

The 1684 agreement at Great Gransden is a good example of the politics of the parish working towards negotiation and halting litigation and riot in its tracks. It was made for the good of the parish in the present and for the future. However, it also illustrates division in the parish between those whose names were on the agreement, and those who were not who appear in the sources to be of equal status until the lists of churchwardens suggests otherwise.

What is revealed in tracing the individuals, included in the agreement or excluded is that even in solely agricultural county such as Huntingdonshire, as will also be shown in the next chapter on agriculture in this book, agriculture was the by-employment of many tradesmen, and that the grazing on the Lammas lands which the agreement is about was an important accessory to their livelihoods. It is also clear that the parish supported a number of 'dynastic' or 'core' families who were recorded in the parish from the 1540s onwards, and perhaps they rather than the parish gentry, were the parish elite holding parish officers, and involved in the day to day governance of the parish and its finances. They were elected/selected for office at parish meetings, and it could be suggested that the early modern parish represented embryonic democracy and governance and that in reply to Collinson's questions, yes the peasants did have politics.

---

[33] J.A. Simpson & E.S.C. Wheeler eds., *Oxford English Dictionary,* Oxford: Clarendon Press, 1989, Vol. V. p.734.

4

FEEDING THE PEOPLE

Ken Sneath

During the early modern period and beyond, English agriculture went through a period of great institutional and technological change. Total farm acreage for both arable and pastoral farming increased. Craig Muldrew estimated that in England, arable acreage increased from 8 to 9 million acres between 1600 and 1700 and pastoral acreage rose from 10 million acres in the early seventeenth century to 12 million acres by the end of the century.[1] Farming started to develop along capitalist lines as small family farms began to be replaced by much larger farms which were more efficient and produced large surpluses for the market. Increasingly, farmers employed wage labourers rather than family members to carry out agricultural tasks. Technological change led to substantial improvements in the efficiency of labour. The rising productivity of the agricultural workforce was achieved by producing far more food with roughly the same number of workers. Urbanisation began to expand as most workers of the growing population of the eighteenth century were employed in the secondary and tertiary sectors in towns and cities rather than villages. Consequently, the *percentage* of workers employed in the primary sector fell significantly although absolute numbers did not. Finally, the process of enclosure continued during the early modern period and was largely completed by Parliamentary enclosure in the late eighteenth and early nineteenth centuries.[2] Total factor productivity increased, and the growing population was fed largely through home production.[3] Together these changes are called an 'agricultural revolution'.[4]

---

[1] C. Muldrew, *Food, Energy and the Creation of Industriousness* Cambridge: CUP, 2011, pp.142-3.

[2] J.R. Wordie The Chronology of English Enclosure 1500-1914 *Economic History Review,* 2nd Series Vol. XXXVI no. 4 1983, 483-505.

[3] J. Burnette, 'Agriculture 1700-1870' in R. Floud, J. Humphries and P. Johnson (eds.), *The Cambridge Economic History of Modern Britain Vol. 1* Cambridge: CUP, 2014, pp.108-113.

[4] M. Overton, *Agricultural Revolution in England* Cambridge: CUP, 1996.

Many of these trends can also be seen in Huntingdonshire. Farm acreage increased substantially following the drainage of the Fenland by the Earl of Bedford and the 'adventurers'. Piecemeal encroachment onto common land was occurring in parishes such as Steeple Gidding and Hamerton.[5] By 1587, the whole of Great Gidding was owned by the Watsons of Rockingham. A map of the manor of Great Gidding for 1641 depicts the village which comprised the enclosed Grove Field used for pasture, 40 closes (enclosed areas of pasture for sheep and cows) and three open fields farmed by tenants. During the seventeenth century, the principal tenant farmers gradually took over many smaller farms. A comparison of farm sizes between 1599 and 1720 showed the increase in larger farms of over 100 acres, from one in 1599 to five in 1720.[6] In St Ives, substantial enclosure took place during the seventeenth century and farms were amalgamated into bigger units. The survey of St Ives by Edmund Pettis, the land assessor, provided details of the common fields, meadow and closes. Analysis of these records by Mary Carter revealed polarisation of land holdings and decline in the number of small farmers who were unable to compete with the growing commercialisation of larger landowners.[7]

Whilst most economic historians concur that an agricultural revolution took place in England, there is little agreement about precisely when it took place, other than it was between 1550 and 1880! These extreme positions were argued by Eric Kerridge who suggested the period 1570-1673, whilst Turner, Becket and Afton argued for the years 1800 to 1850.[8] Robert Allen embraced the entire period and suggested no less than three periods: a Yeoman's Revolution (1520-1739) leading to a doubling in corn yields; followed by a pause between 1740 and 1800 when output grew just 10 percent and finally a Landlord's Revolution during the period 1800-50, which led to a 65 percent increase in the productivity of agriculture.[9] Clearly, in considering agriculture we are entering into a highly controversial arena. The research on which these varying interpretations were given was often based on a limited area of the country. Susanna Wade Martins pointed out that Allen and Kerridge's

---

[5] M. Wickes, *A History of Huntingdonshire* Chichester: Phillimore, 1985, p.68.
[6] P. Ellis and D. Shepherd, *A Millennium History of Great Gidding* Great Gidding: Great Gidding and Little Gidding Parish Council, 2001, pp.45-55. In addition to Grove Field (now Gidding Grove farm) of about 360 acres.
[7] M. Carter ed., *Edmund Pettis' Survey of St Ives, 1728* Cambridge: Cambridgeshire Records Society, 2002, pp.43-57.
[8] E. Kerridge, *The Agricultural Revolution* London: Allen and Unwin, 1967; M. Turner, J. Beckett and B. Afton, *Farm Production in England, 1700-1914* Oxford: OUP, 2001.
[9] R. Allen, *Enclosure and the Yeoman* Oxford: Clarendon Press, 1992.

revolutions were set in the Midland plain and the light chalk sheeplands of the south, so the issue of representativeness looms large.[10]

This chapter considers the extent to which analysis of Huntingdonshire records can shed light on agricultural change in the later seventeenth and early eighteenth centuries. During the early modern period, Huntingdonshire was primarily a rural county with a few small market towns. It was one of the smallest English counties with only Rutland having a smaller population. Agriculture was the single most important production activity of households and the biggest sector of its economy. As well as producing food for the local population, Huntingdonshire's proximity to London meant that the county contributed to feeding the expanding population of the capital. It was also part of a wider network of supply. Stephen Porter found that most sheep and cattle fattened in the county had been bred elsewhere. Some 200,000 head of cattle entered Huntingdonshire along the 'Bullock Road'. Many were headed for the weekly markets and regular fairs at St Ives.[11]

Much of Huntingdonshire comprised clay uplands with heavy soil which had been converted to pasture in many western parishes. The shallow river valleys of the Nene and the Ouse, in the north and south respectively, were predominantly used for arable, with some dairying and rearing of livestock. Draining the fens in the north east of the county enabled an expansion of agriculture, particularly livestock farming.[12] Despite earlier piecemeal enclosures, 80 percent of settlements continued to be farmed as open fields, with 20 percent either fully or partly enclosed.[13] Substantial changes brought about by Parliamentary enclosure did not take place in the county until the second half of the eighteenth century; beginning with Folksworth in 1761.

Mark Overton painted a picture of the agricultural year. The arable year began after harvest in August or September with ploughing and harrowing. Winter cereals, wheat and rye, were sown in September or October. Spring crops, barley, oats, peas and beans were sown from late February to April. Winter grains were harvested before the spring crops and then the annual

---

[10] S. Wade Martins, *Farmers, Landlords and Landscapes* Macclesfield: Windgather Press, 2004, p.6.

[11] S. Porter, 'The Livestock Trade in Huntingdonshire, 1600-1750' in *Records of Huntingdonshire* 1982, Vol.2 p.15.

[12] K. Wrightson, *Earthly Necessities*, New Haven: Yale, 2000 p.161; T. Williamson, *The Transformation of Rural England: farming and the landscape 1700-1870* Exeter: University of Exeter Press, 2002, p.31.

[13] S. Porter, 'An Agricultural Geography of Huntingdonshire, 1610-1749', M. Litt. Cantab. 1973, p.47.

cycle began once more.[14] Wheat flour was used to make bread. Barley could also be used for bread but was more commonly turned into malt to brew ale or beer. Oats were primarily used to feed horses. Peas and beans were used as animal fodder but also consumed by humans. Hay was cut from meadows in summer and used as winter feed for animals. The pastoral year began with lambing and calving in the spring. Sheep were washed and clipped in June and the hay harvest was gathered. Bulls serviced cows and rams serviced ewes in September and October. Pastoral farming was less labour intensive and so by-employment was more commonly associated with pastoral farming, for dairy farmers had spare time for other activities between morning and evening milking.[15]

Historians are faced with major problems in trying to reconstruct and evaluate agriculture during the early modern period. The Board of Agriculture was not established until 1793 and many key records such as crop returns (1801), summaries of livestock kept and crops grown (1866), and census returns (1841) are not available to us. On the other hand, we have enclosure records, parish registers and most importantly probate inventories which provide significant insights into agriculture. Parish Registers cover the great majority of the population as there were relatively few nonconformists in our period. By contrast, probate records were restricted to more affluent members of society and thus do not provide information about approximately the lowest 40 percent of the social spectrum. However, unlike most counties, Huntingdonshire is fortunate in having very considerable numbers of inventories for labourers. This chapter is based on analysis of these records. About a third of the extant probate inventories for the county have been transcribed, including nearly all the labourers' inventories.

Analysis of data from parish registers indicates that the English population rose from 5.3 million in 1661 to 6.3 million in 1761, a rise of 20 percent.[16] Hearth Tax returns can also be used to calculate the population, by counting the number of households and using a multiplier for persons per household. Whilst Hearth Tax lists should record every household, those exempt from paying the tax and paupers were sometimes omitted. The estimated population for Huntingdonshire based on Hearth Tax returns was around 28,200 in 1674. By 1761, the population of the county was approximately 35,300, a rise

---

[14] Overton, *Agricultural Revolution in England*, pp.13-14.

[15] By-employment involves combining agriculture or animal husbandry (or both) with a trade or other occupation. Overton, *Agricultural Revolution in England*, p.18.

[16] E. Wrigley, R. Davies, J. Oeppen and R. Schofield, *English Population History from Family Reconstitution 1580-1837* Cambridge: CUP, 1997, p.614.

of 25 percent.[17] With the exception of items produced in warmer climates like sugar, tea and coffee, the increasing population was almost entirely fed from products of home soil at this time.[18] Rising demand for food was a powerful stimulus for agricultural change and more efficient production.

Parish marriage registers can shed light on agricultural specialism. Ann Kussmaul suggested that seasonal patterns of marriage were an indicator of economic activity. She argued that predominately arable parishes had a high proportion of autumn marriages following the harvest and predominately pastoral parishes had a high proportion of spring and early summer marriages, following lambing and calving. Marriages in parishes with high levels of rural industry had no distinct seasonal marriage patterns. An index number of 100 would indicate no seasonal marriage patterns. Using Kussmaul's methodology, marriage patterns in ten Huntingdonshire parishes, five rural and five with small market towns, were analysed for the period 1701-1725.[19] All selected parishes had marriage peaks in the autumn suggesting a predominance of arable farming over pastoral farming. In Abbots Ripton (227), Eynesbury (220) and Holywell (208), the autumn marriage index was more than double the random index number of 100. In Hemingford Grey, Farcet and Ramsey, marriage patterns peaked in both spring and autumn suggesting that the division between arable and pastoral was much more evenly balanced. (Figures 1 and 2)

---

[17] E. Wrigley, 'English County Populations in the later eighteenth century', *Economic History Review* Vol.60, 1, Feb 2007, p.54.
[18] E. Wrigley, *Energy and the English Industrial Revolution,* Cambridge: CUP, 2010 p.87. One problem in making this assessment is the difficulty of calculating food imports from Ireland.
[19] A. Kussmaul, *A general view of the rural economy*, Cambridge: CUP, 1993, pp.1-4 and 48-52.

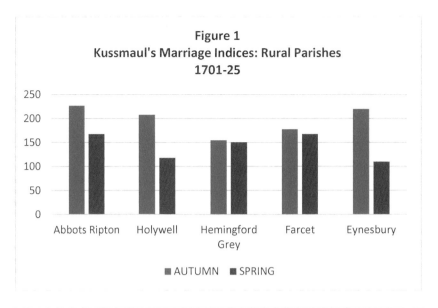

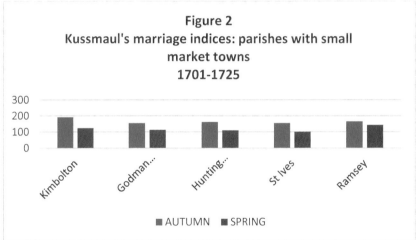

Comparison with Kussmaul's data set for this period suggested that the sampled Huntingdonshire parishes were much more strongly arable in character than Kussmaul's English parishes.[20] Whilst economic activity was not the only reason for seasonality in marriage patterns, the results were reasonably

---

[20] For the period 1701-40, Kussmaul had 531 parishes in observation, of which 136 were market towns and 395 were non-market towns. Only one, Great Stukeley, was from Huntingdonshire. Kussmaul's mean marriage index for non-market parishes was 134 in the autumn ad 140 on spring. For parishes with markets her mean indices were 141 in autumn and 116 for spring. Kussmaul, *A general view of the rural economy*, p.55.

consistent with inventory evidence. For the period 1660-1749, the ratio of the total value of crops to animals in Godmanchester was 62:38, in Kimbolton 45:55 and in Ramsey 29:71. So in fenland Ramsey livestock farming predominated but in Godmanchester arable took precedence. However, as we shall see, inventory evidence also showed that both arable and pastoral farming took place throughout the county and most farmers practiced mixed farming.

Establishing the percentage of the workforce employed in agriculture is a major exercise. Although it was not a legal requirement for fathers' occupations to be recorded in Anglican parish registers until 1813, many parish priests did so before that date.[21] However, when occupations were given they were not always consistently recorded over a sufficiently long period of time to create sequences of robust data. Furthermore, baptism registers only recorded baptisms of children in parish churches and groups such as nonconformists, Catholics and Jews were excluded.[22] If occupational structures of these other religious groups differed significantly from those of Anglicans, then occupational structures calculated from Anglican sources alone would not reflect those of the whole community. However, Bradley found that there was no significant difference between social structures of Anglicans and dissenters.[23] Furthermore, for most of the period covered by this study, non-Anglicans were not large in number. Nevertheless, problems remain. Fathers of baptised children would be biased by age and would not adequately represent occupations predominantly carried out by other age groups. For example, living-in servants rarely appeared in baptism registers as their terms of employment made it difficult for them to marry.[24] Finally, most fathers had more than one child baptised in the same parish over a period of years. Therefore, fathers recorded in baptism registers often represented the same person on more than one occasion. However, there is no reason to believe that certain occupations produced more fertile fathers than others.

---

[21] P. Glennie, *Distinguishing men's trades: occupational sources and debates for pre-census England* Bristol: Historical Geography Research Group, 1990, p.30.

[22] Nigel Yates suggested that in 1720 there were about 115,000 Catholics in England and Wales and nonconformists represented about 6 percent of the population. N. Yates, *Eighteenth-century Britain: religion and politics* Harlow: Pearson, 2008 pp.38 and 56.

[23] J.E. Bradley, *Religion, revolution and English radicalism* Cambridge: CUP, 1990, pp.63-9.

[24] M. Long, 'A study of occupations in Yorkshire parish registers in the eighteenth and early nineteenth centuries', *Local Population Studies,* 2003, Vol.71 p.16.

Leigh Shaw Taylor and Tony Wrigley reported an analysis based on more than a thousand baptism registers that recorded occupations of fathers during the years 1695 to 1729.[25] They found that only half of males (49.8 percent) were employed in the agricultural sector in England and Wales around 1710. Table 1 sets out results of occupational data from baptism registers for five parishes in Huntingdonshire where there was a run of occupational data for at least ten years supplied by the parish priest. Unfortunately, one cannot select a random sample of parishes or the dates for this exercise, as the historian is reliant upon the diligence of parish priests in recording data not expressly required. However, we have at least one representative parish from each of the three *pays* of the county: Ramsey in fenland, St Ives in the Ouse Valley and Broughton, Abbots Ripton and Toseland in the clay uplands. There is also a mix of more urban and rural parishes. Ramsey was a relatively large parish encompassing both a small town and rural areas and St Ives was rather more urban in character. Abbots Ripton, Toseland and Broughton were small rural parishes. Hearth Tax returns for 1674 suggested a population of around 1750 each for Ramsey and St Ives, around 200 for Broughton, and just over 100 each in Abbots Ripton and Toseland.[26] There were only a handful of baptisms a year in Toseland but fortunately a long run of occupational data. As a sample for Huntingdonshire, the five parishes are over representative of those living in market towns, and data for Ramsey is a century earlier than the other parishes. Nevertheless, it still provides some important insights.

---

[25] L. Shaw Taylor and E. Wrigley 'Occupational Structure and population change' in in R. Floud, J. Humphries and P. Johnson (eds.) *The Cambridge Economic History of Modern Britain Vol. 1 1700-1870* Cambridge: CUP, 2014, pp.58-61.

[26] M. Carter, 'Town or Urban Society? St Ives in Huntingdonshire 1630-1740 in C. Phythian-Adams ed. *Societies, Cultures and Kinship, 1580-1850* Leicester: Leicester University Press 1993, p.81.

TABLE 1: MALE OCCUPATIONAL STRUCTURE IN HUNTINGDONSHIRE											
	Inventories 1660-1749		Ramsey Baptisms 1617-1627		St Ives Baptisms 1706-1715		Abbots Ripton Baptisms 1701-1760		Broughton Baptisms 1719-1751		Toseland Baptisms 1702-1746	
	n	%	n	%	n	%	n	%	n	%	n	%
Gent	28	4	9	2	9	2	0	0	0	0	0	0
Profs	28	4	3	1	9	2	17	4	2	1	0	0
Yeomen	120	19	15	4	4	1	174	38	37	14	37	31
Trades	252	40	202	53	282	65	80	18	109	42	20	17
Husb'men	38	6	2	1	0	0	0	0	0	0	0	0
Labs	157	25	147	39	128	30	181	40	114	43	63	52
Totals	623	100	378	100	432	100	452	100	264	100	120	100
Other[27]	351											
Total	974											

Results for St Ives and for even earlier in Ramsey are consistent with Shaw Taylor and Wrigley's data, which indicated a shift from agriculture towards secondary sector employment at a relatively early date. By contrast, the small rural parish of Toseland had quite different results with relatively few tradesmen and 83 percent of fathers working in the agricultural sector.

Perhaps the biggest problem in assessing employment in the primary sector is how to deal with by-employment. Joan Thirsk and Mark Overton *et al.* argue that by-employment was widespread in early modern England.[28] On the other hand, Leigh Shaw Taylor and Sebastian Keibeck suggested that probate inventory evidence overstated the incidence of by-employment amongst farmers and rural manufacturers by a factor of two or three, because males who were by-employed were more likely to be probated because of

---

[27] Widows, spinsters, unknown occupation.

[28] J. Thirsk, 'The Fantastical Folly of Fashion', in J. Thirsk, *The Rural Economy of England: Collected Essays* London: Hambledon, 2003 pp.211, 247-8; M. Overton, J. Whittle, D. Dean, and A. Hann, *Production and Consumption in English Households* Abingdon: Routledge, 2004, p.66.

their additional material wealth.[29] In Huntingdonshire, by-employment reached very high levels amongst the inventoried population. For example, in Ramsey, for the years 1660 to 1749, there was little difference between those designated professionals and tradesmen, of whom 59 percent had crops and animals recorded in their inventories, and all male inventories, of which two thirds (67 percent) recorded crops or animals in their inventories.

Despite obvious limitations of the data, Table 1 also provides some insight into the extent of bias of the selected sample of probate inventories for the years 1660-1749. Nearly all extant labourers' inventories in Huntingdonshire have been deliberately included in the sample. The remaining inventories come from twenty parishes representing both a few parishes with small towns and the remainder being rural parishes. Inventory data can never be representative of the population as a whole because of its under representation of labourers. Data from baptism registers help us to more precisely measure the scale of this bias. In rural parishes, the selected sample for the county had only approaching half the percentage of labourers in the whole community. In small market towns, the social mix was quite different, and most fathers were tradesmen.

ANALYSIS OF THE INVENTORIES

Occupational descriptors recorded in probate inventories are problematic. The four agricultural ranks, gentry, yeomen, husbandmen and labourers each included a broad variety of people. This is explored in much greater depth in chapter 2. Inventory values for agricultural ranks are set out in Figure 3.

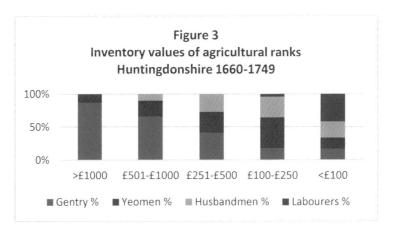

Figure 3
Inventory values of agricultural ranks
Huntingdonshire 1660-1749

[29] S. Keibek and L. Shaw-Taylor, 'Early modern rural by-employments: a re-examination of the probate inventory evidence', *Agricultural History Review*, 61 2013, p.27; Shaw Taylor and Wrigley, 'Occupational Structure and population change', p.60.

As well as representing most of the highest values, 40 percent of gentry had inventories in the lowest value classification (below £100). Those categorised as yeomen could have inventories valued at more than three quarters of gentry but also very low values of moveable goods. Sixteen yeomen (13 percent) had inventory values of less than £20. Labourers consistently had low values with only 3 percent of their inventories exceeding £100 in value. However, it is not always clear the extent to which those designated labourers were agricultural labourers. Even where they were employed in other trades, they might have practiced by-employment by owning a few animals or just a pig. The extent to which labourers owned animals or grew crops is explored below.

Mark Overton *et al.* devised a method for giving an indication of the scale of agricultural activity and the likely amount of land that a householder had available.[30] The first of their four categories (Group 1) had no arable production and livestock was restricted to poultry, bees and/or one or two pigs. These households had no access to land other than a garden, had no common grazing rights and could be classed as cottagers. Group 2 consisted of smallholders with access to grazing but no involvement in arable farming. This group owned 3-10 pigs, and/or 1-10 sheep and/or 1-2 cattle. Group 3 was categorised by Overton *et al.* as 'large-scale pastoral farming'. These represented inventories which recorded more than ten pigs, and/or more than ten sheep and/or more than two cattle. The final category (Group 4) consisted of those whose inventories recorded arable crops.

Table 2 sets out the results of applying this methodology in Huntingdonshire, which can be compared to Overton's study counties of Kent and Cornwall for which we have data. Assembling this amount of data involves literally thousands of hours of work and perhaps more suitable comparative counties would have been preferable. Future research may provide a bigger and more meaningful comparison if a compatible methodology is followed. But the results of this exercise are nevertheless instructive. They show a rise in the percentage of inventories with no agricultural assets in Huntingdonshire by the mid-eighteenth century, (from 33 to 40 percent of inventories) but a smaller percentage change than in Kent. The rise in Huntingdonshire was concentrated in the clay upland parishes, where the percentage of inventories with no agricultural assets rose from 15 percent of inventories in 1660-89 to 35 percent in 1720-49. Pastoral farming in Cornwall both by smallholders and larger commercial farms (Groups 2 and 3) appeared to be rising in Cornwall but falling in Kent.

---

[30] Overton *et al.*, *Production and consumption in English households*, pp.40-41.

TABLE 2: PERCENTAGE OF INVENTORIES IN FOUR AGRICULTURAL CATEGORIES				
	County	1660-1689	1690-1719	1720-1749
		%	%	%
Group 1 (Cottagers: Poultry, bees and one or two pigs)	Hunts	1	1	2
	Corn-wall	5	2	2
	Kent	3	4	3
Group 2 (Smallholders, pigs, sheep and cattle)	Hunts	9	8	7
	Corn-wall	10	13	14
	Kent	9	11	5
Group 3 (Large pastoral farming but no arable crops)	Hunts	11	6	5
	Corn-wall	7	8	10
	Kent	8	7	5
Group 4 (Inventories with arable crops)	Hunts	46	49	46
	Corn-wall	42	40	39
	Kent	46	48	44
All Groups	Hunts	67	64	60
	Corn-wall	64	63	65
	Kent	66	70	57
No agriculture	Hunts	33	36	40
	Corn-wall	36	37	35
	Kent	34	30	43

In Huntingdonshire, the number of persons who practised pastoral farming without also engaging in any arable farming declined. There was a slight fall in smallholding and a bigger fall in larger pastoral farms with no arable crops, which were declining quite sharply, from 11 percent to 5 percent of inventories. This was accompanied by a rise in those who no longer practised agriculture. However, Group 4 is problematic in that Overton *et al.* defined this group as 'all those households where there is evidence of *some* arable production'.[31] Most inventories with agricultural assets in Hunting-

---

[31] Overton *et al., Production and consumption in English households*, p.41.

donshire fell into this group, as they did in both Kent and Cornwall. However, Group 4 includes all inventoried persons who practised mixed farming (arable and pastoral), who were the overwhelming majority. In Huntingdonshire, it was rare (only seven percent of Group 4 inventories) to own crops without animals. Animals were important in producing manure for arable production. On the other hand, many inventories that recorded crops also had considerable numbers of animals. A quarter had animals valued at £50 or more. The median value of animals in Group 4 inventories (£17) was approaching double that of arable crops (£9). Many inventories in Group 4 had relatively few arable crops; the first quartile had crops with a median value of only £2.63, which would represent little more than an acre or two of either wheat or barley. Several people had small amounts of hay or oats that they could have purchased for their animals and thus may not have engaged in arable farming.

Overall, agriculture represented 42 percent of total inventory values in Huntingdonshire during the years 1660-1749 with agricultural assets divided almost equally between arable (22 percent) and pastoral farming (20 percent). Those groups whose principal activity was farming on their own account (yeomen and husbandmen) had the highest percentage (68 percent) of their inventory values represented by animals and crops, divided between arable (37 percent) and pastoral farming (31 percent). There was little difference in the division of arable and pastoral farming between those classified as yeoman and husbandmen.

Yeomen were generally more substantial farmers than husbandmen, who tended to work smaller farms. The median value of total agricultural assets for yeomen (£86) in Huntingdonshire was more than double that for husbandmen, (£41). Whilst this is not a particularly arresting finding, Tables 3.1 and 3.2 show much more precisely how yeomen were different from husbandmen in a county like Huntingdonshire. They highlight how *incidence* of ownership is not the same as numbers of animals and crops owned, which presents a different pattern of ownership. Husbandmen had the highest incidence of ownership of cows, pigs and horses yet yeomen had more cows and pigs, twice the median number of sheep and approaching three times the value of crops of husbandmen. Both had a median of 5 horses which suggested that horses had replaced oxen for draught power. Oxen were rarely recorded in Huntingdonshire probate inventories. Whilst nearly all husbandmen (92 percent) engaged in arable farming, the median value of their crops was only £26 compared to the median value of yeomen (£69). But there were always exceptions to the rule. Thomas Boston from Orton Longueville, designated a husbandman, had crops valued at £391 and animals at £226 in 1738. His crops included wheat, barley, beans and peas. He had 24 cows, 28 pigs,

14 horses, a bull and 237 sheep. Boston's house was also substantial with a parlour, hall, 2 kitchens and 6 chambers.[32]

Tables 3.1 and 3.2 also show ownership patterns of animals and crops by gentry and labourers. Labourers had a higher incidence of ownership of cows, pigs and sheep than gentry, but gentry had greater numbers. This is illustrated most starkly in the size of flocks of sheep. The median size of a flock owned by gentry was 120 but that of labourers was a relatively meagre six sheep. Whilst nearly half of labourers' inventories recorded crops, only five (three percent) had crops valued at more than £10.

TABLE 3.1: OWNERSHIP OF ANIMALS BY RANK IN HUNTINGDONSHIRE 1660-1749

	1	2-5	6-10	11-20	21+	With cows	With-out cows	TO-TAL	With cows	
									COWS	
	n	n	n	n	n	n	n	n	%	Me-dian
Gent	2	6	2	4	1	15	13	28	54	4
Yeomen	7	22	34	28	5	96	24	120	80	8
Husb'men	3	14	10	3	3	33	5	38	87	5
Labs	17	55	14	4	0	90	67	157	57	3
Totals	29	97	60	39	9	234	109	343	68	5
%	12	41	26	17	4	100				

	1	2	3-5	6-9	10+	With pigs	With-out pigs	TO-TAL	With pigs	
									PIGS	
	n	n	n	n	n	n	n	n	%	Me-dian
Gent	0	1	3	2	3	9	19	28	32	7
Yeomen	13	12	18	16	25	84	36	120	70	5
Husb'men	6	8	6	5	6	31	7	38	82	3
Labs	36	11	14	2	1	64	93	157	41	1
Totals	55	32	41	25	35	188	155	343	55	3
%	29	17	22	13	19	100				

---

[32] HA AH18/2/741.

SHEEP									
	1-10	11-20	21-50	51-100	100+	With sheep	Without sheep	TO-TAL	With sheep
	n	n	n	n	n	n	n	n	% / Me-dian
Gentry	4	0	1	0	6	11	17	28	39 / 120
Yeomen	9	4	20	22	23	78	42	120	65 / 61
Husb'men	6	1	4	4	4	19	19	38	50 / 32
Labs	53	9	6	1	0	69	88	157	44 / 6
Totals	72	14	31	27	33	177	166	343	51 / 22
%	40	8	18	15	19	100			

HORSES									
	1	2	3-5	6-9	10+	With horses	Without horses	TO-TAL	With horses
	n	n	n	n	n	n	n	n	% / Me-dian
Gentry	5	2	2	3	3	15	13	28	54 / 3
Yeomen	7	9	31	28	12	87	33	120	73 / 5
Husb'men	1	2	15	6	6	30	8	38	79 / 5
Labs	13	9	5	2	0	29	128	157	18 / 2
Totals	26	22	53	39	21	161	182	343	47 / 4
%	16	14	33	24	13	100			

TABLE 3.2: OWNERSHIP OF CROPS BY RANK IN HUNTINGDONSHIRE 1660-1749								
	£1-10	£11-50	£51-100	£101+	With crops	Without crops	TO-TAL	With crops
	n	n	n	n	n	n	n	% / Med £
Gentry	3	2	0	8	13	15	28	46 / 120
Yeomen	21	12	28	31	92	28	120	77 / 69
Husb'men	9	11	8	7	35	3	38	92 / 26
Labs	68	5	0	0	73	84	157	46 / 3
Totals	101	30	36	46	213	130	343	62 / 14
%	47	14	17	22	100			

Almost half (48 percent) of the 120 yeomen farmers' inventories were from clay upland parishes, with the rest split evenly between river valley parishes (25 percent) and fenland (27 percent). Larger herds of cows (defined as 10+) were found in all three *pays* but were more common in the clay uplands where 34 percent of yeomen had larger herds. In fenland parishes, larger herds were recorded in only 16 percent of yeoman inventories. On larger farms in mainly arable Godmanchester in the Ouse valley, wheat, barley, peas and beans were typically grown but rarely oats. On the clay uplands in Kimbolton the pattern was similar, but some oats were grown. Most inventories which recorded crops in predominantly pastoral Ramsey in fenland, had relatively small amounts of low value (58 percent with crops under £10). Many had just hay or oats for animals, but there were some yeomen farmers growing wheat, oats and peas. However, crops were often grouped together for valuation purposes and were not always specified in probate inventories. Phrases such as 'grain growing in the field' or 'crops' were often employed making precise analysis difficult.

The most valuable animals were cows and horses. Whilst valuation depended upon age of the animal and quality, cows were often valued at around £3 10s each in Huntingdonshire inventories in this period and horses at similar values.[33] Where animals were kept, a cow was nearly always owned. No gentleman in the sample owned a pig or a sheep without owning a cow. Similarly, only one husbandman owned sheep without a cow and no husbandman owned pigs without a cow. Although the majority (57 percent) of inventoried labourers owned at least one cow, those that did not were more likely than other agricultural ranks to have just a pig or a few sheep. (Table 4)

TABLE 4: ANIMAL KEEPING BY AGRICULTURAL RANK IN HUNTINGDONSHIRE				
	Gentry		Yeomen	
	n=28		n=120	
	No.	%	No.	%
Pigs no cattle	0	0	5	4
Sheep no cattle	0	0	4	3
	Husbandmen		Labourers	
	n=38		n=157	
	No.	%	No.	%
Pigs no cattle	0	0	7	4
Sheep no cattle	1	3	18	11

---

[33] Prices of horses recorded in inventories represented a mix of both farm horses, horses for transport and superior riding horses, such as used by gentry. Overton found that inventory prices for horses were considerably lower than those published in the *Agrarian History of England and Wales* (AHEW). Overton believed that inventory prices recorded in his very large database were more accurate than the more limited database of AHEW. M. Overton, 'Prices from inventories' in T. Arkell, N. Evans and N. Goose (eds.) *When Death Us Do Part* Oxford: Leopard's Head Press, 2000, p.131.

Keeping a cow was an important element in a labourer's household economy, for it could be worth a substantial proportion of his wages.[34] However, the inventoried labourer had a median of no less than three cows, which with a total value of around £10 for these three animals, immediately took him to the threshold of the second quartile of inventoried labourers. Cow keeping also facilitated other pastoral activity because skimmed milk could be fed to pigs. Just over two in five labourers owned pigs and sheep. Alan Everitt analysed labourers' inventories in several English regions, including eastern England, in the period immediately prior to the present study. Whilst Everitt found similar results for pigs (42 percent of inventoried labourers with pigs in Eastern England between 1610 and 1640), his results for labourers with sheep were very different (just 16 percent of labourers in Eastern England with sheep, compared to 44 percent in Huntingdonshire, Table 4). Everett also found that flock sizes for labourers were smaller than in the present study, with just 5 percent of labourers with nine or more sheep.[35] The results are consistent with a picture of increasing sheep farming in Huntingdonshire.

In Huntingdonshire, the incidence of animal keeping and owning crops by labourers was related to their inventory values. (Figure 4) A third of labourers (35 percent) in the lower quartile, with inventory values of £10 or less, and three quarters of labourers (75 percent) in the upper quartile of inventory values (£30 or more) owned at least one cow. Upper quartile labourers were more likely to own sheep (68 percent) than yeomen (65 percent) and husbandmen (50 percent). Arable farming by labourers was generally on a small scale. Of the 73 inventoried labourers who grew crops in Huntingdonshire, only 5 had crops valued at more than £10, the highest value being £25.

---

[34] J. Humphries, 'Enclosures, common rights and women: the proletarianisation of families in the late eighteenth and early nineteenth centuries', *Journal of Economic History*, 50, 1990, pp.24-5.

[35] A. Everitt, 'Farm labourers 1500-1640', in C. Clay ed. *Rural Society: landowners, peasants and labourers 1500-1750* Cambridge: CUP,1990, pp.179-80.

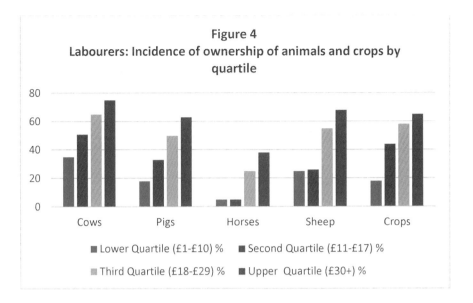

Figure 4
Labourers: Incidence of ownership of animals and crops by quartile

Whilst it was no surprise that ownership of animals and crops by labourers was related to inventory values, the relatively low incidence of ownership of agricultural assets by the lower and second quartiles of gentry was. (Figure 5)

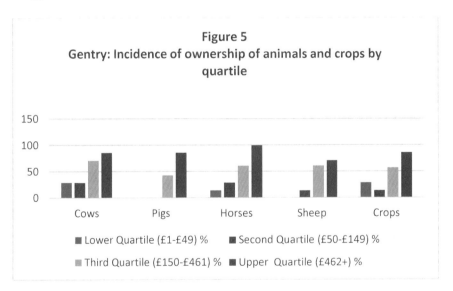

Figure 5
Gentry: Incidence of ownership of animals and crops by quartile

By-employment was common in the early modern period not just in Ramsey but throughout the county. Many tradesmen engaged in arable and pastoral faming. More than a quarter (27 percent) of the value of the 186 selected tradesmen inventories from Huntingdonshire for the years

1660-1749 were represented by their crops and animals. (Table 5) Those in the food and drinks trades had the highest percentage (33 percent) of their inventory values in agricultural assets. Around 40 percent of the 186 selected tradesmen engaged in arable farming also owned cows and pigs, whilst just over a third (34 percent) owned at least one horse. More than a quarter (28 percent) owned sheep. Some tradesmen practised farming on a significant scale. William Creake, a cordwainer from Godmanchester who died in 1747, had significant agricultural interests with 55 acres of arable production. His animals included sheep and lambs valued at £10, pigs, a cow, 2 bullocks and even a bull. Longland, a Buckden blacksmith who died in 1745, had 117 sheep, 5 cows and other animals and crops valued at £114.

Most blacksmiths, butchers, tanners and masons owned a cow and most butchers and bakers owned a pig. Horse ownership was very high amongst bakers (93 percent) tanners (83 percent) and butchers (83 percent) but these horses may have been used for transport rather than agriculture. Evidence for arable farming was highest amongst bakers (93 percent). Whereas a small minority of bakers had just stocks of hay, most were growing wheat for making bread.

TABLE 5: ANIMALS AND CROPS OWNED BY SELECTED TRADESMEN AND CRAFTSMEN HUNTINGDONSHIRE 1660-1749							
	Invento-ries	Horses	Cows	Pigs	Sheep	Ara-ble	Percentage of inventory value
	n	%	%	%	%	%	%
Butchers	12	83	75	67	58	50	39
Bakers	15	93	40	60	20	93	35
Innkeepers	48	40	35	48	31	40	31
FOOD AND DRINK	75	57	43	53	33	52	33
Cordwainers	25	12	28	32	16	36	16
Tailors	16	13	50	37	31	31	17
Glovers	6	17	17	33	0	17	3
Weavers	11	0	9	9	27	9	11
CLOTHING	58	10	29	29	21	28	13
Masons	3	33	67	67	67	67	35
Bricklayer	9	11	11	11	0	0	3
Carpen-ters/Joiners	22	14	54	45	23	36	32
BUILDING	34	15	44	38	21	29	24
Tanners	6	83	67	33	33	67	8
Blacksmiths	13	31	77	38	54	38	25
OTHER TRADES	19	47	74	37	47	47	15
Total	186	34	42	41	28	40	27

Whilst the sample size was small, bakers were one occupational group where pigs (60 percent) were more commonly kept than cows (40 percent). Shaw Taylor found the same pattern of animal ownership for bakers in Northamptonshire inventories in the first half of the eighteenth century.[36] He suggested that bakers may have used pigs to turn bad flour and stale or mouldy bread into bacon.

---

[36] L. Shaw Taylor, *The Nature and Scale of the Cottage Economy*, unpublished paper, University of Cambridge, p.8.

Incidence of sheep ownership was less common than cows and pigs (Tables 3 and 5) and sheep were much more frequently found on farms in the clay uplands than in either the river valleys or fenland. However, sheep farming in the county was changing significantly during the period. Those that practiced agriculture were increasingly keeping sheep. Whilst the majority (53 percent) did not keep sheep in the earliest period, only a third (33 percent) failed to do so by the final period. The size of sheep flocks increased significantly from the end of the seventeenth century. In the period 1660-1689, those with sheep recorded in their inventory had a median of nine sheep. By the mid-eighteenth century, the median had increased to 31 and evidence from later Huntingdonshire inventories showed that it more than doubled again by the end of the eighteenth century.[37] Those with the larger flocks (51+ sheep) were again concentrated in the clay uplands although two of the largest flocks (420 sheep and 347 sheep) were owned by gentry in fenland. The second largest flock (398 sheep) was owned by a butcher from Wyton in the Ouse Valley. His total agricultural assets were valued at £422 in 1747. Sheep were valued at considerably less than other animals in probate inventories although prices were rising in the eighteenth century.[38] There was also a significant difference between prices paid in the spring and after fattening throughout the summer. The rapidly increasing size of flocks meant that the median flock (42) for agricultural ranks was a significant financial asset and could be worth the price of several cows. (Figure 6)

[37] K. Sneath, 'Consumption, wealth, indebtedness and social structure in early modern England', unpublished Ph.D. thesis, University of Cambridge, 2008. https://doi.org/10.17863/CAM.16041.
[38] Overton, *Agricultural Revolution in England* p.116.

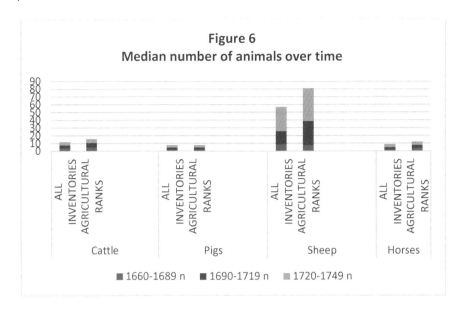

Figure 6
Median number of animals over time

Conclusions

The role of agriculture in Huntingdonshire was vital in feeding both the rising population of the county and London. Whilst the economy was dominated by agriculture, differences in soil type resulted in mixed farming in the county. Arable predominated in the clay uplands and pastoral farming in fenland. This was reflected in parish registers like Abbots Ripton where double the number of marriages took place in the autumn after the harvest was gathered in. In the largest parish, Ramsey in fenland, marriage patterns were quite different, and marriages also peaked in the spring after lambing and calving. Analysis of probate inventories revealed a rather more nuanced picture of agriculture in the county during the early modern period. Whilst the traditional order of agricultural ranks from gentry to labourers prevailed, the assets of each status group varied significantly. Ownership of cows, pigs, horses, sheep was relatively low amongst many gentry. Yeomen could have much greater moveable assets than gentry, and some husbandmen were better off than yeomen. Huntingdonshire is particularly fortunate in the number of inventories that survive for labourers. These inventoried labourers were much more affluent than the average labourer. More than half owned a cow, and even amongst labourers in the lowest quartile of asset values, a third owned a cow. The scale of by-employment amongst the inventoried population in Huntingdonshire was significant. Whilst extreme examples such as the butcher from Wyton who had animals and crops valued at more than £400 can be found, many tradesmen were substantially involved in agricultural pursuits, particularly butchers and bakers in the food and drink sector.

Overall tradesmen held more than a quarter of their movable assets as animals and crops.

Local studies can help to illuminate the nature and extent of structural change in the economy. There was evidence of the beginnings of agricultural change in Huntingdonshire with the reduction in the percentage of employment in the primary sector. The percentage of inventories with no agricultural assets rose from 33 percent of inventories in 1660-89 to 40 percent of inventories by 1720-49. This increase largely took place in clay upland parishes. Whilst those who *only* practised pastoral farming declined, the majority who were engaged in agriculture practiced mixed farming. Some elements of pastoral farming increased. Those that practised agriculture increasingly kept sheep and much bigger flocks were kept. This trend may well have been in response to higher prices. Nevertheless, Huntingdonshire was still very much an agricultural county in which mixed farming was the norm by the mid-eighteenth century. Many of the changes associated with the term 'agricultural revolution' still lay in the future.

5

HUNTINGDONSHIRE FIELDS c.1660-c.1750

William Franklin

Open Field Agriculture

From at least the tenth century the land surrounding the towns and villages of Huntingdonshire had, with the exception of the fen lands, been worked communally with large common arable fields on the higher ground and livestock grazing on the permanent pastures that lay beside the streams, rivers and wetter areas of land. Visually the landscape would have looked surprisingly modern with great open expanses, with few hedges or trees. The pattern of small fields surrounded by hedgerows and ditches that was common until recent times and which is generally considered as quintessentially English was the result of enclosure of the open fields.

Huntingdonshire is for much of its area covered by Pleistocene boulder clay deposits, these overlay earlier Jurassic Oxford Clay deposits which are often exposed on the slopes of the river valleys. In the bottom of these river valleys are alluvial deposits and terrace gravels. The fens of the north east of the county had peat and clayey soils.[1] It is these deposits that have shaped the agriculture and agricultural economy of the area. The soils on the boulder clay are often thin, making arable agriculture very difficult.

The geological profile of much of the county being similar to that of its neighbouring county, Northamptonshire, it is unsurprising that throughout the medieval period Huntingdonshire followed very closely the Midland (Champion) open field system. Villages generally had two, three or occasionally four or more arable fields, each field comprising of a number of furlongs in which occupiers of land produced crops on their respective strips, known as selions. The number of fields in any parish was probably settled by the thirteenth century, and Huntingdonshire like its western neighbours generally on three large open arable fields. Exceptions to this include Great Gransden which retained a (probably) earlier arrangement of two fields, and

---

[1] Geological Survey of Great Britain, (Sixth Edition), Ordnance Survey, Sheets 171, 186, 187, 203, 205. 1977.

Great Stukeley, which by 1750 had seven fields, probably the result of later subdivision.

Table 1 Examples of Townships and number of open arable fields

Township	No. of Fields	Field Names
Great Gransden	2	East Field and West Field[2]
Upton	3	Mill Field, Upper Field, and Lower Field[3]
Great Staughton	4	Conduit Field, Rushey Field, Marsh Field and Moor field.[4]
Bluntisham	4	Gull Field, Colne Way Field, Higham Field and Old Mill Field.[5]
Alconbury	5	Brook Field, Bury Meadow Field, Town Hill Field, Hollows Field, and Stockin Field.[6]
Great Stukeley	7	Down Field, Little Stukeley Field, Little Field, Great Stokkinge Field, East Field, More Field and Allwyncle Field.

Throughout the period from 1660-1750 and into the early nineteenth century, those unenclosed townships practicing open field agriculture produced wheat, barley, oats and peas or beans. Each crop was sown in rotation with those areas sown with wheat in year 1, being sown with oats in year 2 and left fallow in year 3. Similarly, that sown with barley in year 1 was sown with beans and peas in year 2 and left fallow in year 3.[7]

Pasture

Most of the pasture land for the animals of each community lay in the valleys of the various streams and rivers. While prone to flooding, it was these floods that reinvigorated the soil and produced lush meadow land for the

---

[2] H.L. Gray, *The English Field Systems,* London: Merlin Press, 1959, p.469.
[3] HA CON4/2/21/1. Map of Upton Lordship 1659.
[4] TNA MR1/1570. Undated pre-enclosure map of Great Staughton.
[5] HA HP5/3/4/19. Terrier of land in Bluntisham before enclosure.
[6] HA Map 451.
[7] T. Stone, *General View of the Agriculture of the County of Huntingdon* London: J. Nichols, 1793, p.7.

community's animals to graze. Much of this pasture being held in common.[8] Throughout the period 1660-1750 the sight of the town herd being collected about four in the morning from the houses of those with right of common, and taken to the meadow, returning at six in the evening, would have been a common sight.[9]

To ensure enough pasture was available even when the rivers and streams were swollen the system of triennial rotation allowed for each strip of land to be rested after two or three years of arable crops. In the year of rest the fallow strips was be used to produce a crop of hay and then used as pasture for animals; the animals manuring the land in preparation for the next arable crop. All the land, once its arable crop had been harvested, was turned over to the animals of those members of the community who held Right of Common.

A township's permanent meadows were often subdivided, with portions known as doles being allotted to different persons each year in rotation. In Bluntisham cum Earith, the two areas of meadow, one in each township were subdivided, that in Earith into sixteen portions, that in Bluntisham into ten parts. As table 2 shows, these were then subdivided into numerous portions.[10]

[8] Common here is, land subject to communal control, or to the rights of those other than the owner to use the land for specified purposes.
[9] Principally the village farmers, great and small, as not everyone in a township had Right of Common. Rights of Common being old-established rights exercised by the occupiers of farm lands and cottages. There has been much debate about the origin of common rights and it appears that these were created in Saxon England and probably at that time linked to the properties in a village. Later properties may not necessarily have such rights attached to them.
[10] HA HP5/3/4/19. Note Book which includes two undated 18th century terriers.

Table 2 Subdivision of the meadows in Bluntisham cum Earith

Earith Meadow		Portions	Bluntisham Meadow		Portions
1	Short Dartford	31	1	Rock Meadow	41
2	Headmans Meadow	10	2	A bound next the fen there at Lands End	46
3	Swarth Long	32			
4	Cox Dole	28	3	Broad Meadow	67
5	Penny Meadow	16	4	Penny Land	22
6	Bound Stone	23	5	The Gulls	19
7	West side Lords Meadow	3	6	Littleham Hill	54
8	Stitches north of Holt Roods	4	7	Stitches	12
9	Holt Roods	72	8	Wrangland	29
10	Pit Fen Corner	49	9	Bury Fen	35
11	East Howards Swath	8	10	Lents Meadow	6
12	Upper end of this acre	5			
13	North Long	28			
14	Fern Hill South	22			
15	Home Gate	29			
16	Short Dartford	15			

At Brampton, the great flood plain in the curve of the river Ouse, regularly flooded in the winter months, provided both good hay meadow and summer pasture for animals. It remained as permanent pasture, divided into furlongs and doles (the furlongs were themselves split into doles) in 1757 when it was surveyed for the Earl of Sandwich.[11] Prized for its quality, the Portholme was excluded the enclosure of Brampton by act of parliament in 1772.[12]

---

[11] HA 223/5 Estate book of the Earl of Sandwich 1775.
[12] HA HCP/6/1907/2 Enclosure Act.

Figure 1 A Survey and Plan of Portholme Meadow

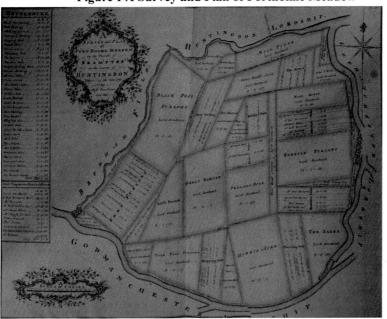

Figure 2 Conduit Field, Great Staughton before enclosure

The field is shown with its furlongs and arable strips, the meadow, divided into portions is shown alongside the stream.

Livestock

Sheep and cattle were the main animals kept by the people of the county. Most households with right of common kept a few cows and other animals and birds for the use of the household, and a few farms kept herds of cattle although outside of the fen areas there is no evidence to suggest any large cattle herds. The fens of Huntingdonshire, like those of Cambridgeshire and Lincolnshire were primarily used for dairy cattle and the production of cheese and butter.

The upland farms, particularly those where wholesale enclosures had taken place favoured sheep. There is no evidence of any particular breed of sheep being favoured by the Huntingdonshire farmers. Stone, writing in 1793 describes the sheep locally as being "very inferior".[13] The account book of John Simpson of Covington 1735-40 shows that sheep were being bought and sold in markets over a wide area without reference to breed.[14]

The Manorial Court

For much of the county this system of farming continued to be heavily managed by the manorial court, which in unenclosed parishes continued to operate through to the second half of the 18th century when for much of the county parliamentary enclosure began at a pace. Although open field land was owned privately, its cultivation was a very community orientated method of agriculture in which everyone, including the lord of the manor had strips in all areas of the township and thus each had a share of the good and poorer soils. The preparation of the land was not only communal in terms of the pasturing of the land after harvest and before ploughing, but in terms of the drainage of the land. In villages on the clay lands across Cambridgeshire, Huntingdonshire, Northamptonshire and Leicestershire the manorial steward required all of the townsfolk to turn out and scour both the drains and gutters on their own lands and the common drains and gutters in the fields ensuring the water ran off the land and was carried away into the streams and rivers. Those failing to turn out were fined by the manorial court.[15] Most parishes held communal equipment for this purpose including

---

[13] Stone, *General View* p.14.
[14] HA 52. John Simpson appears to have been the estate manager for the Prior estate (Stonely?) and his account book details the sale and purchase of animals for the estate from Northampton, Rothwell (Northants), Kettering (Northants) Market Harborough (Leicestershire) and Hallerton (Leicestershire).
[15] H.C. Darby, 'The draining of the English clay-lands'. *Geographische Zeitschrift*, 52. Jahrg., 3. H. 1964 pp.190-201; D.N. Hall, "*Drainage of Arable Land*

a very large drainage plough, often referred to as the Town Plough.[16] As many animals were kept upon the leys (temporary pastures) and upon the hades that often lay between the furlongs, there was always the danger of over grazing. As a result, the field reeve noted any instances of over stocking and the owners presented to the manorial court and fined.[17]

Tenure and Tithes

As in previous centuries, those holding and working the fields generally held their land by either freehold, copyhold or leasehold. Freeholders, as the name implies, were free of services to the lord beyond the payment of a nominal yearly quit-rent. Copyholders could under some conditions be almost as secure. Copyhold of inheritance by 'fine certain' saw the holding passing by inheritance or assignment, and so long as the tenant kept the custom of the manor he had practically a freehold. His rent and fine on admission were trifling compared to the value of the holding, and his services were generally nothing more than suit of court, that is, attendance at the manor courts. Less secure was copyhold by 'fine arbitrary', in other words at the will of the lord. This form of copyhold was more common on the lands of the dean and chapter of Peterborough, and in the case of Bluntisham in the east of the county, the dean and chapter of Ely.

Those working the land continued to pay tithes to the church, the sometimes unscrupulous clergy and impropriators ensuring that everything they could get by way of tithe payments was taken in. When payment was not made action was taken in the ecclesiastical court,[18] for example, between 1660 and 1670 Simeon Paige, the Rector of Hemingford Abbots took a number of cases out against his parishioners for subtraction of tithes. Tithes comprised of two sorts, great tithes, that is a percentage of the crop taken off of the open arable fields, and the lesser tithes, a percentage of a range of other produce such as chickens, lambs, apples, eggs etc. By c 1700 the tithes had frequently been commuted to money payments, although this was not a uni-

---

in Medieval England' in 'Drainage of Arable Land in Medieval England' in H. Cook and T. Williamson eds., *Water Management in the English Landscape*, Edinburgh University Press. 1999. p.34. For a local example of such fines see HA TORK: 15/258. Verdict of the jury of Great Stukeley regarding fines 1662.

[16] W. Franklin, 'Drainage and the town plough'. *Agricultural History Review,* Vol. 63, Part II, 2015, pp.311-320.

[17] HA TORK: 15/258. Verdict of the jury of Great Stukeley regarding fines 1662.

[18] For examples of cases of libel for subtraction of tithes heard between 1660 and 1670 see HA AH4/251/44/3, AH4/251/45/1-3 and AH4/251/46/4.

form practice, and disputes over the payment of tithes sometimes arose between the vicar and the parishioners, for example the vicar of Great Staughton took action against his parishioners in 1711, noting at the front of his tithe book that, "in the month of October, anno Dom 1711. I sent into the court at Huntingdon an exact Terrar of the vicarage of Great Staughton, with an account of the separate rights of the vicar & Parson."[19] As the tithe book of Great Staughton shows, while many of the payments were in money, some payments remained as payments in kind, and this was not always in produce, for example, the tithe of the meadow that lay in the Highway was divided and shared between the tenants of certain houses, "the tythe of which the minister takes in kind: and is marked out for the minister", thus in lieu of monetary payment or payment in produce such as hay, the minister took a portion of the meadow for his own personal use. In Huntingdonshire as almost everywhere else in England the payment of tithe was disliked as it represented a tax on the produce of the farms and fields and the hard work of the farmers.

Enclosure

While the medieval open field system of arable agriculture largely continued to be practiced across Huntingdonshire by 1660, there were changes to the traditional methods of farming. By the middle of the 17th century farmers were coming to recognise that flexibility of land use was a wise measure for increasing productivity. Some clays such as the boulder clays of Huntingdonshire were so poorly drained as to give very poor yields and promised greater yields and profitability if put down to permanent pasture. In the open arable field there had been some flexibility, allowing farmers to lay down some land in the furlongs to temporary pasture, known as leys, and in some instances, where there was communal agreement, a whole furlong might be converted into a temporary pasture.[20] On the higher lands immediately west of the Great North Road, manorial lords were turning over land to pasture, in particular, pasture for sheep. Sheep offered a good profit to the land owner. The cost of the keeping sheep was low, the principle cost being the wages of the shepherds. Grass grew well on the thin soils that overlay the clay deposits, but sheep required space and had to be controlled to ensure they did not over-graze any pasture or wander into arable crops. To facilitate this land was enclosed, that is, areas of land were surrounded by hedged and ditched boundaries.

In this part of Huntingdonshire this was not a new occurrence, sheep in increasing numbers had been pastured on the heavy clay lands, where arable

---

[19] HA HP82/3/1/1.
[20] J. Thirsk, *Tudor Enclosures.* The Historical Association. 1967 reprint. p.16.

tillage was difficult for centuries, and may have been one of the causes of depopulation of some of the villages and hamlets in the west of the county. While such enclosure for sheep may have been practiced before 1660, it certainly continued after that date as the example of the hamlets of Little Gidding and Steeple Gidding show. In 1510 the manors of Little Gidding and Steeple Gidding were in the possession of Christopher Drewell, who died that year. His son and heir, Humphry Drewell commenced enclosing the land in both parishes and by 1549, the poll tax and census of sheep shows that Drewell held 600 sheep on the land in Little Gidding[21] and is said to have destroyed much of that village. In 1596 when Sir Humphrey Drewell sold the estate to Sir Gervase Clifton only one arable field remained.[22] This was subsequently enclosed in the 17th century.[23] Similarly, he enclosed the neighbouring parish of Steeple Gidding. Successive occupants of the manors of both hamlets continued the process of enclosing throughout the 17th century, until both parishes were fully enclosed by c1700.[24]

Figure 3 Steeple Gidding Enclosure

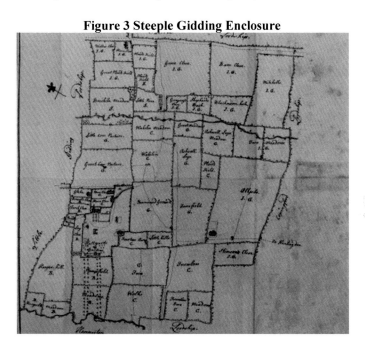

---

[21] TNA E179/122/146 rot. 3.

[22] HA 5806. Map of Little Gidding 1596. For details of the sale see Oxfordshire Archives E6/12/13D/4.

[23] W. Franklin, 'The Ferrars and the Enclosure of Little Gidding, *PCAS,* Vol. CVI, 2017, pp.90-1.

[24] For the progress of enclosure in Little Gidding, HA 5806, Oxfordshire Archives (AO) E6/12/13D/ 4 -16. For Steeple Gidding see, HA Map 120, Map 121 CON 4/2/5/9.

Unlike the later Parliamentary Enclosures, this enclosure by a single mano-rial lord did not involve any act of parliament. The lord of the manor simply came to an arrangement with the church to ensure that it and any freeholder was given land in lieu of their strips in the open fields. Should a dispute occur, or where there was concern about the future legality of the changes made, including the switch to land being held in severalty, the parties would take a case to the Court of Chancery, which upon investigation and a favour-able outcome would give a legally binding judgement.

Enclosure by act of parliament commenced in the county in 1727, with the enclosure of Orton Longueville and Botolph Bridge. In reality, this was not a true enclosure by parliamentary act, but a ratification of what had already taken place. Instead of going to the court of Chancery for a judgement of the legality of the enclosure that had taken place, the land owner, Henry Vis-count Morpeth, with the Dean of Peterborough, Francis Lockyer, Bernard Lewis the rector of Orton Longueville, and the Trustees of Edmond English's charity, used a public petition to bring in a bill and subsequently an act to confirm the legality of their actions. Their petition, "praying leave to bring in a Bill confirming an agreement between the petitioners, to enclose and divide the Common Fields and Common Grounds, lying within the Manors and Parishes of Overton Longville and Butolphsbridge ... and to make sev-eral Exchanges of their respective Properties within the same Parishes, in order to make the said Enclosure and Division more commodious and ben-eficial to the several Parties".[25] The Act was passed on 28th May 1727.[26] After the passing of this act another thirty-three years would pass before the next enclosure by act of parliament in the county.[27]

Despite the wholesale enclosure of some parishes in the west of the county, primarily for sheep husbandry, prior to the enclosure of parishes by act of parliament most enclosure of land was either piecemeal, or as part of the imparkment of estates. The wholesale enclosure of parishes across Hunting-donshire by act of parliament occurred between 1760 and 1864.[28] Piecemeal enclosure generally occurred close to areas of settlement, individual occupi-ers agreeing with the land owner to enclose an area, most often to provide additional grazing for animals. However, on the estates of at least one major

---

[25] Journal of the House of Lords, Vol. 23, pp.220-231. 27 March 1727. *British History Online.* http://www.british-history.ac.uk/lords-jnrl/vol23/pp220-231 (accessed 19 September 2018).
[26] Journal of the House of Commons, Vol. 21, pp.126, 133, 135.
[27] Acts of Parliament to enclose were passed for both Folksworth and Fletton in 1760.
[28] Great Gidding was the last parish in Huntingdonshire to be enclosed in the county, in 1864.

land owner, enclosure took a somewhat different form. Historically, with the exception of some manorial farms and monastic granges, all the farms in a township were located within the bounds of that township, that is along the main streets of the town or village. The Duke of Manchester on his estates allowed at least some of the farms to move out of the main settlement area and into the former open arable fields which were enclosed. This can be seen in the village of Grafham, where by 1750 a significant portion of the land in the parish owned by the Duke was enclosed.[29] Six farms lay outside the village of which only two were former medieval manorial. The Duke's enclosed estate comprised of ditched and hedged enclosures and areas of woodland including small copses. Grafham still had some areas of open field arable and areas of meadow, most of which were owned by the manor of Gaines, the estate centre of which lay at West Perry.

Imparkment

Imparkment is the enclosure of privately-owned land for the primary purpose of pleasure. The creation of a park surrounding a great house was a symbol of status and wealth. The period c1660 - c1750 saw a few such parks created in the county, for example at Kimbolton, the castle purchased by the 1st Earl of Manchester in 1615 was rebuilt by the 4th Earl, Charles Edward Montagu, the 1st Duke of Manchester, between 1690 and 1720. The old castle had surrounding it by 1673 a great park, encompassing four hundred and seventy five acres plus some woodland.[30] Similarly, by the 1750s Hinchingbrooke Park, surrounding Hinchingbrooke House encompassed at least seventy acres (not including the gardens and orchard).[31] These and the many smaller parks created in the period firstly combined the lord's demesne lands into a single block, held in severalty, and took the land out of arable production. The process of imparkment often included some aspect of landscaping such as the creation of vistas achieved by planting of trees to frame a view. To manage such parks animals such as sheep, flocks and cattle herds were used to graze the grass. These being separated from the formal gardens and the house by ha-ha's.[32]

---

[29] HA Map330. Map of the lordship of Grafham, c.1750.
[30] HA Map83. Map of the Great Park by Thomas Stirrup 1673.
[31] HA 223/2. Plan of Hinchingbrooke House, gardens and estate 1757.
[32] Ha-ha, a ditch with a wall on its inner side below ground level, forming a boundary to a park of garden without interrupting the view.

Figure 4 Kimbolton Great Park

Drivers for Change

For any land owner enclosure was not something undertaken lightly. Enclosure for sheep rearing had been a contentious issue since the late 1400s[33] due to the concerns about the impact on the affected poorer members of the communities who found themselves homeless and without land to sustain themselves, although the last commission of inquiry into sheep enclosures had sat in the early 1600s.[34] The costs of enclosing large areas were not insignificant and there was always the danger of civil unrest as had occurred at Newton in the neighbouring county of Northamptonshire in 1607. Despite these concerns there was a shift, particularly in the west of the county away from open field arable farming on the heavy boulder clay to enclosed fields primarily used for sheep farming.

One almost invariable consequence of enclosure was increased rents. Enclosed fields were perceived to provide increased yields, both in terms of animal and arable production. Where enclosed fields on the better soils were

---

[33] The first anti-enclosure measure was taken by parliament in 1489. It became illegal to abandon a farm that had more than 20 acres under the plough. A further Act of 1515 made it illegal to convert land from tillage to pasture. Despite this enclosure of arable land continued in most Midland counties including Huntingdonshire.

[34] J.A. Yelling *Common Field and Enclosure in England 1450-1850* Hamden: Archon Books, 1977, p.20.

used for arable production the actual methods of ploughing and sowing did not change from that used in the open arable fields. For the land owner the additional income from the increased rent was of the greatest benefit, while for his tenant the ability to have all his land in one block held in severalty was beneficial. The tenant paying additional rent clearly hoped that the increased productivity, whether crops or animals would both offset the additional rent and bring an increased income, although this was not necessarily the case as some land was better suited to arable and some to pasture and almost every farm in the period relied upon the mixed economy of both arable and animal husbandry for their income and to feed the family.

A further drive for change was the growth in great estates following the civil war. This has been ascribed to the development of the modern mortgage system, whereby capital could be raised on land without losing control over it.[35] Until the late seventeenth century, if land was mortgaged the person granting the mortgage could immediately enter the land and take possession until the mortgage was paid. This new system of mortgaging allowed money to be raised to purchase land and to make changes to that land such as enclosing it either solely for agricultural purposes or for pleasure.

Summary

1660 was a year which heralded much change in England, a monarch returned to the throne of England, much land taken in the interregnum was restored to its former owners and changes started to occur in banking and money lending that would ultimately lead to an agricultural revolution. However, in 1660s Huntingdonshire the open arable fields and the mode of farming continued very much as it had when the fields were first laid out in the ninth century. For the most part a three-field rotation system of two years of crops and one year of fallow existed as it had since at least the thirteenth century. The majority of field systems that survived into the seventeenth century can be identified, showing most villages had three or more fields as found in other Midland counties such as Northamptonshire and Leicestershire and that one or two parishes retained an earlier pattern of two fields as found in Lincolnshire.

The common field system was a cooperative activity that was reinforced by local by-laws, which were imposed, amended and administered by the villagers in the manorial court. A major limitation of the cooperative nature of this system was that it restricted innovation. There is no evidence to show

---

[35] R.C. Allen, *Enclosure and the Yeoman*. Oxford: 1992, p.102.

that the farmers in the county adopted new arable crops, new breeds of sheep or cattle, or new agricultural practices. However, the common field system did provide the poorer cottager with support through common pasture rights, whose nature and limits were determined by the manorial jury.

It is clear that enclosure of the open arable fields commenced prior to 1660 and continued for a century after 1750. In Huntingdonshire enclosure saw a great increase in the planting of hawthorn hedges together with ditches to divide the fields, and many farmers also took the opportunity to plant trees in the hedgerows. In some villages such as Grafham complete new woods were planted. The cost of creating these new hedges and ditches was by far the largest single item of enclosure expenditure for an individual proprietor.

The dependence of early enclosure on soil type is clearly illustrated by the enclosures at Little Gidding, Steeple Gidding and Coppingford, all of which lay on a boulder clay ridge with thin soils best suited to pasture. In Grafham much of the clay soil area was enclosed and converted to pasture in the early eighteenth century, whereas the areas with soils better suited to able husbandry were retained in common fields until the early nineteenth century.

By the middle of the eighteenth century, large parts of Huntingdonshire had been converted to pasture, fattening beasts destined for the London market. In those villages where enclosure did not take place the number of farmers declined between 1660 and 1750 as the average size of farms grew. A change driven by economies of scale resulted in which land owners charged more in rent and farmers needed to produce more to offset the cost of the increased rent. This increase in the size of farms mirrored the increase in size of the parks surrounding the houses of the wealthiest, made possible by changes in money lending.

All but one Huntingdonshire enclosure, up to 1750, occurred without recourse to Parliament, but after this time the majority of enclosures were enforced by Acts of Parliament. The great period of both enclosure by act of parliament and agricultural innovation would in Huntingdonshire commence after 1760.

6

SETTLEMENT ADMINISTRATION IN HUNTINGDONSHIRE C.1662 TO C.1795

Liz Ford

'There is scarce a poor man in England, of forty years of age...who has not, in some part of his life, felt himself most cruelly oppressed by this ill-contrived law of settlements.'[36]

The Elizabethan Poor Laws stipulated that a locally raised rate would provide for the 'deserving poor', and the underlying assumption was that relief would be given in the parish where people 'belonged'. It was 'generally accepted' that the poor had a right to be relieved in times of 'extreme necessity, or 'indigency'' but this assumption may have encouraged the unemployed to drift to the better-resourced communities, prompting reluctance by rate-payers to fund relief for people who were regarded as 'not belonging' to the parish.[37] The notion of 'belonging', or 'settlement' was clarified under the laws of settlement and removal administration which were enacted between 1662 and 1795, but the effect on the poor's mobility was seen by some critics as harsh. Adam Smith asserted in 1776 that not only was the threat of exposure to instant removal on the suspicion of possibly becoming a potential charge to the parish at some future date an infringement to man's liberty, but also that the settlement laws hindered the free movement of labour and therefore acted as a brake upon economic growth.[38] On the other hand, it was suggested that the reality of economic vulnerability was understood; it was recognised that 'unfortunate circumstances could turn anyone into a beggar', and historians have asserted that the settlement laws were largely supported.[39] Furthermore, they have questioned how rigidly the laws were enforced, given the rapid growth,

---

[36] Adam Smith, *An Inquiry into the Nature and Causes of The Wealth of Nations*, Hampshire: Harriman House, 2007, p.75

[37] 39 Eliz. 1 c. 3 (1598); P. Slack, *The English Poor Law, 1531-1782* Basingstoke: Macmillan, 1990, p.27.

[38] Smith, *An Inquiry*, pp.89-92.

[39] K.D.M. Snell, 'Pauper settlement and the right to poor relief in England and Wales', *Continuity and Change* vol.6, 1991, p.396.

through migration from the countryside, of London and towns such as Manchester, Sheffield and Birmingham.[40] The large numbers of settlement documents in county record offices are a testament to the amount of time and money expended on settlement administration, and this chapter identifies some of the hundreds of people in Huntingdonshire whose lives were directly or indirectly altered by their relationship with the laws of settlement, as administered by parochial officials between 1662 and 1795.

Background to the Act of Settlement and Removal of 1662

The Act of Settlement (1662) was carefully balanced on the twin pillars of providing for the deserving poor in their settled parish, and 'keeping the parish safe' from the non-settled poor. Whilst it had traditionally been accepted that people 'belonged' either to the parish where they had been born, or where they had lived and worked 'for a period of time', following the implementation of Elizabethan poor laws (1598/1601) officials of many towns, manors and parishes issued orders forbidding landlords from renting to newcomers, without first entering into an indemnity bond with the parochial authorities, to 'keep the parish safe' from dispensing relief to the 'unentitled.'[41] This development is evident in Huntingdonshire, for example in 1608, when the officials of Stanground manor issued a manorial order to that effect.[42] The 'Act for the better Releife of the Poore of this Kingdom', which inexorably tied relief entitlement to the notion of 'belonging' to a place of legal settlement, was probably inevitable, because ratepayers' self-preservation required that there should legal methods by which the entitled and deserving poor of the parish were identifiable.[43] The Settlement Act is therefore regarded as the second piece of legislation in the development of the English

---

[40] S. & B. Webb, *English Local Government: English Poor Law History: Part I. The Old Poor Law* reprint by Read Books Ltd. 2011, p.399; R. Wells, 'Migration, the law, and parochial policy in eighteenth- and nineteenth-century southern England', *Southern History*, 15, 1993, p.86. These towns did not gain city status until 1853, 1893 and 1889 respectively.

[41] 13 & 14 Car. II c. 12; P. Styles, 'The Evolution of the Law of Settlement', reprinted in *Studies in Seventeenth Century West Midlands History,* Kinetin: The Roundwood Press, 1978, pp.187-8; L. Charlesworth, *Welfare's Forgotten Past,* p.82, and appendix, p.205.

[42] HA, Transcription of Farcet catalogue, open shelves.

[43] E.M. Hampson, *The Treatment of Poverty in Cambridgeshire* 1597-1834 Cambridge: CUP 1934, revised 2009, pp.125-6; Charlesworth, *Welfare's Forgotten Past,* pp.57-58.

poor law, and established the criterion for settlement in, and removal from, a parish.[44] Philip Styles suggested that the central motive in establishing 'settlement' was to actually facilitate the removal of poor people whose settlement was elsewhere.[45] In other words, the power to remove was the main thrust of the Act of Settlement and Removal, which begged the question, 'What designated a person's settlement?'.

The terms of the Act of Settlement and Removal

After 1662 the concept of 'belonging' was refined to the legal term of 'settlement', which, although intangible, could be acquired, altered, and superseded, by gaining future settlements throughout one's life. Settlement was, in the first instance, attained by birth, but was also dependent upon parents' settlements. For example, if poor relief was needed and the father's settlement could be proved to be in a different parish, removal could be instigated to the place of the father's settlement.[46] The settlement of illegitimate children was subject to legal developments during the course of the old poor law, but in the first instance, their settlement was the parish of their birth.[47] Women could gain a settlement by marriage, because a wife's settlement was automatically linked to her husband's settlement. Owning or renting property worth over £10 per annum conferred automatic settlement.[48] Having established how to gain, or to legally 'belong' to a parish, the Act also included the procedure for removing any person not legally settled in the parish, and who was deemed 'likely to become chargeable to the Parish'.[49]

Non-settled people could be examined (questioned) by overseers and justices about their family and employment history, to establish their place of legal settlement, after which the justices could sign an order for the removal of the

---

[44] Styles, 'The Evolution of the Law of Settlement', p.175.

[45] Ibid., p.187.

[46] Charlesworth, *Welfare's Forgotten Past,* p.82, and appendix, p.49, n.37; R. Burn, *The justice of the peace, and the parish officer. By Richard Burn, ... The eighteenth edition, corrected and considerably enlarged. ... To which is added an appendix, ... In four volumes. Volume 3 of 4* London, 1797, ECCE reprint, ND, pp. 397-406.

[47] Burn, *Justice of the peace,* p.398.

[48] 13 & 14 Car. II c. 12; Styles, 'The Evolution of the Law of Settlement', pp. 187-8; Charlesworth, *Welfare's Forgotten Past,* p. 82, and appendix, p.205.

[49] 13 & 14 Car. II c. 12.

examinant back to their place of legal settlement if necessary.[50] Any new-comer wishing to establish him/herself in the parish could undergo the same process and if judged 'likely to become chargeable' within forty days of arri-val, could face removal. Settlement could therefore be assumed if a newcomer remained unchallenged after forty days.[51] It was, however, very unlikely that the obvious poor would have remained unchallenged for forty days, so settle-ment in another parish was not easy for the relatively poor to achieve.[52]

Settlement legislation between 1685 and 1697

The 1662 Act aimed to restrict the mobility of the poor, and this was tightened even further from 1685 when a newcomer was supposed to give written notice of his arrival to the parochial officers, at which time his forty days of 'proba-tion' began.[53] However, mobility was a normal feature of life in early modern England and in an agricultural economy reliant on seasonal migration for har-vest work, certificates allowing temporary migration were permitted by the 1662 Act. This certification process became a template for future legislation in 1697, but in the meantime some parishes requested bonds, similar to the ones discussed earlier, to 'keep the parish safe' from 'intruders'.[54] Some Hun-tingdonshire bonds agreed between overseers and bondsmen have survived. For instance in 1692, the Kimbolton overseers requested a bond indemnifying the parish against any costs which might arise from John Eaton and his family coming to live in the town, which was signed by the bondsmen John Stokes, a yeoman from Swineshead, and William Eaton, a carpenter from Dean (Bed-fordshire).[55] Occasionally bondsmen were given notice of the overseers' in-tention to enact a bond they had taken previously signed. On October 7th 1695,

---

[50] *Act for the better Releife of the Poore of this Kingdom, 13 & 14 Car. II c. 12;* Brit-ish History online http://www.british-history.ac.uk/statutes-realm/vol5/pp.401-5; Charlesworth, *Welfare's Forgotten Past,* p.47; K.D.M. Snell, *Annals of the Labour-ing Poor: Change and Agrarian England, 1660-1900* Cambridge: CUP, 1985, p.17.

[51] Charlesworth, *Welfare's Forgotten Past,* p.82; J.S. Taylor, *Poverty, Migration, and Settlement in the Industrial Revolution, Sojourners' Narratives,* California: Palo Alto, 1989, p. 19; *Act for the better Releife of the Poore of this Kingdom, 13 & 14 Car. II c. 12.* British History Online http://www.british-history.ac.uk/statutes-realm/vol5/pp.401-405.

[52] *Act for the better Releife of the Poore of this Kingdom, 13 & 14 Car. II c. 12;* Brit-ish History online http://www.british-history.ac.uk/statutes-realm/vol5/pp.401-5; Charlesworth, *Welfare's Forgotten Past,* p. 47; Snell, *Annals,* p. 17.

[53] Ibid., pp.188-9.

[54] Styles, 'The Evolution of the Law of Settlement', p.187.

[55] HA, HP52/18/1/5, indemnity bond dated 14th December 1692.

Stephen Benton, Roger Smith, Joseph Abbott and John Smith had agreed to be bondholders for Robert Mosse and his family who had been resident in St Neots from at least December 1693.[56] Sometime after October 1695 the Mosse family were deemed 'likely to become chargeable', and the bondsmen were warned that the bond would be forfeit unless the Mosse family removed themselves back to their settled parish (Kimbolton).[57] This document represents an intention to enact the bond, rather than an actual order of removal, but subsequent entries in the Kimbolton parish registers indicate the family's removal to Kimbolton.

These sorts of indemnity bonds were usually agreed for parishes a short distance from the settled parish and demonstrate the tradition of short-distance mobility which was a noticeable feature of social and economic life in England.[58] Young adults and adolescents commonly served an apprenticeship, or undertook a year of household or husbandry service away from their birth parish, and much of the mobility and migration in rural areas took place over short distances.[59] In 1697, in recognition of their importance to the economy, the paths to settlement were widened by enabling settlement to be gained either through having worked a complete year of living-in service whilst unmarried, or by having served a fully indentured apprenticeship.[60] The Poor Relief Act of 1697 also legalised the 'bottom-up' indemnity process which had de-

---

[56] HA, HP52/1/1/1 baptism entry in the Kimbolton composite register 1647-1748, 'Robert, son of Robert Moss of St Neots', unpageinated.
[57] HA, HP52/1/1/1 Kimbolton composite register 1647-1748, unpageinated.
[58] C. Pooley & J. Turnbull, *Migration and mobility in Britain since the 18th century,* London: Routledge, 1998, pp.12-17.
[59] P.A. Fideler, *Social Welfare in Pre-Industrial England,* Basingstoke: Palgrave, 2006, p.139; Styles, 'The Evolution of the Law of Settlement', p.188; I.D. Whyte, *Migration and Society in Britain 1550-1830,* Basingstoke: Macmillan, 2000, pp. 22-23; C. Richardson, *Household Servants in Early Modern England* Manchester: Manchester University Press, 2010, pp.74-5.
[60] K.D.M., Snell, *Parish and Belonging: Community, Identity and Welfare in England and Wales, 1700-1950* Cambridge: CUP, 2006, pp.85-6; Hampson, *Treatment* p.129.

veloped 'independently of settlement legislation', by permitting the use of legal settlement certificates. [61] This Act also allowed settlement to be attained by serving a parochial office, or by the payment of rates.[62]

The numbers and types of Huntingdonshire settlement documents

Surviving Huntingdonshire settlement documents for this later period (1697 to 1795) mostly consist of settlement certificates, settlement examinations and removal orders. Although removal orders could be appealed against, scant appeal documentation survived prior to the Quarter Sessions Minute Books of the early 1780's and 1790's. There is also little surviving evidence of paupers' letters to their settled parish, requesting aid, prior to the late eighteenth century. The relevance and importance of the three main sources (certificates, examinations and removal orders) altered during the period (1662-1795) and have accordingly survived in unbalanced numbers (Figure 1). The existence and survival of these documents are a testament to the importance of the legal framework in the execution and history of relief, but the survival of some documents points to the destruction of others. There are 940 settlement certificates, 199 settlement examinations and 175 removal orders (Figure 1). A noticeable aspect of the documents for the town of Huntingdon is the discreet way in which the four parishes– All Saints, St Benedict's, St John's and St Mary's, operated their rating, and therefore their poor relief systems, completely independently from their neighbouring borough parishes. Their settlement policy was operated in the same manner and this can be seen in the issuing of certificates, arranging settlement examinations or removals; the fact that these parishes were situated in the same borough had no bearing on their settlement administration. Certificates were issued from one borough parish to another, and removals and appeals occurred between the borough parishes. Despite the geographic proximity of the parishes, their overseers had the same obligations to the ratepayers as any other overseers - to keep the parish free from 'intruders' who had no legal right to settle themselves there.

---

[61] A. Winter, 'Migration, Poor Relief and Local Autonomy: Settlement Policies in England and the Low Countries in the Eighteenth-Century', *Past and Present,* 2013, 218:1, p.97; Hampson, *The Treatment of Poverty,* p.144; 8 & 9 William III c. 30, Act for supplying some Defects in the Laws for the Relief of the Poor 1697; B. Webb and S. Webb, *English Local Government,* pp.336-7; D. Marshall, *The English Poor in the Eighteenth Century: A Study in Social and Administrative History,* Abingdon: Routledge, reprint, 2007, pp.175-6. This system was found at least in Devon and Cambridgeshire prior to 1697.

[62] Snell, *Parish and Belonging,* pp.85-6; Hampson, *Treatment,* p.129.

Figure 1 Numbers and types of Huntingdonshire settlement documents 1697-1795

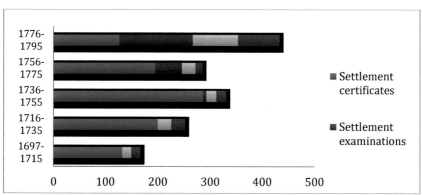

Source HA, All parishes/13/1, /13/2, /13/3, 1697-1795

Settlement certificates were multi-purpose. They offered people the chance to live and work in a parish other than that which was their settled parish; gave them protection from removal on the suspicion of possible chargeability, and an assurance to pay removal costs should their removal be necessary. In issuing a settlement certificate parochial officers understood that it would be virtually impossible for the bearer to gain a new settlement in the host parish.[63] The settlement certificate of Isaac Cuer is a typical example; the overseers of Rothwell (Northamptonshire) admitted to 'owning' the certificate bearer and gave assurances to the parochial officials of the 'host' parish, Kimbolton, that they would:-

'hereby promise for ourselves and our successors to receive the said' bearer and family *'whenever they shall become chargeable (or ask relief).'*[64]

Every certificate was to be additionally signed by one witness (from 1730) and at least one justice, and should have been handed to the host parish's overseer upon arrival in order to prevent a fraudulent attempt to gain settlement.[65] Keith Snell argues that this did not always happen and that many

---

[63] E.M. Hampson, 'Settlement and removal in Cambridgeshire, 1662-1834', *Cambridge Historical Journal,* 2 (1926-28), p.285; Wells, 'Migration, the law, and parochial policy', p.88. A 'host' parish is the term given to a parish where one lived, but one's parish of settlement (settled parish) was elsewhere.

[64] HA, HP52/13/1/32, settlement certificate of Isaac Cuer, 1 November 1736.

[65] Burn, *The justice of the peace,* pp. 295-305; not every certificate included the names of all family members, but after 1730 it was a legal requirement to list each

people travelled without a certificate, but to what extent this was common practice in Huntingdonshire is impossible to say.[66] A certificate holder could not gain a settlement after 1698 'unless he took a lease of a tenement of yearly worth of 10 shillings a year, or by executing a legally obtained parish office.'[67] Leasing a property of this value automatically entailed paying rates but unless he could afford the threshold rent, access to the resources of the parish of settlement was restricted, no matter the length of a certificate-holder's residence in the parish. Until 1795 the cost of removal was the responsibility of the settled parish and their officers were continually balancing the possibility of future removal and maintenance costs, against the possibility that a certificate might offer the bearer the chance of gainful employment elsewhere.

A settlement examination was a prerequisite for every removal order but only 21 removal orders have matching examinations, so the original 154 examinations have not survived (Figure 1). Similar situations have been noted in other counties.[68] An examination lost its purpose if a removal order quickly followed, and the gaining of any future settlement would render the examination redundant, which may explain the loss of the Huntingdonshire examinations. Removal orders were likely to have been retained, to prevent future attempts at settlement, and two copies of removal orders were written; one to the 'host' parish and the other to the 'settled' parish. The most crucial of documents for the parish officers to retain, were settlement certificates, because they could be required at any time to prove the liability of another parish for future generations of the certificate holder. In a sense, their 'shelf life' was infinite. This explains their survival in such large numbers compared to all other Huntingdonshire documents (Figure 1). Numbers of settlement examinations reached their height in the last twenty years of the period, as did removal orders, and this was represented nationally.[69]

The Otteridge case

Although the case of the Otteridge family of Godmanchester (1801) stretches slightly beyond the period, it provides a unique demonstration of the whole

---

member of the household to prevent any of them from gaining a settlement in the parish of habitation.

[66] Snell, *Parish and Belonging,* p.98.

[67] Burn, *The justice of the peace, 12th edition,* vol. 3, p.369.

[68] For example, in Oxfordshire, see B. K. Song, 'Agrarian policies on pauper settlement and migration, Oxfordshire 1750-1834', *Continuity and Change,* vol.13, issue 3, December 1998, p.364.

[69] Snell, *Parish and Belonging,* p.99.

process of settlement administration from certification and examination, to an appeal against removal, a pauper letter, and the paying of non-resident relief.[70] It gives an indication of the intricacies and complexities of settlement law, and shows that even when parochial officers employed an attorney, appeals did not run smoothly for the respondent parish (Godmanchester).[71]

In April 1726, the officers of Holy Trinity, Shaftesbury (Dorset) issued the officers of St Mary, Devizes (Wiltshire) with a settlement certificate in respect of Stephen Otteridge and his family. At some point before 1755, the family moved from Devizes to Godmanchester.[72] Several generations of the Otteridge family continued to live in the parish of Godmanchester.[73] In 1800/01 Stephen Otteridge, a descendant of the original certificate holder, may have asked the Godmanchester overseers for poor relief, which prompted them to enquire into his settlement status.[74] They erroneously judged this to be at St Mary, Devizes, and issued an order for his removal on 14 March 1801.[75] The parochial officers of St Mary immediately, and correctly, issued an appeal against Stephen Otteridge's removal.[76] Settlement legislation had developed since the settlement certificate had been drawn up in 1726; these early settlement certificates included the name of the 'host' parish, and were only valid for removal from that named parish, back to the settlement parish.[77] As the 'host' parish named in the 1726 certificate was not Godmanchester, and the parish of settlement was not Devizes, the removal was quashed (stopped) at the Huntingdon Quarter Sessions on 14th April 1801, and the opinion of the Court of King's Bench was sought regarding the validity of the settlement certificate.[78] It appears that Stephen was allowed to remain in Godmanchester. In 1810 he (or perhaps someone on his behalf) wrote to the overseer at Shaftesbury expressing concern that 'the Parish Officers are timid of his becoming chargeable', and from that point at least, the Shaftesbury overseers assumed

---

[70] Alternative spellings include Ottridge, Otridge and Oatridge.

[71] 'Attorney' was the term used in contemporary documentation. A 'respondent' parish usually instigated a removal, whilst the 'appellant' parish appealed against the removal order at the Quarter Sessions in the county of the respondent.

[72] HA, HCP2/1915/bundle2/11, Settlement certificate of Stephen Otteridge, his wife Mary and son Jonathon, dated April 1726.

[73] HA, Godmanchester parish register transcripts open shelves; various entries.

[74] HA, HCP2/1915/bundle2/11.

[75] Ibid.

[76] Huntingdonshire QS Minute book 1800-08; HCP/2/1179/2; HA.

[77] Snell, *Parish and Belonging,* p.99.

[78] HA, HCP/2/1179/2, Huntingdonshire QS Minute book 1800-08.

financial responsibility for Stephen's maintenance. They assured the God-manchester overseers that they would 'discharge any expences [sic] that may incur by his being relieved' in Godmanchester.[79] This case shows the importance of the liability of a settlement certificate stretching through many generations, and demonstrates the financial motives of the Godmanchester officials in attempting to remove a man whose family had regarded the parish as 'home' for many generations.

Huntingdonshire settlement certificates

Studies of settlement certificates show a steep decline after the 1750's and part of the reason for this is the potentially huge cost of the unlimited liability of the settlement parish.[80] In 1795 legislation altered the settlement procedures whereby the host parish became responsible for paying the cost of removal, in an effort to reduce the chances of indiscriminate removal by the host parish. The legislation additionally effectively curtailed the issuing of certificates; from this point removal was only enforceable if a person had actually become chargeable, meaning that they had requested relief, either from the host, or settled, parish.[81] By limiting removal to chargeable people, rather than including people who were thought likely to become chargeable at some point in the future, there was little point is securing an indemnity certificate, but still relevant to retain those previously issued.[82]

The largest number of surviving Huntingdonshire settlement certificates were issued within the county, which confirms that most certificate holders travelled short distances (Table 1). This is similar to the issuing of certificates in Oxfordshire, and it would have been financially prudent to restrict certificates for short distance migration with the aim of keeping any removal costs as low as possible.[83] The Huntingdonshire certificates issued by officers of settlement parishes in other counties were frequently sent to officials of host parishes in Huntingdonshire with whom they shared a border.[84] Eaton Socon (Bedfordshire) officers certificated some of their parishioners in St Neots and Great Staughton, and the Whittlesey (Isle of Ely) overseers issued certificates for people who had moved to Farcet, Stanground and Fletton. Space does not permit an in-depth analysis of miles travelled between

---

[79] Letter from G. Goddard to the Godmanchester overseers, dated 6th Jan 1810, HP34/13/4/7; HA. Otteridge quote taken as quote from Goddard letter.
[80] Snell, *Parish and Belonging*, p.99.
[81] Certificates continued to be issued sporadically, Snell, *Parish and Belonging*, p. 102.
[82] Snell, *Parish and Belonging*, p.102.
[83] Song, 'Agrarian policies', p.379.
[84] CF; ibid.

every host and settled parish recorded in the county's settlement certificates, but it is evident that no more than one county boundary lay between the settled and host parish of most certificate holders. There were evident exceptions, such as that of Stephen Otteridge's family certificate, but nearly half (49%) the certificates were issued from and to, overseers of parishes within the county. The issuing of the Huntingdonshire certificates reached its height between 1736 and 1755, regardless of the county issuing them, and fell thereafter, which is in line with studies for other counties.[85] Most migration was from villages to the county's towns. The majority of certificate bearers (630) lived in host parishes in the towns of St Ives, Huntingdon, St Neots, Kimbolton, Godmanchester and Ramsey, whereas overseers from these towns only signed 178 certificates for other host parishes within the county. This demonstrates that the village parishes were feeding the towns' populations. Additionally, of all the certificates issued by the six towns, between seventy and ninety per cent of them were issued to people wishing to move to another town, so the village/town migration was mostly one-way. Of the hundred or so parishes in Huntingdonshire in this period, the overseers of nearly eighty four per cent drew up at least one settlement certificate, but only twenty-two per cent of parishes were 'host' parishes. The attractions and possibly more diverse employment opportunities for economic migrants provided a catalyst for migration, and whilst certificate-bearers may not be representative of the Huntingdonshire population, the certification system in Huntingdonshire demonstrates inclination on the part of town officials to accept incomers with certificates, as well as willingness by the settled parish officials, to grant certificates.

---

[85] See n.41 above.

Table 1 County origins of Huntingdonshire settlement certificates 1697-1795

	1697-1715	1716-1735	1736-1755	1756-1775	1776-1795	Total
Bedfordshire	26	26	36	14	11	113
Cambridgeshire	25	22	28	20	15	110
Hertfordshire	1	2	10	4	0	17
Huntingdonshire	53	89	135	111	77	465
Northamptonshire	16	34	49	30	16	145
Lincolnshire	1	7	11	9	2	30
Others	11	20	16	7	6	60
Total	133	200	285	195	127	940

Notes Counties issuing more than ten 'Huntingdonshire' settlement certificates (1697-1795), 'others' are counties which issued ten or fewer certificates. Source; Huntingdonshire Archives settlement records.

Historians have asserted that settlement certificates were typically issued to a man, together with his family.[86] The marital status of around 200 certificate bearers living in St Ives is unavailable.[87] Of the remaining certificates, roughly forty-seven per cent were issued to families (with fewer being given to larger families consisting of three or more children), which is a similar proportion to that in Cambridgeshire.[88] It is axiomatic that the larger the family, the greater any removal costs, so perhaps this indicates unwillingness by parochial officials to grant a certificate in respect of a large family. Forty-five per cent of the certificates were issued to couples, and five per cent to women. The rest (almost three per cent) were issued to men with no given marital status. Given the strict rules for the required information on settlement certificates, it is likely that these men had no dependents. In an agriculturally based economy, single young men who were mobile and healthy were in demand, and as un-certificated men were better placed to gain a set-

---

[86] Hampson, 'Settlement and removal', p.286.
[87] HA, HP72/13/4/1, St Ives settlement certificate records; this compilation was recorded sometime later, the original certificates are missing. There are other examples showing that overseers kept a written record of certificate holders, see Hampson, *Treatment,* p.147.
[88] Hampson, 'Settlement', p.286.

tlement, many single men may have managed to avoid the certification system.[89] This may explain the issuing of few certificates to single men in Huntingdonshire. Historians have suggested that few certificates were issued to single women, because of the possible detrimental effect upon the rate-payers, if a poor, single, woman were to become pregnant, and a charge on the settled parish.[90] This is probably the reason why so few certificates were given to single women in Huntingdonshire. On the other hand, certificated women might have experienced better employment or marriage opportunities elsewhere, whilst losing their old settlement in the process. In April 1741, the officers of Wellingborough (Northamptonshire), issued a certificate to two dressmakers, Dorothy and Ann Wainwright (possibly sisters) after they became resident in All Saints, Huntingdon.[91] Dorothy married Henry Nettleton in All Saints on 18th October 1742, thereby taking her husband's settlement.[92] The marriages of several single women certificated to St Ives during this period may indicate that the St Ives overseers were particularly vigilant in demanding certificates in respect of single women.

Parishioners could sometimes play the 'settlement system' to their advantage. Temporary work undertaken elsewhere might confer an unwanted settlement. A request to their parish of settlement for a settlement certificate would circumvent the possibility of gaining a new settlement, and Snell suggests that parochial officers were content to issue certificates to 'good' workers whom they wished to retain.[93] Working the system to a parishioner's advantage becomes noticeable if admitted by an examinant, or when a particular individual is identifiable in several sources. King Ruff was born in Stilton in 1757 and acquired his Huntingdon settlement through apprenticeship to a cordwainer in the parish of All Saints.[94] Following the completion of his apprenticeship in Huntingdon, he worked in Stilton, and subsequently returned to Huntingdon, where he was examined regarding his settlement, and he told the justice questioning him that he had:-

---

[89] Snell, *Parish and Belonging*, p.102.
[90] Hampson, 'Settlement', pp.277 & 286; Landau, 'Laws of settlement', p. 412; Snell, *Parish and Belonging*, p.98.
[91] HA, HP46/13/1/58, Settlement certificate for Dorothy and Ann Wainwright, 20th April 1741.
[92] HA, HP46/1/1/2, All Saints Huntingdon composite register, 1678-1783.
[93] Song, 'Agrarian policies', p.368.
[94] HA, Settlement examination of King Ruff, 21 September 1779.

*'paid rates to that parish [Stilton] but before he paid any Rates he procured
a Certificate of his settlement from the parish officers of All Saints in the said
Borough [of Huntingdon].*[95]

He appears to have acted to protect his favoured Huntingdon settlement,
which could have been superseded by paying rates to the parish of Stilton. He
was apparently able to navigate his way around the legal intricacies of the
settlement system in order to retain his preferred settlement. The parochial
officers of All Saints, Huntingdon, were therefore unsuccessful in their attempt to prove a settlement had been gained away from their parish.

A slightly different example is that of William Cole. William was a glover and
breeches maker from Kimbolton, who had probably been born, and almost
certainly married, in the town. It may be the case that the Cole family had a
stronger emotional attachment to Kimbolton, than King Ruff had towards Stilton, his place of birth.[96] William Cole and his family were issued with consec-
utive settlement certificates to two different parishes, firstly in 1760 to the
parish of Riseley (Bedfordshire) and then in 1769, to the parish of All Saints,
Huntingdon.[97] The family subsequently returned to live in Kimbolton.[98] It is
very unusual to find a person with multiple certificates, and it probably
demonstrates proactivity on William's part due to his reluctance to lose his
Kimbolton settlement, rather than gaining a subsequent, unwanted settlement
in either Riseley or Huntingdon.

The act of marrying occasionally prompted a settlement examination, which
provoked the examinant to seek a settlement certificate from their parish of
settlement.[99] Norma Landau found that most of the childless married men
who were 'subjected to the settlement laws' during this period, had recently

---

[95] HA, HP83/13/1/22, settlement certificate for King Ruff, 14th December 1778; HA,
HP46/13/3/26, Settlement examination of King Ruff, 21 September 1779.
[96] HA, HP52/1/1/1 Kimbolton composite register 1647-1748; William Cole was baptised on August 15th, 1735, and William Cole, glover, married Esther Ireland on Jan
21st 1760.
[97] Bedfordshire Archives, P50/13/1/11, settlement certificate for William Cole and
Esther his wife, 8th April 1760; HA, HP46/13/1/120, settlement certificate for William Cole, Esther his wife, and their children; Esther, Mary, Elizabeth and Martha,
14th October 1769.
[98] HA, AH16/39, will of William Cole, glover of Kimbolton.
[99] N. Landau, The regulation of immigration, economic structures and definitions
of the poor in eighteenth-century England', *The Historical Journal* 33:3, 1990, pp.
541-571, p.554.

been married and asserted that the cost of a potential family was the reason to check the man's settlement.[100] The Kimbolton parochial officers often requested proof of the settlement of recently married couples, which does imply that single men were not targeted to request a certificate from their settled parish. For instance, William Barley married Catren Shepard in the summer of 1747 and they were certificated in December of that year; James Brickford married Elizabeth Plowman in October 1751 and their settlement certificate was dated April 1752; Thomas Willows married Elizabeth Brown in October 1757 and their certificate was issued six weeks afterwards.[101] Between 1782 and 1795 four other couples living in Kimbolton were issued with a settlement certificate from their settlement parishes, all had recently married in Kimbolton.[102] Kimbolton overseers sought a removal order from the justices in respect of Thomas and Susannah Briggs on 20th November 1790, following their earlier marriage in Kimbolton on 5 November.[103] The Eaton Socon overseers must have been happy to grant the Briggs' certificate, which was issued just seven days later, even though it is a fairly late example of certification; only thirty Huntingdonshire certificates were issued between 1790 and 1795.[104]

Few women were ever given settlement certificates.[105] The certificate issued by Huntingdon All Saints in 1771 to Huntingdon St Mary in respect of Mary Snodle unusually acknowledged that she was 'a poor woman', but neglected to include her marital status and so the presumption is that she was single.[106] The host parish overseers would have been assiduous in obtaining this settlement certificate due to her poverty. However, both parishes were in the borough therefore any removal costs should have been slight. The inference however, is that some sort of future financial support would probably become necessary, and perhaps the unusual wording was an acknowledgement of that. As a wife gained her husband's legal place of settlement upon mar-

---

[100] Landau, 'The regulation of immigration', p.549.
[101] Kimbolton Parish Registers Transcript, open shelves; HA.
[102] HA, HP52/13/1/73, James Putterall 1782; HP52/13/1/74 Richard Mott 1782; HP52/13/1/75 Thomas Brown 1786; HP52/13/1/76 Thomas Briggs 1790.
[103] HA, HP52/13/3/22; HP52/13/1/76; Removal order and settlement certificate of Thomas and Susannah Briggs; HA, Kimbolton Parish Registers, open shelves.
[104] HA, HP52/13/3/22; HP52/13/1/76; Removal order and settlement certificate of Thomas and Susannah Briggs.
[105] For example, see S. Williams, *Poverty, gender and life-cycle under the English poor law, 1760-1834*, Woodbridge: Boydell, 2011, p.82.
[106] HA, HP46/13/1/125, Mary Snodle, settlement certificate, dated 1771.

rying, and this usually persisted into widowhood; a widow might be removed somewhere completely unfamiliar.[107] Widowed Emma Stocker was due to be removed to Huntingdon from Great Chesterford (Essex) on 4 March 1741 but she must have contacted the Huntingdon overseers to ask for their help; they agreed to send a settlement certificate to the Great Chesterford overseers.[108] Perhaps it is possible to detect humanitarian overtones when officers did (unusually) agree to grant a certificate to a widow - even if their prime motivation was financial. In weighing up the immediate removal costs and likely resulting maintenance costs, against only a potential future threat of removal costs, the overseers may have decided that the latter choice was the better risk.

Officials understood the liability carried with every certificate, and they had an obligation to certificate-holders and their families if they were unfortunate enough to be removed back to their settled parish. It was usually the very vulnerable, and actually chargeable certificated parishioners, who were removed prior to 1795. In 1732 William Neave and his wife Lettes had been granted a certificate from Huntingdon St John for the parish of Brandon (Suffolk).[109] In early 1744 their three children Thomas (four years old), Mary (nine) and William (twelve), were orphaned.[110] Their certificated father had been unable to earn a new settlement in Suffolk in the intervening twelve years since leaving Huntingdon, therefore the orphans were removed to Huntingdon, their father's last legal place of settlement. They probably had no familiarity with Huntingdon but its officers became responsible for their maintenance costs. It is very likely that the children were 'boarded out' until old enough to be apprenticed, at the town's cost.[111] The fate of the eldest child, William, is unknown, but the two youngest children were apprenticed at the age of 10 by the borough in 1745 and 1750.[112]

---

[107] Hampson, 'Settlement', p.285.

[108] HA, HP46/13/2/2, Removal order for Emma Stocker, 4 March 1741; note in Huntingdon All Saints Vestry book 1731-1776, HP46/8/1/2, unpageinated.

[109] Suffolk Record Office at Bury St Edmunds, FL536/7/3/1/33, Settlement certificate of William Neave.

[110] HA, HP46/13/2/3, 11th January 1744; HP46/13/2/4, 21st March 1744.

[111] There are no surviving St John's overseers' accounts books for this period but the Kimbolton overseers' accounts books include contemporary costs for the 'boarding out' of orphans, see HA, HP52/12/12/4, 1741-1753.

[112] HA, HP46/13/2/3-4, Removal orders for Thomas, Mary and William Neave, 11 January 1744; HA, Huntingdon Apprenticeship Card Index.

Huntingdonshire settlement examinations

Settlement examinations represent the parochial officers' most immediate influence during this period, over the fate of the poor who lived away from their parish of settlement. An examination established which parish shouldered responsibility for future poor relief by ascertaining how a settlement had been attained. The reasons for arranging a settlement examination have been hotly debated by Snell and Landau. Snell asserted that settlement examinations were a fairly accurate guide to the dating and commencing of unemployment and chargeability, and also suggested that one-year service contracts gradually gave way to weekly, monthly, or fifty-one week hirings.[113] In contrast, Landau argued that in Kent officials used the settlement laws for the precautionary surveillance of migrants whom they regularly examined. [114] A removal frequently followed the examination, but it might otherwise provoke a settlement certificate from the parish of settlement.[115] Furthermore, Landau maintained that parochial officers monitored migrants 'vigilantly' in Kent.[116]

Most of the Huntingdonshire village parishes for which settlement examinations survive, had just one or two dating from pre-1795, whereas the towns experienced a higher frequency of examinations. Towns drew the population from the countryside and offered a greater range of employment opportunities than those usually found in villages, particularly in service industries. Sixty-two examinations were arranged in Huntingdon and forty-one in Kimbolton between 1744 and 1795 (Figure 2) with the number rising in both towns up to 1785, and then tapering off in Kimbolton. The highest number of settlement examinations took place between 1776 and 1785 in both towns, due to a large number of 'group' examinations. The Kimbolton overseers appeared to be concerned about a small influx of wool sorters into the town and organised for the examination of five men on 14th June 1783 and 15 men on 14th January 1784. All the deponents were male, with an unrecorded marital status. More than half had served apprenticeships in the woollen trade, mostly in other counties. Although many other examinants in Kimbolton can be connected to Kimbolton parish register entries, most of the group examinants cannot, and appear to be strangers in Kimbolton. Their settlement examinations are unusually brief, and several examinations were recorded on one piece of paper. Only one justice signed these group examinations, which

---

[113] Snell, *Annals*, pp.75-76.

[114] N. Landau, 'The laws of settlement and the surveillance of immigration in eighteenth-century Kent', *Continuity and Change,* 1988, p.391.

[115] Landau, 'The laws of settlement', p.400.

[116] Ibid., p.392.

was highly irregular, but it possibly indicates a sense of urgency in examining a number of people quickly.[117] Three of Kimbolton's leading townsmen supported a movement to petition parliament to legislate against abuses and illegal trading practices in the woollen trade; John Luccock and Edward Smith were involved in the manufacture of worsted, and Neville Tomlinson was a 'gentleman-investor'.[118] The organising of these examinations might indicate that the leading townsmen were concerned that the worsted business was being undercut in Kimbolton, by an influx of worsted workers. This is possibly an isolated example of pressure being brought to bear upon people whose presence in the town was a source of concern to the rate-payers, rather than demonstrating a differentiated attitude towards the settled and non-settled in a parish.[119]

Figure 2 Dates of settlement examinations in Huntingdon and Kimbolton between 1744 and 1795

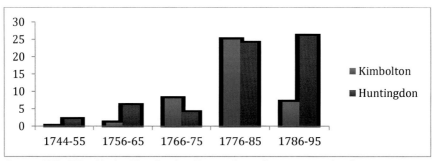

Source HA, HP46/13/3, Huntingdon Borough settlement examinations, 1744-1795; HP52/13/2, Kimbolton settlement examinations 1756-1795

---

[117] Two justices should have signed all settlement papers; Burn, *The justice of the peace, 12th edition,* vol. 3, pp. 434-77. After 1730 any signed by just one justice were invalid. Styles, *Evolution,* p.198.

[118] Northampton Mercury, cited by K. Sugden, The Occupational and Organizational Structures of the Northamptonshire Worsted and Shoemaking Trades, circa 1750-1821 (M.St. in Local and Regional History, Cambridge, 2011), pp.31-33; will of John Luucock, woolstapler, draper and grocer of Kimbolton, will dated 23 March 1787 prob/11/1151/266; will of Neville Tomlinson, gentleman of Kimbolton, will dated 3 July 1809, prob 11/1501/11; http://www.discovery.nationalarchives.gov.uk

[119] Snell, *Parish and Belonging*, pp.97-98.

More than a third of all the surviving borough examinations took the form of a group examination, which occurred on at least five occasions and were therefore more common in Huntingdon than the rare event described in Kimbolton. The majority of the deponents were either currently serving, or had served, in the militia, and had recently married. This might suggest that the Huntingdon officers did sometimes use examinations as a precautionary surveillance tool to establish settlements, a practice suggested by Landau. There was an awareness of a high rate of military family desertion, which was concerning for overseers, because the parish took responsibility for any allowance paid to the chargeable wife of a man who served in the militia on the parish's behalf.[120] Overseers were therefore always keen to establish a militiaman's settlement because they formed a highly mobile cohort of society, frequently called upon to serve away for up to five years at a time.[121] It is therefore not surprising to note that the settlements of some of the examined militiamen were established as being in Essex, Hertfordshire, Middlesex, Northamptonshire and Yorkshire. Whenever possible, overseers would track down the putative father of an illegitimate child, and examine him as to his place of settlement. For instance, the settlement examination of Mary Lee noted that her settlement was in All Saints, Huntingdon, that she was a pregnant, single woman likely to be chargeable to the parish. Included with the examination, was a note of the warrant for the arrest of Edward Seabright, 'serjeant in the Plymouth Division of Marines now quartered at Huntingdon' together with an instruction to 'find security to indemnify the parish.'[122]

The majority of examinants in both towns appear to have gained their settlement from apprenticeship, of from a year of service (Figure 3). Ann Kussmaul makes the point that between thirty-three and fifty per cent of agricultural workers in early modern England were servants in husbandry, and accordingly 'most ... youths in rural England were servants in husbandry'.[123] Given the agricultural nature of Huntingdonshire's economy it is quite likely, and where no evidence suggests otherwise, that the majority of examinants who had gained their settlement by service, had been engaged in husbandry. The validity of settlement gained through a service year was one of the most difficult to disprove because it could have occurred anywhere.

---

[120] Williams, *Poverty, gender and life-cycle* p.53.
[121] D. Kent, 'Gone for a soldier': Family breakdown and the demography of desertion in a London parish, 1750-91, *Local Population Studies*, 45, 1990, pp.27-42.
[122] HA, HP46/12/2/uncatalogued, examination of Mary Lee, 17 October 1780.
[123] A. Kussmaul, *Servants in Husbandry in Early Modern England,* Cambridge: CUP, 1981, pp.3-5.

The subject encompassed most space in settlement manuals and was the most debated cause of appeals against removal, probably because more people had gained settlement through service than by any other route.[124] According to Snell, as the period of the Old Poor Law continued, employers increasingly ended hirings a few days before the end of the contracted year of service, which prevented a hired person from attaining a settlement.[125] The examinants living in Huntingdon and Kimbolton gave very few examples of employment being cut short, but shorter periods of hiring were becoming more evident.[126]

Figure 3 Attaining of settlement by examinants living in Huntingdon and Kimbolton 1744-1795

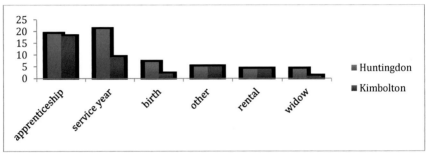

Source HA, HP46/13/3, Huntingdon Borough settlement examinations, 1744-1795; HP52/13/2, Kimbolton settlement examinations 1756-1795.

The gaining of settlement through apprenticeship remained steady for Huntingdon examinants, but declined towards the end of the period for Kimbolton examinants. Few examinants had served their apprenticeship in the town where they were examined, and this might explain why they were examined – to evaluate where their place of settlement was, if not in the town. Place of birth was usually included but the age at examination was not usually included, neither were many employment dates, therefore in most cases it is impossible to gauge the length of time between gaining the settlement, and being examined. The statement resulting from the examining in Huntingdon of Charles Patrick on 14th November 1775 is fairly typical, and ambiguous as to his age or marital status, but the overseers' aim was to have proved his place of settlement to their satisfaction.

---

[124] For example, R. Burn, *The justice of the peace,* contains nearly 200 pages detailing settlement case law, of which 97 concern settlement by service.
[125] Snell, *Annals,* pp.75-76.
[126] Snell, *Annals,* pp.74-77.

'This examinant saith that he was born in Little Oakley in the county of Northampton and that he afterwards served his father as an apprentice for seven years by indenture in the same parish as a mason and that he hath done no act whatever since to gain him a settlement elsewhere.'[127]

Some examinants may have not admitted all the facts about their settlement, perhaps to maintain some control over their fate after examination. Charles Patrick had previously been examined in Kimbolton (13th March 1775) and the details on each of his examinations do not concur.[128] According to the examination in Kimbolton, his father had been certificated to Little Oakley from Burton Latimer (Northamptonshire) therefore the apprenticeship Charles had served at Little Oakley did not qualify him for settlement there. Following the Kimbolton examination, Charles was removed to Little Oakley.[129] Charles' motives for disguising the truth of his settlement are unknown, and perhaps his circumstances were more widely known in Kimbolton than in Huntingdon, but the two examinations shed more light on the mobility of examinants.[130] Taylor suggests that of the poorer parishioners, those who left their parish of settlement were the 'most competent of the poor' and perhaps Charles Patrick was simply unlucky in being examined twice, but it may indicate the difficulties of attaining a settlement post-apprenticeship.[131] Few male examinants in Kimbolton or Huntingdon appear to have obtained their settlement post-apprenticeship by paying rates, or by serving a parochial office, and the conclusion to be drawn is that attaining a new settlement after reaching their mid-twenties, became hard to acquire for the type of people being examined – which might explain why they were examined.

In determining the facts of a settlement issue the officials occasionally used family settlement papers, and called witnesses to give evidence during ex-

[127] HA, HP46/13/3/12, Settlement examination of Charles Patrick, 14th November 1775.
[128] HA, HP52/13/2/6, Settlement examination of Charles Patrick, 13th March 1775. Photo of Charles Patrick's examination on p.134.
[129] HA, HP52/13/3/15, Removal order for Charles Patrick, 13th March 1775.
[130] Entries in the Kimbolton composite register indicate that the Patrick family lived in Kimbolton at least from June 1773; HA, HP52/1/1/3, Kimbolton composite register 1749-1799, unpageinated.
[131] J.S. Taylor, 'Voices in the Crowd: The Kirkby Lonsdale Township Letters, 1809-36', in T. Hitchcock, P. King, & P. Sharpe (eds.), *Chronicling Poverty: The Voices and Strategies of the English Poor 1640-1840*, Basingstoke, Macmillan, 1997, p.114.

aminations, who were often family members or employers. Thomas Horseford worked for a year in Kimbolton for his brother, Edward, as a 'bricklayer as often as he could find Employment- but not as an apprentice.'[132] Edward was then questioned by the justice and agreed that apprenticeship indentures had not been signed.[133] Thomas, his second wife and two daughters were subsequently removed from Kimbolton.[134] Thomas Cross's settlement examination of 1783 was used in 1816 to establish that his daughter Hannah, a pregnant, single woman, had no settlement other than one derived from his settlement in Hunsdon, Hertfordshire and so she was removed there.[135] Her father had served a year in Hunsdon over 25 years previously and it is almost certain that she had never lived there. Hannah's situation was not unusual as single women were much more likely to undergo a settlement examination than single men.[136] Pregnancy was the cause of over half the settlement examinations of single women; if a paternity order proved unable to be enforced, the mother's and child's parish (or parishes, if different), would have to fund their maintenance, which could be expensive.[137]

Single women comprised 14 per cent (Huntingdon) and 13 per cent (Kimbolton) of deponents compared to only 4 per cent of single men in each town. Families and single mothers were most often examined and/or removed.[138] Other studies have found that the 'majority' of examinants were married labourers with one or two children which concurs with the picture in Huntingdon.[139] At least three quarters of the Huntingdon deponents were married, but only about half the Kimbolton deponents; the figure for Kimbolton might be unrepresentative because of the scanty marital information recorded on the group examination. Barring examinations identified as having

---

[132] HA, HP52/13/2/11(1), settlement examination of Thomas Horseford, 7th February 1782.
[133] HA, HP52/13/2/11(2), settlement examination of Edward Horseford, 7th February 1782.
[134] HA, HP52/13/3/18, removal order, Thomas Horseford, 7th February 1782.
[135] HA, Settlement examination of Thomas Cross, uncatalogued and attached to the removal order of Hannah 28 February 1816, HP52/13/3/61.
[136] Marshall, *The English Poor,* p.164; A. Levene, 'Poor Families, removals and 'nurture' in late Old Poor Law London', *Continuity and Change,* 25:2, 2010, pp. 233-262.
[137] For example, Williams, *Poverty, gender and life-cycle,* p.51.
[138] H. Woledge, and M. A. Smale, 'Migration in East Yorkshire in the Eighteenth Century', *Local Population Studies,* 70, 2003, pp.29-48, p.35, table 2; Hampson, 'Settlement', p. 277; Hampson, *Treatment,* p.140.
[139] J.S.Taylor, 'The Impact of Pauper Settlement, 1691-1834' *Past & Present* 73, 1976 p.57; Hampson, 'Settlement', p. 277; Woledge and Smale, 'Migration in East Yorkshire', p.35, table 2.

been arranged for a specific purpose, those of groups, single women, widows and recently married men, there is not evidence contained in the settlement examinations held in Kimbolton or Huntingdon during this period, to either corroborate or disprove Snell's assertion that many examinations were caused by recent unemployment.

Evidence of non-resident relief in Huntingdon-shire

It has been suggested that some examinants were underemployed, rather than unemployed. Parochial officials understood that when a justice signed a removal order it was tantamount to an order of maintenance, and it may have been financially prudent, if strictly illegal, to relieve in the host parish rather than to remove the person back to their settlement.[140] Furthermore, Burn asserted that any relief paid by host parish officials without agreement from the settled parish overseers, equated with acceptance of responsibility of the pauper's settlement.[141] Naturally overseers were reluctant to allow this, just as non-settled people were unwilling to ask for help from the host overseers, as this was an admittance of chargeability. However, in a bid to reduce costly removals, or perhaps on humanitarian grounds, there is evidence that overseers in host and settlement parishes increasingly saw the mutual benefits in discussing the situation of certificated and chargeable paupers before arranging their removal. For instance, the Raunds (Northamptonshire) overseers wrote to the Kimbolton overseers in March 1778 regarding the Widow Pack and her two children. Her husband had been a 'certificate man' from Kimbolton which was therefore their legal place of settlement. Widow Pack had requested aid from the Raunds overseers, who wrote to the Kimbolton overseers in March 1778:-

> '*You must relieve or fetch them home, she is very troublesome and has asked for relief several times but we have refused to give this without letting you know.*'[142]

Some relief was then paid by the Kimbolton overseers, probably via the Raunds overseers, because it was not until March 1780 that a removal order

---

[140] M. Nolan, *A Treatise on the Laws for the Relief and Settlement of the Poor*, Vol. 2, London, 1814, 3rd edition, p.188.

[141] Burn, *The justice of the peace*, p.815.

[142] HA, Letter from Raunds overseers to Kimbolton overseers dated March 1778.

was issued for the Packs to be returned to Kimbolton.[143] The cost of the meeting held between the two sets of overseers and a justice to discuss the case amounted to nearly £3, most of which was spent on their meals, and the removal order was signed the same day.[144] The evidence demonstrates that the Raunds overseers were communicative, and amenable to helping the widow and her family, provided that they were reimbursed, but perhaps the Kimbolton officers decided that it was financially beneficial (and less trouble) to bring the Pack family home to Kimbolton.

Although operated alongside settlement law, non-resident relief was not strictly legal, as under the terms of the Elizabethan Poor Law, relief was only permissible in the parish of settlement, but its growth was due to the increasing conviction that it was a pragmatic and potential method of saving money.[145] Officers in both Huntingdon and Kimbolton cooperated with parochial officials in other parishes to effectively act as banking agents in paying non-resident relief from at least 1756 (Kimbolton) and 1777 (Huntingdon). For instance, the Kimbolton overseers paid non-resident relief via host overseers of 1s. per week from 1763 to Widow Wood in Woodford (Northamptonshire), and 2s. per week to the widow of James Bull in Hartford (Huntingdonshire).[146] Widow Bull had at least two children therefore 2 shillings per week was insufficient for the family's maintenance and she probably had alternative means of making a living.[147] Legally both families should have been removed but possibly their wish was to remain in the host parish where they may have lived for very many years, and where they were perhaps able, with some aid, to maintain themselves and their family. The Kimbolton overseers presumably hoped a small amount of aid would forestall their removal back to Kimbolton, where perhaps their maintenance costs would have been much greater. The administration of non-resident relief was very time consuming as well as requiring the acquiescence of the host overseers, but in situations where non-resident relief was not an option that officers were prepared or able to give, removal was the probable outcome.

---

[143] HA, box HP46/12/1/1, uncatalogued, letter from Raunds overseers to Kimbolton overseers dated 31 December 1779; box HP46/12/1/1, removal order for Martha Pack and her two children dated 28 March 1780.

[144] HA, box HP46/12/1/1, uncatalogued, bill from Raunds overseers to Kimbolton overseers dated 28 March 1780; HA; box HP46/12/1/1, uncatalogued, removal order for Martha Pack and her two children dated 28 March 1780.

[145] Williams, *Poverty, gender and life-cycle'*, p.82.

[146] HA, HP52/12/5, Kimbolton Overseers Account Book 1753-1774, unpageinated.

[147] By 1797 the average weekly allowance as calculated by Eden was between one shilling a week to two shillings and sixpence per person, quoted in D. Marshall, *The English Poor,* pp.100-101.

Huntingdonshire removal orders

The syntax employed in removal orders was straightforward, designed to accentuate the lack of entitlement to settlement by the person being removed from the host parish. The early handwritten orders, mostly dating from the pre- 1750's, were clearly taken from a legal template and include phrases such as 'lately intruded into your parish, and 'having attempted to settle himself as an inhabitant not legally qualified so to do.' To have been removed during this period was a rare event, but must have been isolating and frightening, often following a catastrophic personal event in one's personal circumstances, such as the death of a family member, illness or perhaps a pregnancy whilst unmarried. There are 176 Huntingdonshire removal orders dating from 1698 to 1795, which is an average of less than two a year, but a few removals for which the orders have not survived, occurred much earlier than this. The earliest evidence of a removal organised by the Kimbolton overseers is in the account book for March 1668, with a payment for a warrant for the removal order of Thomas Clarke.[148] In 1671 the payments for Mary Polter's three days of lodging with meals, and her removal back to St Neots, were also recorded.[149] These examples of removals indicate that settlement administration was well organised from a very early date after the 1662 Act, and it raises the possibility that the paperwork for early removals in other parishes has also been lost.[150] The surviving 176 removal orders indicate that most removals were organised from the county's towns. Officers in thirty-five Huntingdonshire parishes initiated removals, but twenty-five of these parishes only undertook three or fewer removals throughout the whole period. For the ratepayers in most Huntingdonshire village parishes, a removal would have been a very rare occurrence and expense. Five parishes organised ten or more removals; Godmanchester, Huntingdon, Kimbolton, Ramsey and St Neots; removal administration for the towns of Kimbolton and Huntingdon has been assessed in greater detail.

---

[148] HA, HP52/12/1, Kimbolton Overseers Account Book 1649-1689, unpageinated.
[149] HA, HP52/12/1, Kimbolton Overseers Account Book 1649-1689, unpageinated.
[150] Few Huntingdonshire overseers' accounts survive pre-1700.

Figure 4 Removals from and into Huntingdon and Kimbolton by demographic type

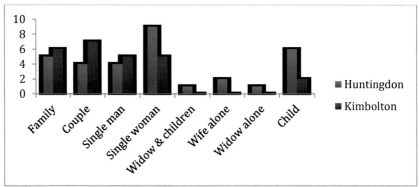

Source: HA:HP46/13/2; Huntingdon borough removal orders, 1709-1793; HP52/13/3; Kimbolton removal orders, 1703-1790.

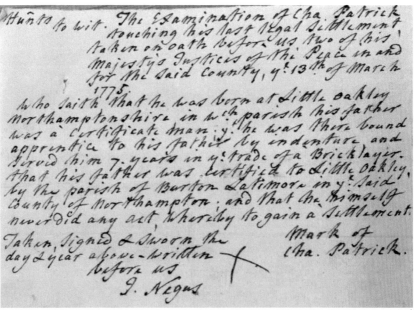

Figure 5 Settlement examination of Charles Patrick, dated 13th March 1775[151]
(Courtesy Huntingdonshire Archives)

Fifty-seven removals were organised into and away from, Huntingdon and Kimbolton, during this period. This is relevant because even when the removal was not at the instigation of the town's parish officers, they had to

---

[151] HA, HP52/13/2/6

administer their settled poor who had been removed to the town from a host parish. Removal orders precipitated by the Kimbolton parochial officers between 1735 and 1795 were predominantly directed at families and single women. Of the ten surviving removals out of Kimbolton, four each were in respect of these groups whereas only one single man and one couple were removed. At least one single woman was removed to give birth in her parish of settlement.[152] Three of the four families consisted of both parents, and one or two young children, aged between one and five years old. This equates well with Hampson's findings for Cambridgeshire where, at least up to the mid-eighteenth century, the majority of removed families in Cambridgeshire included an average number of two children.[153] Details given in the four family settlement examinations suggest that three of the household heads were not in regular work; two of them had been apprentice bricklayers, and a third had kept an alehouse and had been a rate-payer in Rushden (Northamptonshire).[154] The assumption is that these removals were related to chargeability caused by lack of employment; married craftsmen, unskilled workers and tradesmen, especially those with children, were often examined and removed in Kent, as opposed to single men.[155]

Historians have noted officers' efforts to remove pregnant, single women to avoid the conferring of settlement upon their unborn child, and it has also been suggested that it was sometimes easier to remove a pregnant single woman rather than to pursue a putative father for an affiliation order.[156] The latter seems to have been Mary Enfield/Infield's experience. She was issued with a removal order from Brampton to St John's, her parish of legal settlement, with her illegitimate child, in September 1776.[157] St John's overseers then paid Mary one shilling per week for several months after she had given birth to a second illegitimate baby.[158] Perhaps these officers were not as assiduous as the overseers of All Saints in pursuing putative fathers. It was not

---

[152] HA, HP52/13/3/21, removal order of Elizabeth Smith, 24 September 1784.

[153] Hampson, 'Settlement', p.277

[154] HA, HP52/13/2/6, 11, 8, settlement examinations of Charles Patrick, Thomas Horseford, and William Hooper; HP52/13/3/5, 18, 16, removal orders, Charles Patrick, Thomas Horseford, and William Hooper.

[155] Landau, 'The regulation of immigration', at p.549.

[156] Woledge and Smale, 'Migration', p.35, table 2; Hampson, 'Settlement', p. 277; Hampson, *The Treatment of Poverty,* p.140; C. Vialls, 'The Laws of Settlement: their impact on the poor inhabitants of the Daventry area of Northamptonshire, 1750-1834', unpublished Ph.D. dissertation, University of Leicester, 1998, pp.164-5.

[157] HA, HP46/13/2/12, removal order for Mary Infield, 1776.

[158] HA, HP46/12/2/5, Huntingdon St John Overseers' Account Book, 1776, unpageinated

unusual for the pregnancy of a single woman to provoke a settlement examination and removal, but a forced marriage was rarer.[159] Sarah Truss, a pregnant, single woman, was examined in the borough parish of All Saints 20th September 1793 as to her legal settlement, which was St John's parish, Huntingdon. The All Saints overseers immediately executed a removal order, to shift the financial burden of an illegitimate child away from the parish of All Saints, on to the mother's settled parish of St John's.[160] The parish officers of St John's also examined Sarah, on 30 September 1793, when she admitted that she was single and pregnant, that her unborn baby would be chargeable to the parish of St John's, and that the father was Thomas Bells of Grafham, five miles away.[161] The St John's overseers were slightly more proactive on this occasion; they tracked down Thomas Bell and examined him on December 28th 1793. It was categorically established that he had gained his latest settlement by serving a fully indentured and completed apprenticeship to a shoemaker, William Mayes, in Grafham.[162] The parish officials of St John's then organised a marriage licence, and Thomas and Sarah were married in St John's the same day, with the overseers paying £1 18s for the licence and marriage fees.[163] Presumably they regarded this sum to be a fraction of the trouble and cost which they would have been responsible for, had Sarah given birth to an illegitimate child whose settlement would have been St John's.[164]

The majority of removals into the borough of Huntingdon (six) occurred between the four Huntingdon parishes. Given their proximity to each other, removals would certainly have been relatively cheap and easy to organise, but perhaps these removals demonstrate the acute awareness of financial accountability the overseers (who were also rate-payers) felt towards the rest of the parish rate-payers. There is also an absence of retaliatory removals between the parishes, and where details are given, the inter-parish borough removals seem straightforward. Two single women who were removed within the borough were both pregnant, therefore it is understandable that

---

[159] Williams, *Poverty, gender and life-cycle* pp.108-9.
[160] HA; HP46/13/2/23, Mary Infield's removal order, 20th September 1793.
[161] HA, HP46/13/3/53, Sarah Truss' settlement examination.
[162] HA, HP46/13/3/54, Thomas Bells' settlement examination.
[163] HA, HP46/12/2/6, Huntingdon St John Overseers' Account Book, 1793-4, unpageinated.
[164] Thomas Turner gives a first-hand account of the difficulties he experienced as a parish overseer in a similar incident, see D. Vaisey, ed. *The Diary of Thomas Turner, 1754-1765,* Oxford: OUP, 1985.

they were removed to their parish of settlement.[165] James Ransom had been examined on two occasions in the previous two years before being removed with his family.[166] The rarity of undergoing two examinations in Huntingdon possibly implies that he had either asked for poor relief or had been identified as being close to becoming a charge on the parish, in which case this removal seems understandable.

After 1795 removals could be suspended due to sickness, but illness was rarely recorded on a removal order, or as the cause of removal, prior to 1795. It is occasionally indicated by the survival of linked correspondence such as a bill from the host overseers. James Longland broke his thigh when working in Great Staughton (Huntingdonshire) in 1793 but was not examined or removed to Huntingdon St John, his settled parish, until 24 July that year, when he had recovered and could safely travel.[167] His medical and maintenance costs had been paid by Great Staughton parish during his illness, which were presumably recouped from Huntingdon, and upon being removed to Huntingdon he was paid a weekly amount of 3s. into September.[168] It is suggested by Alannah Tomkins that contemporaries may have contested a straightforward link between illness and poverty, preferring 'to view poverty as a personal failing'.[169] Perhaps, therefore, any sickness causing unemployment, poverty and chargeability, was no more noteworthy to record on a removal order than any other cause of chargeability. The implication from the Huntingdon settlement documents is that the administration of settlement documentation prior to 1795 has probably disguised the number of removals caused by illness, whereas sickness as a cause of removal is easier to detect after 1795.

Removals in Huntingdonshire can usually be associated with direct economic or physical vulnerability, but some of the saddest cases involve children who faced removal from their family, because of their illegitimacy.

---

[165] HA, HP/46/13/2/12 removal order for Mary Infield, 28 September 1776; HP46/13/2/23, removal order for Sarah Truss, 20 September 1793.

[166] HA, HP46/13/2/7, removal order for James Ransom, March 1760.

[167] HA, HP46/13/2/22, removal order and examination of James Longland with associated correspondence, 24 July 1793.

[168] HA, HP46/8/1/3, Huntingdon All Saints with St John, vestry minute book 1776-1818, unpageinated.

[169] A. Tomkins, "Labouring on a bed of sickness': The material and rhetorical deployment of ill-health in male pauper letters', in Gestrich, A., Hurren, E., and King, S., *Poverty and Sickness in Modern Europe: Narratives of the Sick Poor, 1780-1938,* Continuum International: London, 2012, p.52.

Thomas Carr, aged eight, was issued with a removal order in 1776. [170] Thomas was the blind, illegitimate son of Elizabeth James and had been born in Huntingdon St John's. He subsequently lived with his mother and stepfather in Holy Trinity, Cambridge. Until the age of seven, a child was a 'nurse' child, and if his/her settlement was different from his mother's he/she was legally protected from any removal which involved separation from his/her mother. [171] In 1776 Holy Trinity's parish officials executed a removal order in respect of Thomas, alone, back to Huntingdon St John's. [172] A removal order was not unusual in these circumstances. [173] There is no surviving settlement examination but given Thomas' disability, perhaps the parish officials had judged him to require parochial support, if not at that time, then most probably in the future. The cost of bringing up a child was not an insignificant amount, and the Huntingdon overseers later examined Thomas' mother to identify his father, presumably for maintenance. [174]

Appeals against removal orders at Huntingdon Quarter Sessions

Appeals against removal were heard at the Quarter Sessions in Huntingdon, which usually took place at the Fountain, or the George, Inn. Proceedings of the court were recorded in Minute books, which are almost complete between 1782 and 1791 and which include thirty-eight appeals. [175] The names of the appellant and defendant parishes were listed, together with the names of the justices who had originally heard the case, and the date that had occurred, together with the name(s) listed on the removal order. Little information was usually included to explain the appellant parochial officers' grounds for appeal, and some appeals were simply noted as 'abandoned.' Just over half (52.5%) of the appeals against removal orders were confirmed, 31.5% were reversed or quashed, and 16% were either abandoned by one of the parties, waiting a judgement following a referral to the Court of King's Bench, or

---

[170] HA, HP46/13/2/13, removal order for Thomas Carr, 25 November 1776.

[171] Levene, 'Poor Families', pp.233-262.

[172] HA, HP46/13/2/13, removal order for Thomas Carr, 25 November 1776.

[173] Hampson, 'Settlement', p.280.

[174] P. Crawford, *Parents of Poor Children in England, 1580-1800,* Oxford: Oxford University Press 2010, p.127: HA, HP46/15/10, examination of Elizabeth James, 12 August 1777.

[175] HA; HCP/2/1030/1 January 1782 - January 1787; HCP/2/1030/2 April 1787 – October 1790); HCP/2/1031/1 July 1784 – January 1788); HCP/2/1031/2 January 1788 – January 1792; Huntingdon Quarter Sessions Minute Books.

adjourned.[176] Confirmation was given in six cases as no appeal was prosecuted. In other words, an appellant parish roughly stood a one-in-two chance of being successful in their appeal against a removal order.

Apart from 1783, which saw eleven appeals against removal orders, appeals seem to have been a relatively rare occurrence and there were usually no more than four appeals per year, with the average number being 3.8 per year. It is not surprising that a majority of appeals featured the demographic types who were most costly to maintain - women, either on their own, or with dependents, formed the largest group of appeals against removal, followed by families (Figure 6). If single women were unable to maintain themselves, their parish faced high costs. Where children were involved, the cost steeply rose. It is clear to see that the removal of single women was likely to provoke an appeal, which is not surprising, given the proportionately higher number of removals of single women in Huntingdonshire (see Figure 4). The couples, particularly where their ages and state of health is unknown, may have been removed due to old age as well as under employment. The lone appeal in respect of a single man underlines the importance of male labour to the economy – and illness may have played a part.

Figure 6 Demographic type of appeals against removal orders heard at Huntingdon Quarter Sessions, 1782-1792

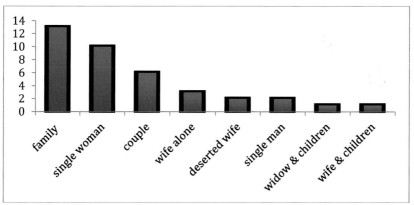

Source:- HA; HCP/2/1030/1 (January 1782 - January 1787); HCP/2/1030/2 (April 1787 – October 1790); HCP/2/1031/1 (July 1784 – January 1788); HCP/2/1031/2 (January 1788 – January 1792); Huntingdon Quarter Sessions Minute Books.

For the people they affected, removals must have been a traumatic experience. Once a removal order was issued, parochial officers quickly set about

---

[176] Successful appeals were recorded in the Minute Books as 'reversed', 'overturned', 'discharged' or 'quashed'.

putting the removal into practice. The parish of settlement then had the opportunity to appeal against the order. In November 1781 Isabella Craddock, a widow with one small daughter, was removed from St Mary's Huntingdon, to the parish of St Giles, Northampton. Her husband Joseph had been a 'serjeant in the 3rd Regiment' when they married at St Mary's in January 1779, but his recent death was the catalyst for Isabella's removal. Following Isabella's arrival in St Giles, Northampton, the St Giles parochial officers lodged an appeal at the Huntingdon Quarter Sessions on 15th January 1782 against her removal order, and this was respited until the next sessions, on 5th April. Upon hearing the appeal in April, the Quarter Sessions justices ruled that the order 'should be discharged', but the reasons for this decision were not minuted.[177] It was also ordered by the court that the sum of 'twenty-one shillings and six shillings be paid forthwith' by the churchwardens and overseers of the poor of the parish of St Mary to the parochial officers of St Giles for their

'costs in prosecuting their appeal and for the maintenance of the said paupers between the time of their undue Removal and the Determination of this Appeal, to be recovered by due course of Law.'[178]

The maintenance element of this bill would have been small, but the total amount would have been a huge proportion of the annual poor relief expenditure of the parish. As an illustrative comparison, the poor relief expenditure of all four Huntingdon parishes in 1776 was reported to have been £330.[179] The personal cost to Isabella and her daughter is incalculable. Although the parochial officers of St Giles had a duty to 'provide for them according to law', they may have been placed in the parish workhouse for the five months they spent in Northampton from the time of their 'undue Removal' until the result of the appeal.[180]

Appeals against removal could occur between the closest of parishes, and all the borough parishes were concerned in at least one appeal with their neighbour. Firstly, a dispute over Richard Lamb's settlement in the borough caused an appeal against his and his family's removal from St John's to St Benedict's. The family were removed on July 22nd 1785 and the appeal was

---

[177] HA; HCP/2/1030/1 January 1782 - January 1787, unpaginated.

[178] HA; HCP/2/1030/1 January 1782 - January 1787, unpaginated.

[179] *Abstract of the Answers and Returns Made Pursuant to an Act passed in the 43[d] Year of His Majesty King George*, House of Commons, Parliamentary Papers, 1804, p. 214 col. 7b.

[180] A parliamentary report of 1776-7 reported the St Giles Workhouse had space for fifteen inmates, http://www.workhouses.org.uk

not heard until October 4th, when it was confirmed due to Richard's 'fraudulent' attempts to gain a new settlement in St John.[181] This was unusual but not unexpected as he claimed settlement through service, which was notoriously hard to prove. The second borough appeal involved the other two parishes in the borough. The cost of a failed appeal in Huntingdonshire averaged at around £6 during this period, a substantial sum, and the decision to appeal was sometimes discussed at vestry meetings. Cambridgeshire appeals during the late eighteenth century averaged 'over £10'.[182]The vestry of All Saints, Huntingdon, met to discuss appealing against the removal from St Mary's, Huntingdon, of William Stears and his wife Mary, on 30 June 1788.[183] Perhaps the proximity of the parishes provoked the meeting, but the appeal was ultimately quashed. All Saints had to pay litigation and court costs of £2 12s. 6d, with added maintenance costs of £2 3s. 10d, so the officers had probably been wise to obtain the backing of the vestry members before appealing the order. As with the inter-borough removal orders, there is no available evidence to suggest that the second appeal was retaliatory.

The un-prosecuted or abandoned appeals probably resulted from later and more accurate information from settlement examinations, or specialist advice regarding legalities of settlements. In December 1782 Martha Hartley was removed from St Ives to St Clement Danes, whose parish officers initially lodged an appeal at Huntingdon Quarter Sessions against the removal.[184] They subsequently changed their minds, and chose to not prosecute the appeal, which was subsequently confirmed at the Huntingdon Quarter Sessions in January 1783. The protocol of a removal dictated that upon Martha's arrival in St Clement Danes in December 1872, the parochial officers would have examined her, to determine her legal place of settlement. From an entry in the St Clement Danes workhouse register in April 1785, it appears that Martha was the widow of Richard Hartley, whose last legal settlement had been gained through keeping 'the Bell in Little Shire Lane' in St Clements Dane.[185] There is no further detail as to when Richard gained his settlement, or when he had died, and Martha's reasons for being in St Ives are unknown, but the Hartleys did not have any children.[186] Martha was placed into the workhouse soon after her removal from St Ives in December

---

[181] HA, HCP2/1030/1, Quarter Sessions Minute Book 1782-1787, unpageinated.
[182] Hampson, 'Settlement', p. 288.
[183] HP46/8/1/3, Huntingdon All Saints with St John, vestry minute book 1776-1818, unpageinated.
[184] HA; HCP/2/1030/1 January 1782 - January 1787.
[185] https://www.londonlives.org/
[186] ibid.

1782 and died at the age of sixty-two, in April 1785. This removal demonstrates the vulnerability to removal of an aged and poor woman, without immediate family to offer help and support.

The justices were possibly frustrated when appeals were timetabled into the Quarter Sessions, but the appellant's parish officers neglected to appear for the hearing at the court. In July 1791 Thomas and Elizabeth Brown were removed, with their two children, from St Neots to Eynesbury. There is no detail as to the reasons for this removal, but the Eynesbury officers lodged an appeal against the removal. On the scheduled day of the appeal, the officers from St Neots did not arrive. Regardless of the legalities of Thomas's last settlement, the justices' decision at the sessions was to quash the removal order, and to fine the parochial officers of St Neots £5 10s 9d, for their non-appearance, and for costs.

Conclusion

The underlying concept of settlement administration lay in the strong belief of officials and ratepayers that the parish boundary should be kept safe from intruders. Entitlement to poor relief was loosely tied to the notion of 'belonging' to a parish until 1662, when the Act of Settlement and Removal refined this notion into a legal definition of 'settlement'. Informal 'settlement' administration had a long history in Huntingdonshire, beginning with the manorial orders forbidding the renting of property to strangers, without having first given financial security to the town officials, thereby circumventing charges to the parish. Formal settlement administration dates from soon after the Settlement Act of 1662, with the first removal from the town of Kimbolton having been organised in 1668. Settlement administration in Huntingdonshire appears to have been organised most strongly in the county's towns. Around two thirds of the certificate holders lived in the county's towns, many of the examinations occurred in the three towns of Godmanchester, Huntingdon and Kimbolton, and removals mostly concerned officials in the towns. The small distances between Huntingdonshire host and settled parishes are obvious throughout the archive of settlement documentation, particularly within the borough of Huntingdon. The independent operation of the four parishes with regard to rating, poor relief and settlement administration processes in the borough, indicate the importance for the overseers in identifying and 'owning' the poor who were deemed entitled to relief through settlement, whilst satisfying their accountants – the parish ratepayers. Certification was an important part of settlement administration until the realisation by ratepayers and officials that parochial liability of the certificate holder could continue through the generations, as seen in the Otteridge case. Examination was time consuming, and possibly used as a screening process, but always with the aim of establishing a liability for poor relief elsewhere. Surviving overseers' accounts indicate the gradual acceptance by officials of the implementation of non-resident relief as a cheaper alternative to removal during this period in Huntingdonshire, but when threatened with a removal which could incur large maintenance costs, parish officials would consider appealing against the removal at the quarter sessions. The driver behind settlement administration in Huntingdonshire during this period was financial, not humanitarian.

7

CAN'T PAY, WON'T PAY

Evelyn Lord

The hearth tax was a response to a shortfall in the income allotted to Charles II for his personal expenses and to enable him to govern the country. Parliament were anxious to prevent him from levying unconstitutional taxes without their consent as his father had done, and when the income from the Excise and other funds granted to him at the Restoration did not meet his needs, they looked for another source of income. The extra amount required annually was £120,000, and Parliament wanted it from a tax which included the whole population, paying according to their means; it cast around for a commodity they could tax which was common to all. The Speaker of the House of Commons described the process of elimination and the resulting tax. 'We pitched at last upon those Places where we enjoy our greatest Comfort and Security, Our Dwelling houses, and considering even the Security for us by Your Majesty's Vigilance and Care in the Government we have prepared a Bill whereby we desire it may be enacted That all Houses in the Kingdom which are not worth in yearly value Twenty Shillings and not inhabited by Almsmen, must pay your Majesty, your Heirs and Successors, Two Shillings a year for every chimney-hearth forever.'[1]

The model chosen for the tax came from the United Provinces of the Dutch Republic (now The Netherlands) where at least three provinces had levied a tax on hearths, Friesland, Gelderland and Utrecht.[2] The two shillings per hearth a year was to be paid in two instalments; one shilling at Lady Day (25th March) and one shilling at Michaelmas (29th September). In choosing these dates for payment of the tax Parliament used the customary dates for paying rents and renders and changing tenancies. This was a new tax, but given a traditional setting for its payment, and as a further nod to custom it would be administered by the machinery of local government already in

---

[1] Commons Journal. The Speaker, quoted in C. Meekings ed., *The Surrey Hearth Tax 1664*, Kingston upon Thames: Surrey Record Society, Numbers XLI, XLII, vol. XVIII, 1940, p.xi.
[2] M.C. Hart, *The Making of a Bourgeois State,* Manchester: Manchester University Press, 1993, pp. 77, 96, 122,132. This was a provincial tax rather than a national tax, and in the province of Holland (now South Holland) was an extraordinary tax levied in times of crisis.

place. The petty constable was responsible for assessing the number of hearths in each household, collecting the tax, and delivering the cash to the high constable of the Hundred. The hundredal constable had the assessment and the amount collected verified by the Justices of the Peace, and the county sheriff would be responsible for getting the tax return to the Treasury. A complicated administrative arrangement which soon fell apart.

Even before the Bill had completed its course through the Commons it was realised that apart from those living in dwellings worth less that 20s a year automatically exempt, no provision had been made for those unable to pay. Hastily cobbled together exemption clauses were added to the tax at the Report stage of the Bill, and approved on the Bill's third reading. Only one clause gave exemption for poverty. 'No persons who by reasons of poverty, or the smallness of his estate, is exempted from the usual payments or contributions to church or poor shall be charged or chargeable with any duties imposed by act imposed.'[3] Exemption for living in a house with the value of less than 20s a year on the full improved rent was formalised and added to with the phrase 'nor having land, tenements, goods and chattels worth £10.[4] Further clauses exempted hospitals and alms houses worth less than £100 a year and industrial hearths. Nowhere in the act were those on poor relief mentioned and poverty as defined by the hearth tax is a legal construct based on property qualifications. A further clause made the onus of paying the tax the responsibility of the occupier of a dwelling rather than the owner or landlord.

In practice in the early stages of collecting the tax in Huntingdonshire the statutory reasons for exemptions were either ignored or misinterpreted. Petty constables added 'taking collection', 'not able to pay', 'not worth anything' 'house visited by the plague' 'poor and in prison' or 'living in a town house' as valid causes for exemption.[5] Those claiming exemption needed an annual certificate signed by the minister, churchwardens and other parish officials and endorsed by the Justices of the Peace, additional time-consuming bureaucracy.

The 'Act for establishing an additional revenue upon His Majesty, his heirs and successors for the better support of their Crown and Dignity' passed

---

[3] T. Arkell, 'Printed instructions for the administration of the hearth tax.' in K. Schurer and T. Arkell, eds., *Surveying the People*, Oxford: The Leopard's Head Press, Local Population Studies Supplement, 1992, p.39.
[4] Arkell p.39.
[5] TNA E 179/122/226

through the Commons and Lord, but did not receive royal assent and come onto the statute book until 19th May 1662. This meant that it had missed the date for the 1662 Lady Day collection. Instead petty constables were given until 31st May to complete their assessments, and the collection was to be with the Justices of the Peace by midsummer. [6]

The length of time that it took for the return of monies to reach the Treasury was huge, and by 1663 it was clear that the tax was not going to achieve the hoped for £120,000; £80,000 was paid in from the 1662 Lady Day collection, and £59, 000 from the Michaelmas 1662.[7] A Parliamentary Committee was formed to investigate the disappointing yield of the tax, and the king demanded a revising act to deal with anomalies in the original act and recover debts owing on the tax. Arrears of payment were to be listed and a punishment of one month's imprisonment was enacted on violence towards tax collectors, and powers of distraint for non-payment were given to the constables.[8]

The tax yield continued to fall, and another revising Act in 1664 tightened up the regulations and changed the way in which the tax was collected. The sheriff was discharged and receivers of the tax money were appointed by the Exchequer Commission. The petty constable still had to go from door to door to make collections, but now he was accompanied by chimney-men, 'his Majesty's officers.'[9]

The receivers were no more successful in collecting the tax than the sheriffs, and arrears on the tax grew. The lists of the Huntingdonshire arrears TNA E 179/331 part 3 was 'probably compiled in response to the 1664 revising Act,' and it covers the hundreds of Normancross, Leightonstone and Toseland; only the borough of Huntingdon represents arrears in Hurstingstone Hundred, and this records those who had died following the assessment but before the collection.[10]

---

[6] Meekings, Surrey Hearth Tax, p.xii.
[7] C. Meekings ed., *Dorset Hearth Tax Assessments 1662-1664*, Dorchester: Friary Press, 1951, p.ix.
[8] Meekings, Dorset Hearth Tax, pp.xi, xii.
[9] E. Parkinson, *The Establishment of the Hearth Tax 1662-1666*, London: List and Index Society, Special Series, Vol. 43, 2008, pp.24, 25.
[10] TNA E179 data-based document details. E 179/331 part 3. Originally parts 1 and 2 were exemption certificates, which have now been re-catalogued as E 179/231/ff. 1-192.

Circular letters sent between 1662 and 1665 from the Treasurer the earl of Southampton to the county sheriffs and justices of the peace show that central government perceived the local administration as being negligent in collecting the hearth tax and even putting obstacles in the way of its collection. In February 1662/63 the Treasurer demanded 'an examination into the behaviour of the petty constables collecting the tax and 'that all vigilance be made against false and short returns and improper exemptions.' Schedules were drawn up for each county. Schedules of Hopeful Arrears, the Constables' Arrears and Desperate Arrears. The first aim of the schedules was to focus on those responsible for assessing and collecting the tax from the sheriff down to the petty constable. The Huntingdonshire sheriff was reckoned to be in arrears of £1545 and on 6th December 1665 a warrant was issued for the arrest of the sheriff of Cambridgeshire and Huntingdonshire 'for the arrears of hearth tax money.' The receivers who took over the collection did no better, legal process was started against John Perryn the receiver for Huntingdonshire and his deputy Thomas Terry in 1667 and both were arrested on 10th March 1667/8. The process against Perryn was not finished until 10th July 1668, and on 26th November 1667 warrants for the arrest of Samuel Fox, Mr Walker and Thomas Drawater constables of Godmanchester were issued. Samuel Fox was imprisoned and not released until 11th June 1668.[11]

Won't Pay

The arrears list for 1662-1663 was obviously based on the assessment made for the Lady Day 1662 tax, as the list of arrears mirrors the 1662 assessment and the 1665 return added to it. Comparing the two documents helps to show why some of those listed were in arrears, and what happened next in 1665.

The arrears lists include those who could have paid the tax, but did not. Like all taxes the hearth tax was unpopular. There was opposition to it as the Bill went through the Commons. Sir Richard Temple complained that this was a tax on a necessity rather than a luxury, and that those paying the tax received no benefit from it as the money disappeared into the royal coffers.[12]

The institution of the chimney-men, who could invade private households added to its unpopularity and provoked violence. In Michaelmas 1666 at St Neots 'the constable, although he was required thereunto, did flatly refuse to assist the collectors in collecting the said duty. Encouraged by this part of

---

[11] M.A. Shaw ed., *Calendar of Treasury Books 1660-1666*, London: HMSO, 1907, p.694; M.A, Shaw ed., *Calendar of Treasury Books, 1667-1668*, London: HMSO, 1905 p.205.

[12] C.D. Chandaman, *The English Public Revenue 1660-1688*, Oxford: Clarendon Press, 1975, p.79.

the town stood upon their guard in opposition to His Majesty's officers…'
Elsewhere people gathered to prevent the chimney men entering houses, and
the constables refused to hand over the lists of assessments to the receivers
and were backed by the local Justices; riots followed passive resistance in
many towns. This outbreak of violence against the hearth tax coincided with
a period of general poverty, and the stopping up of a loop-hole that allowed
legal evasion of the tax. It also coincided with the introduction of yet another
set of collectors, a consortium of London businessmen who purchased collection of the tax, known as tax 'farmers'.[13]

In Huntingdonshire Robert Auberry of Alconbury was a serial refuser. His
probate inventory assessed when he died in 1673 shows that he could afford
to pay, as his goods, chattels and livestock were assessed at £156-12s 8d, and
the inventory indicates that he lived in a substantial two hearth house with
at least five rooms.[14]

Others who refused to pay included Thomas Drawater of Alwalton, Robert
Archdeacon of Southoe, Stephen Goby of Fenstanton, Thomas C[blank] of
Offord Darcy, and Widow Smith of Bottlebridge an owner of a divided tenement which she shared with Ralph Taylor, and 'she refuseth to pay the
duty.' This was individual resistance, but without any of the collective action
as seen at St Neots.[15]

Some practised less violent but more creative ways of avoiding payment.
Chimneys were pulled down, hearths blocked up, some left a parish and disappeared without trace, houses stood empty, and many claimed that they had
been assessed with too many hearths in the first place.[16]

Arrears Michaelmas 1662, Lady Day 1663 and Michaelmas 1663

The list of arrears for this period includes the Hundreds of Leightonstone,
Normancross and Toseland, but not Hurstingstone Hundred, although it includes a list of those who had died in the Borough of Huntingdon since the
1662 assessment. It shows that 73 percent of those assessed in 1662 were in
arrears by the end of 1663. The break-down for arrears in each Hundred was

[13] TNA Privy Council 2/59, 2/60 quoted in M. Braddick, *Parliamentary Taxation in the Seventeenth Century*, London: Royal Historical Society, 1994, p.255;
L. Marshall 'Levying the Hearth Tax, 1662-1668', *English Historical Review*,
Oct. 1936, pp. 628-648.
[14] TNA E 179/122/226; HA AH 18/1/11.
[15] TNA E 179/122/226.
[16] TNA E 179/122/226.

76 percent of 1662 assessments in arrears in Leightonstone, 73 percent for Normancross, and 71 percent for Toseland. By the end of 1663 three-quarters of those assessed in 1662 in these three hundreds had not paid the tax. If the same percentage of arrears ran across the whole of England it is not surprising that the king and the government were worried about the shortfall.

Nevertheless, the 1665 return added to the 1662 assessment shows that many of those in arrears in 1663 paid for their original assessment in 1665. This was made possible because the recovery of arrears was limited by the 1664 revising act to two years.[17] In Leightonstone Hundred 71 percent of those in arrears in 1663 paid for the original assessment in 1665, 79 percent in Normancross, but only 60 percent in Toseland.[18] However, in some parishes over half of those in arrears in 1663 had still not paid the tax in 1665. In Easton and Buckworth 57 percent of those in arrears in 1663 remained in arrears in 1665, 54 percent at Covington and Buckden, 50 percent at Thurning and Coppingford, but 79 percent at Godmanchester, a percentage that will be discussed later.

The arrears were not always paid by the original householder assessed. A feature of the 1662 assessment coupled with the 1665 Lady Day return is that it illustrates a considerable amount of mobility in each parish, as householders moved from house to house. Overall 468 payments of arrears in 1665 were made by a different householder to the original assessment, 18 percent of the total arrears. In Leightonstone Hundred 16 percent payments were made by others than those assessed, 14 percent in Toseland, but 2 percent in Normancross, and more detailed research on the Huntingdonshire fenland shows that movement within and out of parishes suggests an almost itinerant population. For example, at Stanground between 1662 and 1665 there were 27 moves within the village, and 20 in its daughter village of Farcet, plus a further 21 at Farcet with exemption certificates dated 1666 that do not appear in the hearth tax return or the arrears.

Lack of settling the accounts could be linked to the social and economic structure of the three hundreds. In Normancross substantial arrears were recorded in only 3 of the 27 parishes, in Leightonstone in 5 of the 30 parishes recorded, and in Toseland 12 of the 23 parishes listed in the arrears schedule had substantial arrears. Normancross was dominated by fenland, and although by 1658 the drainage of the Middle Level was deemed complete and Jonas Moore's map of the drained fens shows that land had been allotted in

17 Parkinson, pp. 78, 80.
18 TNA E179/122/226.

the Huntingdonshire Fens to Adventurers, it also shows that some commons such as Holme Common shared between a number of parishes remained open and available, and other sources such as the Stanground rate books show that land was available to rent even for those with only one hearth, or exempt from the tax. More enclosure had taken place in the west and south of the county, and where arable was enclosed it was put down to pasture, which would have depressed the labour market.[19]

It is useful to consider what being in arrears meant to those on a limited daily wage. Those with one hearth with arrears from 1662 to Michaelmas 1663 kept 3s in their pockets, and those with 2 hearths 6s; additional resources for their domestic economy. Saving this to pay the tax would not have been possible, but it might have helped to find the 1s or 2s tax in 1665.

Most of those in arrears were recorded as having one or two hearths, but they included a social mix from labourers, husbandmen, and yeomen through to the clergy and gentry.[20] Clergy in arrears include Anthony Berridge clerk of Yaxley, Nathanial Gibson of Woodston, and Ferdinando Berridge of Great Paxton. At least 13 gentry were in arrears. These included Lord Devonshire in arrears on a 4 hearth empty house in Sawtry Moynes, Castell Sherrard esquire on a 4 hearth empty house in Folksworth, Thomas Gregory gentleman for his two hearth house in Alwalton, Sir John Browne on an empty two hearth house in Spaldwick, The Earl of Manchester for two, two hearth empty houses in Kimbolton, Robert Clapton gentleman for his one hearth house in Eynesbury and in Godmanchester Robert Baker, John Mayle and William Harte all described as gentlemen.[21] Many of those designated as gentry were in arrears as owners of empty houses, a situation which was to continue in a later list of arrears.[22]

It is with Godmanchester in the Toseland Hundred arrears list that the actual compilation of the schedule has to be considered. The lists of all three Hundreds are almost identical to the 1662 assessment and the 1665 return, but Toseland Hundred is slightly different in that it includes a class of exemptions 'taken off by certificate', which are rare in the other Hundreds. It would appear that the constables compiling the return and the arrears for Toseland had access to documentation that the other constables did not, perhaps because Toseland was compiled at a later date. What the exemption certificates

---

[19] Jonas Moore, Mapp of the Great Levell of the Fenns, facsimile edition, Cambridgeshire Records Society, 2017; HA HP 80/11/2/1-2 Stanground Rate Book.
[20] TNA E179/331 part 3.
[21] TNA E 179/122/226; TNA 179/331 part 3.
[22] TNA E 179/331 part 3.

tell us is that there were many listed as in arrears in Toseland who were actually exempt from paying the tax.

Can't Pay

Those with exemptions from paying the tax appear on the schedule without any mention of why they were considered to be in arrears. This only becomes clear when the arrears are compared with the assessment and return. In Leightonstone Hundred this amounted to 14 percent of those listed as being in arrears but exempt from paying the tax, 7 percent in Normancross but 25 percent in Toseland, of which over half were in Godmanchester and were 'taken off by certificate', which suggests that the Godmanchester constables had view of the certificates, which other constables did not. Those unable to pay the tax but recorded as being in arrears in Normancross were all in single figures the most being 6 at Orton Longuville, in Leightonstone there were 14 instances in Brampton and 13 for Alconbury, in Toseland as well as 129 for Godmanchester there 24 exemptions recorded as arrears in Buckden and 13 in Hemingford Grey.

The 1662-1663 arrears also reveal a number of people listed as being in arrears who did not actually exist and appear on the tax return as 'no such man', others were listed on arrears but on the return as 'gone' leaving no trace of where. There were also at least 11 entries on the arrears for Normancross that do not appear on the tax return, 9 in Leightonstone, and 16 in Toseland Hundred. Clearly they had slipped through the tax net at some point, perhaps recorded by the constables but not entered on the final tax return, or perhaps in receipt of poor relief and automatically excluded from the return.

Arrears Michaelmas 1664, Lady Day 1665, Michaelmas 1665

This was a 'Schedule of Sperate Debts upon the account of the hearth money in the county of Huntingdon being a return of several houses which are tenantless and no distress to be taken.'[23]

The list is of the owners of the house and the name of the late occupier who should have paid the tax but had now moved on leaving an empty house. The hearth tax statutes put the onus of paying the tax on the tenant rather than the owner, and stated that empty houses were to be recorded on the

---

[23] TNA E 179/331 part 3.

assessments and returns but were not classed as non-payers. Andrew Wareham suggests that defining a house as empty was a device used to save time, and that the house might not have been empty, but the constable could not trace the owner.[24] Parkinson states that the original wording of the act meant that hearths in empty houses were chargeable, and that as many of the empty houses were owned by the gentry the constables were reluctant to press for charges.[25] However, the occupier was liable for the tax and not the owner, and most of the empty houses on the Huntingdonshire schedule of arrears were not only empty but tenantless, and the hearths unused.

While the numbers of hearths mentioned in this particular schedule for Huntingdonshire shows that these were often substantial houses left unoccupied, and indeed owned by members of the aristocracy or gentry who seem to have preferred to leave large houses they owned tenantless. In favouring owners over occupiers the hearth tax shows a glimmer of the ideal of property ownership inherent in the 20th and early 21st centuries, and a tenantless house meant a loss of rent for that property, and there may have been underlying reasons for leaving these houses empty.

Owners listed on the schedule include those with inherited wealth. For example, Sir John Cotton baronet of Conington who owned houses in Conington and Huntingdon, the Earl of Devonshire who owned property in Sawtry Moynes, Sir Thomas Proby of Elton who owned an eight hearth empty house in Yaxley, his nearest town and another in Old Weston, Sir Thomas Dacres owned a house in Woodwalton, the Duke of Lennox and Richmond with two houses in Buckworth and another in Leighton Bromswold, Sir Gilbert Pickering baronet who owned and had occupied a house in Brampton, but had let it fall, and the Earl of Manchester with empty houses in Alconbury, Kimbolton and Winwick, and property across the shire.[26]

Other owners appear to have inherited a family property. Francis Glover gentleman of Water Newton who when he died occupied an eleven hearth house, but whose executors could not be traced, Thomas Gardner of Easton who occupied a 3 hearth house left to unknown heirs, William Thompson of Buckworth who before his death owned and occupied a two hearth house now owned by his heirs, Anne and Elizabeth Jellings of Knapworth Cambridgeshire who were left property now empty in Fenstanton. It is also possible that owners from outside the county had inherited family property in

[24] A. Wareham, 'The hearth tax and empty properties in London on the eve of the Great Fire', *The Local Historian*, Vol. 41, No. 4, November 2014, p.286.
[25] Parkinson, pp.133, 134.
[26] TNA E 179/331 part 3.

Huntingdonshire. For example, James Sawyer of Caldecote in Hertfordshire owned an empty property in Brington, John Williams of March in the Isle of Ely owned a two-hearth empty property in Stowen Catworth, Thomas Botham of Newton in Bedfordshire owner of an empty one hearth house in Great Staughton, [blank] Stacher of Deadman's Place, Southwark who owned a three hearth house in Godmanchester, and Richard Pagett, Esq of Westminster in Middlesex who owned a one hearth house in Pidley cum Fenton. Pagett is listed in the Hearth Tax volume for London and Middlesex of 1664 for three houses in Petty France, St Margaret's Westminster with 7, 9, and 11 hearths each.[27]

Of course, how those listed became property owners needs more research on sources such as Feet of Fines, conveyances, and probate material. What can be said is these were likely to be freehold properties or in the case of the Earl of Manchester and other peers and gentry part of a manorial holding.

The numbers listed on this schedule were 38 for Leightonstone Hundred, 24 for Normancross, 46 for Toseland, and this time Hurstingstone Hundred is included with 47 empty houses. The amount of arrears for which no distraint could be taken came to £75-9-0.

The text of the schedule shows that not all those on it were actually owners of empty houses, and that there were still those refusing to pay, as well new entries which were not on the earlier arrears schedule. In Leightonstone Hundred there were four new refusers, Thomas Porteshoyle of Swineshead was assessed for 8 hearths in his own occupation paid 3s but refused to pay the rest. John Killingworth of Keyston assessed for 2 hearths paid for only one, John Bradshaw of Ellington had stopped up his hearth 'to defraud the King's Majesty of his revenue'. He was assessed for 7 hearths but paid for one, John Stanke's tenant William Dodd refused to pay for a two hearth house before leaving, and Robert Auberry still refused to pay 'distress was taken, which opposing the Constable and his officers [Auberry] did gesend [snatch] out of their hands.'[28]

In Normancross Hundred there was one new arrears not on the earlier schedule, and in Toseland Charles Caesar gent appears for a one hearth house late occupied by Annis Kidman. In Great Stoughton Robert Gutteridge an owner-occupier assessed on one hearth but now standing empty refused to

---

[27] M. Davies, C. Ferguson, V. Harding, E. Parkinson, A. Wareham eds., *London and Middlesex 1666 Hearth Tax*, The British Record Society, 2014, Part 2, p. 1704. The date at the head of the page is 1664. It is probable that he originated locally, or in the Fens as Paget and Padgett are local fenland surnames.
[28] TNA E 179/331 part 3.

pay. In Somersham in Hurstingstone Hundred Sir Kenelm Digby was the owner of an empty 16 hearth house late in the occupation of James, Earl of Suffolk. The 1662 assessment was for 21 hearths, occupied by the Earl of Suffolk, and in 1665 Anthony Hammond paid for that amount. It is probable that the house was divided with Suffolk occupying a part with 16 hearths, and that later on his departure Hammond occupied the whole house.

Other anomalies between the arrears and the return include Edward Raby of St Ives on the arrears as an owner of a 4 hearth house let to Henry Bassett, whereas the hearth tax return gives the owner as Henry Wilson and that the tax was paid in 1665. Similarly, in Woodhurst the arrears list Thomas James as the owner of a 9 hearth house, with Thomas Colston as the tenant, but in the hearth tax return Colston has paid tax on the 9 hearths. In Alconbury William Bone is given as the owner of a 2 hearth house occupied by Richard Cockerell but the return makes Cockerell the owner rather than a tenant, and in Ramsey Thomas Wilcox is listed as an owner of a 6 hearth house late tenanted by Thomas Stimpson, whereas the hearth tax return gives the owner as Henry Williams esquire, the Lord of the Manor.

The return also shows that not all empty houses were on the arrears list. For example, there are 6 empty houses on the arrears for Ramsey but 11 on the return, and there are 14 empty houses on the return for Godmanchester but 20 on the return. It is possible that it was hoped that the extra empty houses on the return were where it was thought that the tax could be paid.

Property and the Hearth Tax

The hearth tax and the exemptions for those who could not pay were based on property, and in the early modern period property and its absolute rights were part of a package of ideals reflecting the shift from manorial tenures and collective, family owned property to individual ownership or leaseholds. Harold Perkins has suggested that the individualistic idea of absolute ownership of property 'was bequeathed to the late seventeenth-century by the landed aristocracy which had fought for three centuries to establish it.'[29] However, it is clear from the hearth tax that the majority of householders in Huntingdonshire were tenants without individual property rights.

Establishing individual property rights in the face of manorial tenure, free-holds and probate could be difficult. A good example of this is Samuel Pepys

---

[29] A. Macfarlane, *The Origins of English Individualism*, Oxford: Basil Blackwell, 1978, pp. 57,58,80, 89, 90.

who struggled to obtain individual rights to his freehold property in Brampton and copyhold land elsewhere in Huntingdonshire, left by his uncle to Samuel's father with reversionary rights to him, but challenged by other relatives and his uncle's stepsons.[30]

John Locke's *Two Treatises of Government* written in c 1680-1683 is a mixture of Calvinism and collectivism. Once deeply conservative by the 1680s Locke was a Whig and a liberal accused of sedition. In the section on property Locke states that property could be acquired by hard labour and moral standing and although there should be no restraints on the acquisition of property, enough should always be left for others. Private property would increase productivity, and therefore he promoted the enclosure of commons as resulting in greater productivity. Property to Locke was not just the material world, but liberty, religion and estates, which were all part of God's property. Perhaps most importantly Locke insisted that the purpose of the political society is to protect private property, while elsewhere he supports right of resistance. [31] In Lockean terms Robert Auberry's refusal to pay was a righteous act against tyranny, as was the riot at St Neots against chimney men entering houses.

To the king and government the hearth tax was a list of names and hearths equalling revenue for the crown. It was a list of householders, but not of houses as there is no way of telling from the tax return if the householder is living in a single or divided property. It is not a sure estimate of the population of village, town or county owing to under-registration and the excluded. It is only when other sources are factored in that if can be used as socio-economic document. The number of exemptions do not represent the extent of poverty, and the number of hearths do not in themselves represent wealth and status.

The arrears discussed in this essay go down to a level below the assessments and returns, and show that across the shire collecting the hearth tax was fraught with difficulties; there were those who could not pay and those who would not pay, and the 1662-1663 arrears list suggests whole scale evasion or collusion with the constable to avoid payment. What happened actually happened in each parish is not known, but the constables must have received

---

[30] E. Lord, 'Samuel Pepys and Huntingdonshire', *Huntingdonshire Hearth Tax*, London: British Record Society and Cambridgeshire Records Society, forthcoming.
[31] J. Locke, *Two Treatises of Government*, ed. M. Goldie, London: Everyman, 1993, pp. 127-139.

written or verbal instructions about making assessments and returns and who could have exemption, but in 1665 how did the parishioners realise that there was a two-year limitation on their debts?[32] Like most areas of the hearth tax there is always more to be uncovered. Despite this it remains the most important source for life in post-Restoration Huntingdonshire, and the people who lived it.

---

[32] Parkinson illustrates an example of a notice which was pinned to the door of an empty house warning that payment of the hearth tax was due, and suggests that each collector was given a paper book of notices to use. She also reproduces a copy of a self-assessment for hearths. Parkinson p.136. Nothing similar has been found for Huntingdonshire, partly because there are no appropriate quarter sessions records surviving. Constables' account for the hearth tax period record the constable taking the collection to the Justices of the Peace, but not how and when the collection was made.

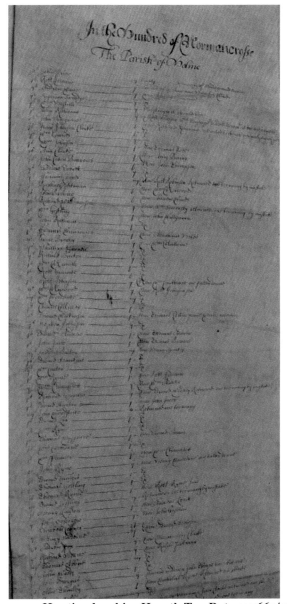

Figure 7.1 Huntingdonshire Hearth Tax Return 1662/1665

8

THE CLERGY IN POST-RESTORATION HUNTINGDONSHIRE AND THE HEARTH TAX

Liz Ford

On Sunday 16th July 1662, fifty-one Huntingdonshire clerics signed their agreement to the Act of Uniformity at the Bishop of Lincoln's Palace at Buckden.[1] By the 25th August (St Bartholomew's Day) 1662, eighty-one Huntingdonshire rectors, vicars and curates had complied with the Act of Uniformity.[2] The Church of England had been dis-established during the Commonwealth period and this Act was central to its restoration. The Act set down strict and narrow principles for Church of England clerics and it was viewed as a harsh settlement, partly because any clerics who refused to comply with the Act faced the prospect of ejection from their living.[3] Whilst the religious settlement was being put in place, the government sought new methods by which the restored monarchy could be financed, as the tradi-tional means had become obsolete during the Commonwealth years. The re-sulting Hearth Tax became law on 19th May 1662, remaining in force until the accession of William and Mary in 1689, but was unpopular from its in-ception.[4] The format of the hearth tax provides a wealth of information and this chapter tracks the post-restoration clergy of the county through the

---

[1] LA, DIOC/SUB/3, Bishop's Subscription Book 3, 1662-77. I am indebted to Alan Richardson for indicating this source.

[2] The Act of Uniformity 14 Car 2 c 4 1662.

[3] J. Spurr, *The Post-Reformation: Religion, Politics and Society in Britain, 1603-1714* New Haven: Yale, 2006, p.145; S. Doran & C. Doran, *Princes, Pastors and People, the Church and Religion in England 1529-1689* London: Routledge, 1991, p.158; see also S. Clemmow's chapter 9, p.189.

[4] 1 Gul. & Mar., c. 10 1689; Arkell, T. ed. with Alcock, N. *Warwickshire Hearth Tax Returns: Michaelmas 1670 with Coventry Lady Day 1666* Stratford on Avon and London: Dugdale Society 43 and British Record Society 126, Hearth Tax Se-ries 7, 2010, pp.18-19.

hearth tax sources, highlighting differences between the hearth numbers and likely size of dwelling inhabited by parish rectors, vicars and curates.[5]

Clergy were members of one of the most articulate, well-educated groups of men and Huntingdonshire clergymen, virtually all of whom were university educated, have left a paper trail in contemporary documents which can shed light on non-religious aspects of their life.[6] Sources such as tithe disputes heard at the court of the Archdeaconry of Huntingdon demonstrate the clergy's actions and motivations in attempting to defend a prime source of their income. Other disputes and parish records can illustrate their wider involvement in parochial life, and glebe terriers may include a description of the type of home they inhabited. Probate documents such as wills and inventories can help to provide evidence of the clergy's financial affairs and concerns. It may be an accident of survival, but the fiscal nature of many of these sources demonstrates the importance with which the clergy viewed their pecuniary concerns, despite their spiritual calling. Using all these sources in addition to the hearth tax, a broader understanding can be gained of the lives of the clergy in post-restoration Huntingdonshire.

---

[5] Buckden Palace (Bishop of Lincoln) with 33 or 36 hearths is excluded from this study of the parish clergy. For transcripts see E. Lord, K. Sneath & L. Ford, *The Huntingdonshire Hearth Taxes* London & Cambridge: British Record Society and Cambridgeshire Records Society, forthcoming. This includes transcripts of the TNA 1662/1665 Assessment/Return, the 1674 Lady Day Return, and exemption certificates E179/231. Householders were listed in three types of taxation record. Hearth tax assessments list householders' names together with their hearth numbers; returns denote payments made by householders; and exemption certificates name householders who were excused from payment. Most of the latter were exempt on the grounds of their poverty but certificates occasionally include other categories of householders, even clergymen, whose hearth numbers had decreased. Additional original hearth tax sources; TNA, E179/249/1, the 1666 Lady Day Return for Huntingdonshire and E179/122/227, probable 1664 Lady Day Return for Huntingdonshire. Additional other sources include the clergy database, http://theclergydatabase.org.uk and W.M. Noble, 'Incumbents of the County of Huntingdon' in *Transactions of the Cambridgeshire and Huntingdonshire Archaeological Society*, vol. 2 part 3 Ely, 1909.

[6] Qualifications information accessed from the clergy database, http://theclergydatabase.org.uk and http://venn.lib.cam.ac.uk/Documents/acad/2018/search-2018.html

Identifying the clergy in the Hearth Tax in Huntingdonshire

The hearth tax was created for taxation purposes but the resulting information also offers a partial post-restoration census of the county, if caution is used.[7] The hearth tax recorded relatively few people by their status, but because the clergy were sometimes described as 'clerkes', they have been described as 'probably' the only 'traceable status group' other than 'gentlemen, esquires and titled' individuals.[8] That being said, identifying all the Church of England incumbents in the Huntingdonshire hearth tax documents is not as straightforward as it might seem, for several reasons. The 1662/1665 Huntingdonshire hearth tax documents include sixty-one men described as a 'clerke', but these men were not necessarily the incumbent of the parish where they lived.[9] The assessments for the newly introduced hearth tax were carried out during the summer of 1662, which was too early for the effects of all the clergy ejections (resulting from a refusal to sign the Act of Uniformity) to have been put into effect. The hearth tax assessment of 1662 accordingly included incumbents whose ejection was imminent, but who had not yet departed their previous living; incumbents who were unaffected by the Act; and any clergy who had recently been ejected from their living but had relocated. All these men retained their clerical status. James Bedford (five hearths) was listed as the 'clerke' in Bluntisham, but he would soon be ejected.[10] William Dell (four hearths) in Hail Weston had already been ejected from his living in Yelden (Bedfordshire) and Thomas Readman

---

[7] For example, see T. Arkell, 'A Student's Guide to the Hearth Tax: some truths, half-truths and untruths', and C. Husbands, 'Hearth tax exemption figures and assessment of poverty in the seventeenth-century economy', both in N. Alldridge ed. *The Hearth Tax: Problems and Possibilities* Hull, Humberside Polytechnic 1974. see Lord et al, *The Huntingdonshire Hearth Tax,* forthcoming.

[8] W. Jacob, *The Clerical Profession in the Long Eighteenth Century 1680-1840* Oxford: OUP, 2007, pp.1-3; N. Evans (ed.), *Cambridgeshire Hearth Tax Returns Michaelmas 1664* London: British Record Society, 2000, pp.xxxiv – xxxvi; widows were indicated and people with identical names were occasionally differentiated by occupation.

[9] TNA E179/122/226, Huntingdonshire Hearth Tax Assessment 1662/Return 1665 A copy of the 1662 assessment document was used as the template for the completed 1665 Michaelams return, hence its description as '1662/1665'.

[10] Ibid.; A.G. Matthews, *Calamy Revised, being a revision of Edmund Calamy's Account of the Ministers ejected and silenced, 1660-2* Oxford: OUP, 1934, pp.43-44.

(six hearths) in Bury, from his living in Claypole (Lincolnshire).[11] The two latter clerics did not live in a benefice property. Additionally, the description of 'clerke' included curates, schoolmasters, non-practising ministers, and occasionally men employed in the legal profession.[12] William Garfield (three hearths) in Alwalton and William Sell (four hearths) in Godmanchester, were described as clerkes but were respectively a non-practising cleric and a schoolmaster.[13] Other incumbents were not described as clerics in the hearth tax schedules. Some were awarded the honorific status of 'gent', without any additional acknowledgement of their clerical status, such as Charles Wilson (seven hearths), the rector of Kimbolton, whilst a minority of other clerics such as Luke Grosse (two hearths), the rector of Great Gidding, had no description.[14] A few clergymen such as Giles Allen in Stibbington (nine hearths), or Peter Gunning in Somersham (eight hearths) were qualified to be described as a 'Doctor of Divinity'. By the time of the 1674 Lady Day hearth tax return, most incumbents were simply either described as 'Mr', or very occasionally 'gent' – along with many other men in the parish, who were not clergymen.[15] Furthermore, some incumbents were found in additional sources, even though they were absent from the hearth tax, for example, the perpetual curate of Ramsey, John Robins, who was not included in any schedule.

The awarding of status in the hearth tax might be as a direct cause of high hearth numbers, but other evidence in the hearth tax suggests not.[16] Stephen Anderson, rector of Catworth (five hearths), was described as a clerke in 1662/65 but the status of Thomas Whitehand, rector of Swineshead, and Samuel Morton, rector of Haddon, both with five hearths, was not recorded. Edward Flud, rector of Denton (three hearths), was awarded the status of 'gent', as was Barnabas Oley, vicar of Great Gransden (four hearths).[17] Most

---

[11] Ibid., pp. 161; 502; 406. 'Readman' is also listed as 'Redman'; many surnames have alternate spellings in the hearth tax documents and the most frequently occurring spelling has been used.

[12] TNA E179/122/226, Huntingdonshire Hearth Tax Assessment Michaelmas 1662/Hearth Tax Return Michaelmas 1665.

[13] A.G. Matthews, Calamy Revised, p.433.

[14] A university degree was supposed to confer the status of gentleman; see also K. Sneath's chapter 2 'Changing Social Structure in an Agricultural County.'

[15] TNA E179/249/2, 1674. This was also the case in Cambridgeshire; Evans & Rose eds. *Cambridgeshire Hearth Tax Returns* p.xxxv, and in Warwickshire; Arkell, T. ed. *Warwickshire Hearth Tax Returns* p.39.

[16] Ibid.

[17] TNA E179/122/226, Huntingdonshire Hearth Tax Assessment 1662/Return 1665.

rectors, vicars and curates were entitled 'clerke', just over a quarter of rectors were described as a 'gent', whereas few vicars were; and around half the vicars, but only five per cent of rectors, had no description.[18] There appears to be no overt relationship between hearth numbers and the awarding of a gentleman's status, but rectors were given the honorific 'gent' status to a far greater extent than vicars and curates, in the Huntingdonshire hearth tax. It is impossible to account accurately for this disparity, as it is not known whether the status was self-awarded, or annotated by the constable, at the drawing up of the 1662 assessment.

Numbers and types of Huntingdonshire clergy in the hearth tax

There were just over ninety parishes located entirely within Huntingdonshire, and with reference to the additional sources, clergymen of eighty-six parishes (fifty-six rectories; twenty-three vicarages; and seven perpetual curacies) were identified on at least one hearth tax schedule between 1662 and 1674.[19] It is difficult to identify a clergy house with certainty in the hearth tax but the tenure of a vicarage or rectory house (and glebe) formed part of the incumbent's right of appointment, and it is likely, unless there is information to the contrary, that the dwelling occupied by the incumbent, and who was taxed as its householder, equated with the benefice house.[20] A few entries in the hearth tax schedules indicate that occasionally a tenant, rather than an incumbent, occupied the clergy house, or that the clergy house was empty, and some parishes, notably many curacies, do not always appear to have had a clergy house.[21] In 1662 the rector of Holywell, Francis Wilford, was assessed for seven hearths but in 1665 William Carrey, who was not a

---

[18] This analysis is based on the TNA E179/122/226, Huntingdonshire Hearth Tax Assessment 1662/Return 1665.

[19] The Compton Census of 1676 gives a higher number which included Huntingdonshire parishes partly in other counties, see S. Clemmow's chapter 9, 'Dissent in Post-Restoration Huntingdonshire'. Differences between the endowments and tithing rights of Rectories and Vicarages are found in the Glossary; although perpetual curacies were not formally recognised as benefices by the Church authorities until 1838, in practical terms they had the tenure of a benefice, being recommended by the patron and licensed by the bishop, but their living was often comparatively small and possibly without a clergy house. They were differentiated from the type of curate employed directly by a rector or vicar as an assistant.

[20] Spurr, *The Post-Reformation*, p.246; an example is William Dell of Hail Weston.

[21] See note 19 above.

cleric, paid tax on seven hearths and was recorded as the tenant.[22] Spaldwick vicarage was recorded as 'empty' in 1665, and the likely situation of the curate, John Robins, has already been noted. A core of twenty-five clergy whose incumbency continued throughout this period probably fostered a feeling of stability within the county's clergy after the turbulence of recent times, but thirty-four clergy houses had two or more changes of incumbent during the hearth tax years. This was either because of the death, or the removal due to some other reason, of the incumbent. Where hearth numbers remained constant in subsequent hearth tax schedules, even with a change of incumbent, this is taken to indicate the continued occupancy of a designated clergy house. However, hearth numbers in a specified building were not necessarily constant, and might increase or decrease.[23] A good example is the recording of the Bishop of Lincoln's hearth numbers at the Palace of Buckden, which varied between thirty-three and thirty-six.[24] Richard Newman, rector of Hamerton, was assessed for six hearths in 1662, and following his death the new rector, Ferrar Collett, paid tax on six hearths in 1665.[25] By 1674 Ferrar Collett paid tax for seven hearths, in the same house, and this addition is possibly due to house improvements.[26] Variance in hearth numbers is more likely to be attributable to building alterations rather than to a subsequent incumbent occupying a different clergy house.

Within the eighty-six parishes, approximately one hundred and thirty Huntingdonshire clergymen can be identified as having paid hearth tax, or having been involved with hearth tax administration via their endorsement of exemption certificates between 1662 and 1674, although not all clergymen who endorsed exemption certificates were necessarily identified as paying the hearth tax themselves. Henry Hickuck was the curate of Toseland from 1672 to 1685. He married Lucy Berridge, the daughter of Ferdinand Berridge, vicar of Great Paxton, in July 1673, and signed the exemption certificate for Toseland in 1673, but he is not listed as a payer of the hearth tax in any Huntingdonshire parish at Lady Day in 1674.[27] This possibly illustrates, together with the earlier example of John Robins, the lack of provision of a clergy house in curacy benefices. There are other examples of curates endorsing an exemption certificate without any evidence of paying the tax themselves, for instance, Robert Dickman, curate of Upwood, and John Pearson, curate of Warboys. Ministers who were away from their parish may

[22] TNA E179/122/226, Huntingdonshire Hearth Tax Assessment 1662/Return 1665.
[23] T. Arkell, 'Introduction, Part I', p.39.
[24] TNA E179/122/226, 1662/1665; E179/249/2, 1674.
[25] TNA E179/122/226, 1662/1665.
[26] TNA E179/249/2, 1674.
[27] TNA E179/331/107, Exemption certificate for Toseland, 20th March 1673.

have been under pressure to find a proxy cleric to complete the necessary certification, and occasionally a minister who had previously been ejected from a different parish was drafted in to endorse a certificate. John Laughton had been ejected from the curacy of Brington in 1662, but moved to Catworth where he was listed as a hearth tax payer in 1665. He continued preaching independently, and later signed an exemption certificate for Old Weston.[28] Nathaniel Bradshaw had been ejected from his living at Willingham (Cambridgeshire) in 1662, and by 1674 was living with members of his family in Hemingford Grey.[29] He endorsed the Hemingford Grey exemption certificate for Lady Day 1674, but was not the incumbent, and he was not recorded as paying the hearth tax in 1674.[30] The incumbent, John Raban pluralistically held the livings of Hemingford Grey and Penn (Staffordshire), which were about sixty miles apart.[31] In theory, pluralistically held parishes were to be no more than thirty miles apart, and a curate should have been instituted to cover for Mr Raban, but this does not seem to have been organised.

Rectors outnumbered vicars by more than 2:1 (Table 1) in the eighty-six parishes. This is a larger difference than that found in other counties, for example in Warwickshire and Leicestershire, where the ratio was about 60:40, but it fits the general pattern of the greater distribution of rectories throughout the Church of England at this time.[32] Throughout the period from 1662 to 1674 the average number of hearths per Huntingdonshire rectory was 4.7, and for vicarages, 3.7, whilst the mean hearth number was four for both types of house. Huntingdonshire rectors were in a beneficial position in comparison to the county's vicars, and to curates (Table 1). Twenty-one rectors inhabited homes in the six to ten hearth group whilst only three rectors lived in homes with one or two hearths. Only three vicars were in the former, higher category, one of whom was William Foster (eight hearths), the vicar of Stanground. He was additionally entitled to receive the tithe rights of Farcet, as well as the commuted tithes to land previously reclaimed by the draining of the fens in the 1630's. The latter were valued at £25 per annum, so Stanground would have been an unusually attractive vicarage benefice.[33] Six of the seven curates lived in a home with only one or two hearths, which put them on a par with eighty per cent of Huntingdonshire's

---

[28] TNA E 179/122/231/93, undated exemption certificate.

[29] Matthews, *Calamy Revised,* pp.69-70.

[30] TNA E 179/122/231/179.

[31] Bishop's Subscription Book 3, 1662-77.

[32] J. Spurr, *The Restoration Church of England, 1646-1689* New Haven: Yale, 1991, p.174; J.H. Pruett, *Parish Clergy Under the Later Stuarts: The Leicestershire Experience* Chicago: University of Illinois, 1978, p.7.

[33] https://www.british-history.ac.uk/vch/hunts/vol3/pp212-217#highlight-first.

householders, whereas the seventh curate, Samuel Coney, minister of Little Paxton, had five hearths. Samuel Coney is an anomaly as a curate, being the only Huntingdonshire curate described in any hearth tax document as a 'gent'.[34]

Table 1: Clergy houses and hearth numbers 1662-1674[35]

Hearths	Rectory		Vicarage		Curacy		Totals		All Hunts Hearths	
	n	%	n	%	n	%	n	%	n	%
1	1	1.8	1	4	1	14	3	3	**3516**	55
2	2	3.6	5	22	5	72	12	14	**1600**	25
3 to 5	32	57	14	61	1	14	47	55	**1052**	16
6 to 10	21	37.6	3	13			24	28	**255**	4
Total	**56**		**23**		**7**		**86**		**6423**	

Comparisons with a different county can be useful. Ryan states that hearth numbers in clergy homes recorded in the Essex hearth tax, ranged from three to twelve hearths.[36] This appears to be a different range of hearth figures to those in Huntingdonshire, where three clergy houses had one hearth, eleven had two and none had more than ten hearths.[37] However, sources additional

---

[34] TNA E179/122/226, Huntingdonshire Hearth Tax Assessment 1662/Return 1665.
[35] Data is compiled from the Huntingdonshire Hearth Tax documents, all TNA; 1662 Assessment/1665 Michaelmas Return, E179/122/226; 1664 Lady Day Return, E179/122/227; 1666 Lady Day Return, E179/249/1; and the 1674 Lady Day Return, E179/249/2.[1] Data extracted from John Price's tables, E. Lord, K. Sneath & L. Ford, *The Huntingdonshire Hearth Taxes*, London & Cambridge: British Record Society and Cambridgeshire Records Society (forthcoming).
[36] P. Ryan with D. Stenning & D. Andrews, 'The Houses of Essex in the Late Seventeenth Century' in C. Ferguson, C. Thornton & A. Wareham, *Essex Hearth Tax Returns, Michaelmas 1670* London: British Record Society, 2012, p.92.
[37] Ryan *et al*, 'The Houses of Essex', p.92.

to the hearth tax were used to identify the maximum number of Huntingdon-shire clergy, and that procedure may not have been followed for the identi-fication of clergy houses in the Essex hearth tax. Notwithstanding this, there is a lot of consistency between the two counties, with a greater number of Essex and Huntingdonshire clergy paying tax on four hearths than on any other number.[38]

Clergy hearth numbers as an indicator of wealth

The extent to which the hearth tax can indicate poverty or wealth has been the subject of much discussion amongst historians. Margaret Spufford as-serted that hearth numbers might be used as a very general guide to wealth, and although other historians are less certain that hearth numbers can be used to equate to a measure of 'wealth', there is a consensus among historians that a general indication of poverty and wealth is best assessed relative to, and within, a local area.[39] There are further problems associated with esti-mating the relative or comparative wealth of clergymen from their hearth numbers. In theory the benefice provided the means to sustain the incum-bent, together with the clergy house, and this was dependent upon the terms of its foundation - whether it was a rectory, vicarage or curacy. There may have been an additional source of income from a generous patron or bene-factor, such as a stipend or augmentation, and some tithes may have been commuted to cash payments (moduses).[40] All these factors differed from parish to parish, and although it would generally be expected that a vicarage would have had fewer hearths than a rectory, it has been shown that this was not always the case, due to diverse social, geographic and economic condi-tions in each parish, as well as the personal circumstances of the incumbent. It is therefore challenging to put forward a meaningful comparison other than in very general terms.

---

[38] Ibid.; Lord *et al*, *The Huntingdonshire Hearth Taxes*, figures extrapolated from John Price's data sheets.

[39] M. Spufford, *Contrasting Communities, English Villagers in the Sixteenth and Seventeenth Centuries* Cambridge: CUP, 1974, pp.36-45. For further interpretations of this argument, see C. Husbands, 'Hearths, wealth and occupations: an explora-tion of the Hearth tax in the later seventeenth century', in K. Schurer *et al*, *Survey-ing the People,* pp.65-77; T. Arkell 'The incidence of poverty in England in the later seventeenth-century', *Social History* 12, 1987, pp.23-47; C.M. Ferguson, 'The hearth tax and the poor in post-Restoration Woking' in E. Vallance, T. Dean & G. Parry eds. *Faith, Place and People in Early Modern England* Woodbridge: Boydell, 2018, pp.111-132.

[40] J.H. Pruett, *Parish Clergy Under the Later Stuarts*, p.85.

Evelyn Lord suggested that whilst there were many Huntingdonshire parishes with houses of three to five hearths, few of the county's parishes contained houses with hearth numbers above this level, therefore for Huntingdonshire, '3+ hearths has been taken as an indication of relative wealth.'[41] In very generalised terms, this would indicate that the eighty-three per cent of the Huntingdonshire clergy who paid tax on three or more hearths, possibly lived in a state of comfort only enjoyed by the twenty per cent of all householders in the county who were taxed on three or more hearths. At the other end of the scale, in Huntingdonshire as a whole, eighty per cent of householders had only one or two hearths, compared to seventeen per cent of the county clergy.[42] Occasionally the number of a cleric's hearths recorded in one hearth tax schedule had decreased in a subsequent taxation schedule, and any reductions should have been recorded on an exemption certificate. Surviving exemption certificates include reductions, often due to 'chimney downe', in the hearth numbers of Wolstane Chicheley (Kings Ripton), Barnabas Oley (Great Gransden), and Richard Carrier (Orton Longville) but at least six other clerics claimed fewer hearth numbers in 1665 than they had in 1662.[43] It is clear that the clergy did not want to be over taxed on their hearths, but it is impossible to know whether exemption certificates were completed for the latter clergy, or whether the clergy were paying tax on all their hearths.

When the hearth numbers of clergymen are compared to those in the other households in the parish, trends across the county become more noticeable. In most rural areas of England, houses of clergymen, rectories in particular, generally had either the highest, or second-highest, number of hearths, in the parish.[44] Huntingdonshire rectories follow this trend (Table 2). Of the forty-three clergy houses having the highest, or second highest, number of hearths compared to the other houses in the parish, thirty-six (eighty-six per cent) were rectories. It has been noted that, frequently lacking the rights to great tithes, vicarages were less likely to have the greater hearth numbers, whereas the (usually) higher income from a rectory would go hand in hand with

---

[41] E. Lord, 'The Hearth Tax and the Distribution of Wealth in Huntingdonshire', in E. Lord, *et al, The Huntingdonshire Hearth Taxes*, forthcoming.

[42] Figures extrapolated from John Price's data sheets, E. Lord *et al, The Huntingdonshire Hearth Taxes.*

[43] TNA E179/331/132/21, Exemption certificate, Kings Ripton, 1664; TNA E179/331/132/121, Exemption certificate, Great Gransden, 1666; TNA E179/331/132/135, Exemption certificate, Orton Longville, 1664; Huntingdonshire Hearth Tax Assessment 1662/Return 1665.

[44] D. Spaeth, *The Church in an Age of Danger, Parsons and Parishioners, 1660-1740* Cambridge: CUP, 2000, p.36.

higher hearth numbers.[45] Spurr suggests that by this period many vicarage benefices, being dependent only on small tithes, would not have supplied a living wage, and the vicarage of Stanground is, of course, an obvious exception to this generalisation.[46] The reality and accuracy of his suggestion is difficult to assess for Huntingdonshire during the hearth tax period, because of lack of information. However, it is clear to see that of the fifteen Huntingdonshire clerics with the lowest or second lowest number of hearths, i.e., one or two hearths, within their parish, eighty per cent were vicarages or curacies (Table 2). A county wide survey of benefice income was not undertaken until the early eighteenth century, and although the majority of benefice value was usually concentrated in tithes (lesser and greater), and a record of parochial tithing customs was often recorded in glebe terriers, few vicarage terriers have survived which could supply adequate financial details. At best it could be suggested that although income comparisons cannot be made, vicarages were less likely than rectories to contain the highest or second highest number of hearths, and were twice as likely to contain the lowest or second lowest number of hearths as a rectory, in Huntingdonshire.

---

[45] The technical differences between rectories and vicarages are fully explained in the glossary.

[46] Spurr, *The Post-Reformation*, p.236.

Table 2: Number of hearths in clergy houses relative to all other houses in the parish[47]

Number of hearths in clergy house	Highest hearth number	2nd highest hearth number	Lowest hearth number	2nd lowest hearth number	Others	Totals
1			1 R 1 V 1 C			3
2				2 R 5 V 5 C		12
3 to 5	5 R	15 R 3 V 1 C			12 R 11 V	47
6 to 10	10 R 1 V	7 R 1 V			4 R 1 V	24
Total	16	27	3	12	28	86

Notes: R = rector, V = vicar, C = curate.

Glebe terriers and clergy houses

After 1603 'a true note of all the glebes, lands, meadows, gardens, orchards, houses, stocks, implements, tenements and portions of tithes', belonging to any parsonage or vicarage' should have been included in the glebe terrier.[48] This included chapel possessions. Tithing arrangements were intricate and complex, hence they were included in glebe terriers for future consultation and reference.[49] For instance, tithes were due on honey, and on hearths in the parish of St Cleer (Cornwall).[50] Details in terriers can be useful to compare with hearth numbers, if the terrier includes relevant information, but it has been noted that few relevant terriers date exactly from this period. The Diddington Glebe Terrier (c.1663) simply acknowledges 'A dwelling house' and continues to describe the associated land, and tithing customs.[51] Some

---

[47] Data compiled from TNA E179/122/226, Huntingdonshire Hearth Tax Assessment 1662/Return 1665. This excludes the Bishop of Lincoln's Palace at Buckden.
[48] R. Potts, *A Calendar of Cornish Glebe Terriers 1673-1735* Torquay: Devon & Cornwall Record Society, vol.19, 1974, p.ix.
[49] For example, see S. Hindle, 'The Sad Fortunes of the Reverend John Perkins', in E. Vallance, T. Dean, & G. Parry, G. eds. *Faith, Place and People in Early Modern England* Woodbridge: Boydell, 2018, p.75.
[50] Potts, *A Calendar of Cornish Glebe Terriers 1673-1735*, p.xviii.
[51] LA, Diddington Terrier 16/28; TNA E179/122/226; E179/249/2.

sources expand upon the details given in earlier ones. For example, the 1668 glebe terrier of Hemingford Grey indicated the presence of a vicarage, without any detail as to its condition, but in 1697 the vicarage was described as 'having been ruined in the recent rebellion'.[52] The vicar in 1666, John Raban, was one of a small number of vicars who instigated court actions against parishioners for their substraction of tithes.[53] It has been noted that Raban pluralistically held a living in Penn (Staffordshire) and may have been absent part of the time (he is not listed in the hearth tax) but perhaps his absences were extended due to the possibly ruinous nature of the vicarage.[54] Other glebe terriers are more detailed. Two terriers for Eynesbury dated 1607 and 1709 contain many similarities in their descriptions of the clergy house.[55] The 1607 terrier lists twelve rooms including 'a parlor, an hall, a kitching', with three further rooms consisting of a buttery, wash house and milk house on the ground floor, and six rooms above. The 1709 terrier similarly describes a hall, kitchen and parlour, with three or four further rooms on the ground floor, and 'four or five good chambers with boarded floors and one very good garrett'.[56] The houses seem almost identical, with the main point of contrast being the materials used for building. In 1607 the house was described as 'bilt with timber and covered with thatch' whereas by 1709 it had become 'a tiledhouse' with 'Ruffcast walls'. It seems very likely that the footprint of the house had remained unaltered, but cosmetic improvements had been made to the building. John Turner was the rector of Eynesbury from 1649 to 1689 and was taxed on six hearths in 1662/65 and 1674.[57] John Turner's house probably had a hearth in the parlour, the hall, and the kitchen, with some of the remaining hearths likely to have been in upstairs rooms. From the description in the terrier, he lived in a substantial, probably twelve-roomed house. By this point, many rectories of this size will have had brick chimneys, allowing for the provision of hearths in some upstairs chambers.[58]

---

[52] LA TER12/81, Hemingford Grey Terrier 20th March 1668; British History Online, https://www.british-history.ac.uk/vch/hunts/vol2/pp309-314#fnn3.

[53] HA AH4/251/45/1-3, 1666, Citations v. Hemingford Grey parishioners.

[54] http://theclergydatabase.org.uk

[55] HA AH/30/5, Terriers of Eynesbury, dated 1607 and 1709.

[56] Ibid.

[57] Noble, 'Incumbents of the County of Huntingdon', p.203; E. Lord et al, Huntingdonshire Hearth Tax.

[58] P. S. Barnwell, 'Houses, hearths and historical enquiry', in P.S. Barnwell, and M. Airs, eds. Houses and the Hearth Tax: the later Stuart house and society York: CBA Research Report 150, 2006 pp.178-179.

The glebe terriers of Fletton also survive from 1607 and 1709.[59] Thomas Rannier, rector of Fletton between 1652-1694, consistently paid tax on five hearths.[60] The description of 'the Parsonage', with five chambers upstairs, two parlours, a hall, a kitchen and sundry utilitarian rooms downstairs, is similar in both terriers. As implied in the Eynesbury terriers, whilst the footprint of the house may not have been altered since 1607, the outside appearance of the house had been improved; by 1709 the greater part of the thatched roof had been slated. Comparing the likely number of rooms indicated on the terriers of Fletton and Eynesbury, with the hearths enumerated in the hearth tax, implies that around half the rooms had a hearth. However, both these rectories were substantial buildings, with the rectors paying more hearth tax than many of their peers, and a minority of other terriers describe more humble clergy dwellings. For Cambridgeshire, Margaret Spufford suggested that a house with one hearth probably consisted of three rooms (typically a hall, lower chamber, and service room) and a house with two hearths was likely to consist of four or five rooms (a hall, parlour or bedchamber, two service rooms and one upper chamber).[61] The terriers for Great Gidding terriers of 1607 and 1709 contain almost identical descriptions of the 'Vicarage House', which was much smaller than the rectories detailed above.[62] The house was constructed from wood and clay, covered with thatch, and consisted of five rooms; a hall and parlour with a chamber above each, plus a kitchen. The 1709 terrier is more detailed, and described the flooring as 'boarded' upstairs, the rooms below as 'bricked' and the kitchen as 'slabbed'.[63] Luke Grosse was the vicar of Great Gidding between 1616 and 1667, and the hearth tax documents of 1662 and 1665 show that he had two hearths, which would fit well with Spufford's analysis.[64] There are not, however, enough surviving terriers which would prove that all vicarages consistently had a lower ratio of hearths to rooms, compared to rectories.

Other Huntingdonshire glebe terriers describe the origins, the destruction, or the absence of a clergy house, and sometimes offer an insight into parochial life. The terrier for the chapelry of Hilton (1709), whose mother church was Fenstanton, sets out the history of the clergy house in Hilton. There was no

[59] HA AH/30/5, Terriers of Fletton, dated 1607 and 1709.
[60] E179/122/226, Huntingdonshire Hearth Tax Assessment 1662/Return 1665; W.M. Noble, 'Incumbents of the County of Huntingdonshire, p.51. Rannier was alternatively listed as Rayment in the schedules.
[61] M. Spufford, 'The Significance of the Cambridgeshire Hearth Tax', *Proceedings of the Cambridgeshire Antiquarian Society,* LV, 1962, p.58.
[62] HA AH30/5, bundle 1, Terriers of Great Gidding 1607 & 1709.
[63] Ibid.
[64] E179/122/226, Huntingdonshire Hearth Tax Assessment 1662/Return 1665.

provision for such a house until 1641, when the inhabitants of Hilton were so 'desirous of having a teacher reside among them' that they bought an 'old house' and improved it to make 'two low rooms and two chambers' for the curate to live in.[65] This house was probably the residence of Richard Wood, who was described as a 'clerke', with two hearths, on the 1662 assessment. He subscribed to the Oath of non-resistance in July 1662 as 'curate of Hilton'. Richard Wood's hearth numbers and the description of the house in the terrier also equate well with the type of dwelling described by Spufford. It was noted earlier that not every parish had a clergy house, and a glebe terrier might list the reason for this. For instance, the Barham terrier of 1668 explains the destruction of the clergy house, which had previously been 'blowne downe and the poor having carried away the materials abutting the churchyard'.[66] A different example is that of the tiny hamlet of Little Gidding, which consisted of just three houses in 1662.[67] Although the rector, Ferrar Collett, is not included on the hearth tax assessment list, his father was assessed as a householder with twenty-three hearths in Little Gidding, and the assumption is that Ferrar Collett probably lived with his father.[68] According to the Little Gidding terrier (1708), there was 'no Parsonage-house; nor hath bin any within the memory of man'.[69] Ferrar Collett resigned the incumbency of Little Gidding in 1663 when he was appointed to the living of nearby Hamerton, following the death of the rector Richard Newman. Hamerton had the attractions of being a larger parish, with a clergy house, but Mr Collett continued to 'suppy the cure' in Little Gidding until the following year when James Wildbore was pluralistically appointed to the benefice, in addition to Steeple Gidding. Ferrar Collett had difficulty in securing payment for having supplied the cure at Little Gidding, however, and had to apply to the Archdeacon's court to be reimbursed for his expenses.[70] This was unusual, as Huntingdonshire clergy most frequently resorted to the courts in order to recover tithes from the laity, rather than for serving the cure in another parish.

Disputes between clerics and the laity

Disputes between the laity and clergy can demonstrate tension in the parish, but actions brought by the laity against the clergy which ultimately escalated

---

[65] HA AH30/6, Hilton terrier, dated July 9th 1709.
[66] HA AH30/5, Barham terrier dated 1668.
[67] E179/122/226, Huntingdonshire Hearth Tax Assessment 1662/Return 1665.
[68] For further information on the Ferrar family, see for example, http://littlegidding.org.uk/nicholas_ferrar
[69] HA AH/30/5, Terrier of Little Gidding, dated 1708.
[70] HA AH/4/251/31/1, 'Mr Farrar's Accompt, 1663'.

to the ecclesiastical or secular courts, were seemingly rare in late seventeenth-century Huntingdonshire. There may, of course, have been other episodes of tension where a resolution was found prior to a formal court action, and which are less likely to have left a documentary trail. Furthermore, these court actions mostly concerned 'instance' cases where a libel, a citation, and finally a judgement would be made, which were time consuming and expensive.[71] Not all cases always proceeded through every stage, which may explain the seemingly abrupt end to many libels. The minority of late seventeenth-century court cases brought by the laity against an incumbent were usually the culmination of a religious disagreement, or concerned clerical misdemeanours.

In 1674 John Merriton, rector of St Ives, was accused by Daniel Parnell, one of his churchwardens, of behaving in an un-clerical manner. It was purported that Mr Merriton's unacceptable behaviour included 'frequent swearing and cursinge', being 'a common talebearer and backbiter', having 'blasphemed the name of God' and calling his parishioners 'rogues'.[72] Apparently this dispute stemmed from a long-held belief of Daniel Parnell's that Mr Merriton had 'turned out Mr Bradshaw' from his living at Willingham (Cambridgeshire) in 1662.[73] Mr Merriton defended himself from these accusations which were judged to be 'not proven', but he had subsequent problems within his parish, albeit of a different nature. In 1682 John Acton withheld tithes, as did Thomas Sutton in 1693 and both men were taken to court by Mr Merriton.[74] In spite of many witnesses speaking on Sutton's behalf, Merriton was successful in proving his case, and Sutton was ordered to pay the rector fifty shillings in lost tithes.[75]

The duty of each clergyman was to 'supply the cure of the soul' to his parishioners, and this required either his presence, or that of a surrogate, in the parish. In a rare case Bartholomew Mountford, rector of Covington, was accused of 'not supplying the cure'.[76] In 1668, William Love, one of the

---

[71] Spurr, *The Post-Reformation*, p.243.

[72] HA AH4/251/64/3, 1674, Parnell v. Merriton, 1674.

[73] HA AH4/251/64/4, Interrogatory questions, Parnell v. Merriton, 1674; M. Carter, *'An urban society and its hinterland: St Ives in the seventeenth and early eighteenth centuries',* Unpublished PhD, University of Leicester 1988, pp. 241-2.

[74] HA AH/4/251/64/9, Citation against John Acton re substraction of tithes, 1682; AH/4/251/68/58, Citation against Thomas Sutton re substraction of tithes, 1693.

[75] HA, AH/4/251/64/63, sentence of Thomas Sutton, 1694.

[76] Bartholomew Mountford is incorrectly listed as 'Mr Blumford' in 1674 and John Mumford in 1665.

churchwardens in Covington, accused Mr Mountford of anticlerical behaviour. The charges against the rector included 'immoderate drinking', spending two days and one night at the yearly feast at Offord Darcy, not administering the sacrament (giving communion), being non-resident, and living in Brampton nine miles away.[77] Any of these misdemeanours caused a minister to be ineffective but Spaeth asserts that drunkenness was often the catalyst which caused churchwardens to present a minister at court; drunkenness was viewed as being particularly 'inappropriate to the clergy's spiritual position'.[78] It could be suggested that Mr Mountford's absence from the parish was partially explained by the condition of the rectory, which was the only Huntingdonshire rectory recorded as just having one hearth in the hearth tax.[79] The previous rector, William Turner, had chosen to live in the town of Kimbolton, where he had been assessed for eight hearths in 1662.[80] Subsequent seventeenth-century rectors frequently held an additional living and in 1712, Samuel Taylor (rector between 1698-1738) stated that he lived in Kimbolton, the 'Parsonage House being very bad, and the Rector not able to build a better'.[81] Whatever the cause of Mr Mountford's absence, several witnesses were called to speak against him in 1669, which could indicate the depth of negativity towards the rector within the parish, or it might be evidence of an organized campaign by the churchwarden. Mr Mountford did manage to convince the Archdeacon in 1669 that:-

'if any other time the said Cure was neglected by [me] it was by reason that [I] was sick and so much involved in debts that [I] could not with safety supply the said cure as [I] would have done.'[82]

Any clergyman would have been anxious not to lose his living or his livelihood and Mr Mountford additionally defended himself by stating that on several occasions he 'did procure' Mr Boundy, rector of nearby Shelton (Bedfordshire) and Mr Anderson, rector of Catworth, to 'supply the cure of Covington', and he asserted that he had administered communion 'several

---

[77] HA AH4/251/18/1-3, March 1669 - March 1670, Articles v. Bartholomew Mountford.
[78] Spaeth, *The Church in an Age of Danger*, p.125.
[79] TNA E179/249/1.
[80] Ibid.
[81] E179/122/226, Huntingdonshire Hearth Tax Assessment 1662/Return 1665; J. Broad (ed.), *Bishop Wake's Summary of Visitation Returns from the Diocese of Lincoln, 1706-1715: Part 1, Lincolnshire* and *Part 2, Outside Lincolnshire* Oxford: OUP, 2012, p.522; the visitations are discussed in Simon Clemmow's chapter 9.
[82] HA AH4/251/18/1-3, March 1669 - March 1670, Articles v. Bartholomew Mountford.

times' during his tenure at Covington Church. Canon law required that a sacramental service (communion) should be held just three or four times annually, with Easter being the most important, and churchwardens' accounts from other Huntingdonshire parishes indicate that purchases of communion wine were generally confined to Easter and Christmas.[83] Mr Mountford's responses to the accusations seem to have convinced the Archdeacon and he was issued with an admonishment in March 1670 'to conforme himself to a better life'.[84] Unfortunately he was not ultimately successful in achieving this, and in April 1674 he was deprived from the living, his sentence of deprivation being 'affixed to the door of the parsonage house'.[85] This type of friction between minister and congregation was infrequent, and Bartholomew Mountford's deprivation appears to be the only such example in post-restoration Huntingdonshire.

Tithe disputes between the clergy and laity

A frequent cause of friction between the clergy and the laity in the late seventeenth-century Church of England was the substraction (non-payment) of tithes.[86] These cases demonstrate the important financial implications of tithes to both parties, and between 1661 and 1685, clergy in a quarter of Huntingdonshire parishes cited lay-people for the non-payment of tithes, which is a very similar proportion to that found in Leicestershire.[87] Tithing customs were complicated and varied, and a working knowledge and understanding of agricultural practice was desirable, for instance, differentiated rates of tithes were applied to a range of crops.[88] There was a clear association between supplying the cure, and receiving tithes.[89] The incumbent provided 'the cure' and acted as a good landlord by keeping the glebe in order, whist the parishioners paid a tenth of their crops and animals to the incumbent, either in kind, or as a commuted payment. The Incumbent was reliant upon, and expected to receive, these tithes as part of his due income.[90] In compar-

---

[83] Spaeth, *The Church in an Age of Danger*, p.4, & p.182, n. 44; HA, for example, HP27/5/1-19, Fenstanton CA; HP36/5/1, Great Gransden CA; HP82/5/1, Great Staughton CA.

[84] HA AH4/251/18/4, March 1670, Instructions to Bartholomew Mountford.

[85] HA AH4/251/18/6, April 1674, Deprivation of Living, Bartholomew Mountford.

[86] Spaeth, *The Church in an Age of Danger,* p.133.

[87] HA AH/4/251, various parishes, 1662-1690; Pruett, *Parish Clergy Under the Later Stuarts*, pp.89-90.

[88] For instance, HA AH4/251/10/2, John Robinson v parishioners, 1666.

[89] Spaeth, *The Church in an Age of Danger,* pp.153-54.

[90] Spaeth, *The Church in an Age of Danger,* p.151.

ison to rectors, only a small minority of vicars instigated court cases for substracted tithes, and this is probably because rectors faced the larger loss of great tithes, whereas vicars were usually only entitled to small tithes.[91] This type of legal action demonstrate the clergy's readiness to defend a crucial source of their income, but Pruett asserts that clerics who believed themselves to have been cheated out of their tithes resorted to court action reluctantly, due to the burdensome costs involved in a failed case.[92] However, other factors may have increased a cleric's resolve. Simon Paige, rector of Hemingford Abbots, had previously suffered the sequestration of his tithes in the Commonwealth years, and this may have strengthened his determination in pursuing several parishioners for non-payment of tithes between 1659-1663.[93]

Although Spaeth asserts that tithes were harder to collect from non-resident substracters, and consequently they were less frequently targeted by the clergy, there are instances where this did occur, and again, this probably demonstrates the clergy's determination in pursuing 'their rights'.[94] Additionally, another cause of concern was the falling value of land in the late seventeenth-century, which caused heightened tension for both the receiver, and the payer, of monetary tithes.[95] Richard Alfeild, rector of Grafham (1667-1689), must have felt that he had no option other than to cite Thomas Beadles of Great Staughton for substraction of tithes, after unsuccessful attempts to discuss the matter with him, and John Slade, a witness, described seeing an argument between the two men.[96] The dispute centred on the 'worth of the close', rather than on the unwillingness of Beadles to pay; Beadles argued 'the close' was 'not now worth three shillings per acre', which he had offered to pay, rather than the four shillings Mr Alfeild maintained was the tithe payment due to him.[97] Richard Alfeild took advantage of the opportunity in court to additionally press Thomas Beadles for the payment of the previous four years' Easter offerings, at the rate of 4d per adult and 2d for the others in his household.[98] Other clerics chose to forego these

[91] Pruett, *Parish Clergy Under the Later Stuarts*, pp.82-87.

[92] Pruett, *Parish Clergy Under the Later Stuarts*, p.89.

[93] W.A. Shaw, *A History of the English Church During the Civil Wars and Under the Commonwealth*, London: Longman, 1900, p. 314; HA AH4/251/40/2-7, 1664, Citations v. Hemingford Abbots parishioners.

[94] Ibid.

[95] Spaeth, *The Church in an Age of Danger*, pp.133, 136-40.

[96] HA AH4/251/35/2-3, 21st February & 24th April 1677.

[97] HA AH4/251/35/1, Articles v. Thomas Beadles, 1676.

[98] This is similar to Easter offering values in Leicestershire; Pruett, *Parish Clergy Under the Later Stuarts*, p.94.

payments, regarding them to be an 'offering, rather than their due', as noted by Ferdinand Berridge, vicar of Great Paxton, in the parish register.[99] Tithe arrangements could be complicated, tree timber for example, was titheable at different rates depending upon the age of the tree when felled, and custom and memory played an important part.[100] Some incumbents faced the problem of reinstating rent or tithe payments that had lapsed during the Civil Wars and Commonwealth years.[101] John Robinson, the vicar of Buckworth, cited George Smith, from Woolley, for the non-payment of his tithes for the 'meadow of Woolley' in 1666.[102] It was usual to call witnesses in tithe cases, and in this case, witnesses were asked how they knew that tithes had not been paid, or that 'during ye tymes of Rebellion' the payment of such tithes were ever controverted by 'any usurping power then extant', or, on the other hand, that tenants had been compelled to pay, and did pay, the tithes.[103] Most tithe cases in Huntingdonshire were pursued against a single substractor, sometimes on multiple occasions, but occasionally a multitude of parishioners were taken to court due to withholding tithe payments.

The absenteeism of subsequent rectors of Somersham provoked large numbers of parishioners to withhold their tithes in the post-Restoration period. The Rectory of Somersham (with Bluntisham, Colne & Pidley-cum-Fenton) was a living additionally annexed to the holder of the position of Regius Professor of Divinity at Cambridge, and was worth in the region of £300 per annum in tithes; this was the most valuable benefice in Huntingdonshire by the beginning of the eighteenth century.[104] Peter Gunning (rector between 1662 and 1667) appointed curates for Somersham (William Hicks), for Colne (Samuel Fuller), and for Pidley cum Fenton (Thomas Thurlin), and these four clergymen all duly signed the Subscription Book on 16th July 1662. Peter Gunning was assessed for eight hearths in Somersham in 1662 but his other commitments rendered his continual presence in Somersham very unlikely, and by 1665 he was absent from Somersham, leaving his curate, William Hicks, to pay the hearth tax, but Samuel Fuller and Thomas

[99] HA HP64/1/1/1, Great Paxton Composite Register, 1583-1702, unpaginated.
[100] HA AH30/6, Haddon Terrier, dated 1709; HP64/1/1/1, Great Paxton Composite Register, 1583-1702, unpaginated.
[101] D. Dymond, 'The Parson's Glebe: Stable, Expanding or Shrinking?' in C. Harper-Bill, C. Rawcliffe, R. Wilson (eds.), *East Anglia's History*, Woodbridge: Boydell, 2002, p.89.
[102] HA AH4/251/10/2, John Robinson v parishioners, 1666.
[103] Ibid.
[104] Broad (ed.), *Bishop Wake's Summary of Visitation Returns,* p.522.

Thurlin are not listed in any hearth tax schedules.[105] Peter Gunning and Joseph Beaumont (the successive Regius Professor of Divinity at Cambridge) instigated a total of fifty-eight libels between 1663 and 1684 for the withholding of tithe payments by parishioners living in several parishes.[106] Joseph Beaumont faced a much stronger challenge from a greater number of parishioners unwilling to pay tithes, who argued that because Beaumont had never been instituted as Rector at Somersham, he was not entitled to tithe income. Beaumont appealed the case to the Court of Arches, where it was finally ruled in 1691 that a vicar had not been endowed at Somersham, and therefore the Regius Professor should either 'serve the cure or should allow £100 per annum for the support and maintenance of a curate obliged to constant residence.'[107] The amount of £100 per annum was much higher than the income of most Huntingdonshire benefices – even by the time of Bishop Wake's visitations in the early eighteenth century, when the benefice income of more than thirty parishes was reported to be less than £50 per annum.[108]

Clerical poverty and debt

Clerical poverty and debt are hinted at in a few instances in seventeenth-century Huntingdonshire, and although exact details are hard to discover, evidence suggests that the vicar of one of the poorest benefices seems to have been living in poverty. Although it was taken some time after the hearth tax years, Bishop Wake's valuation (1712) of £27 per annum for the benefice of Great Stukeley was the lowest valuation of all the vicarage benefices in the county, but gives an indication that it was probably not a wealthy living during the earlier period.[109] The vicar, James Seabourne, had been instituted in 1618, and probably died in the late 1660's.[110] He was the sole Huntingdonshire vicar to be assessed for just one hearth in 1662, but there was no vicarage for him to inhabit; the vicarage had been 'taken down in the Civil War and never rebuilt' which implies that this had occurred during his

[105] E179/122/226, Huntingdonshire Hearth Tax Assessment 1662/Return 1665.
[106] HA AH4/251/69, dated 1663- 1684; one of these men, Micapher Alfray of Warboys, was either the son or grandson of the eponymous vicar of Woolley who is discussed below.
[107] British History online, History of Somersham parish, pp. 223-230, fn. 81 *Hist. MSS. Com. Rep.* xiii (v), 467.
[108] Broad ed. *Bishop Wake's Summary of Visitation Returns,* Huntingdonshire section, pp.473-547.
[109] Ibid., p.525.
[110] The parish registers are incomplete but James Seaburne (sic) signed the Bishops' Transcripts until 1664; HA AH/28/85/1, Great Stukeley Bishops' Transcripts, 1604-1673. Whilst the date of James Seabourne's burial is unknown it is assumed to have been prior to the sequestration order in 1669.

incumbency.[111] This provides further evidence that several Huntingdonshire clergy houses had suffered during the Commonwealth years. In 1665 it was noted on the hearth tax return next to James Seabourne's name that he was 'not worth anything'.[112] This comment has to be treated with caution as it would be extremely unusual for a serving vicar to be 'not worth anything', and there is always the possibility that a contemporary error created an incorrect hearth tax entry. However, the churchwardens' accounts show that they were forced to sequester the living in 1669 in order to pay visiting clerics 'to provide the cure.'[113] Tithes amounted to slightly more than £17 for five months in 1669, and nearly £11 was expended on ministers to 'serve the cure' during the year.[114] The minsters who were regularly paid to serve the cure included John Bush, the vicar at Hartford, and Benjamin Gery, the rector of Little Stukeley. There was a sliding scale of 'pay', dependent upon qualifications and experience. For example, John Bush and Benjamin Gery were each paid five shillings on every occasion whereas Avery Wagstaffe, who was not ordained until 1675, received just four shillings each time he served the cure.[115] Great Stukeley appears to have been a poor, unattractive prospect for clerics. The living was vacant, certainly from 1669, until 1673, and by 1712, the vicar reported to the Visitation that he ' has to have another parish,' (Hemingford Abbots) 'where he resides, because the living [is] so poor.'[116] Where a living was inadequate, a minister occasionally had a second living, but this did not necessarily solve debt problems.

John Dixon was the rector of Offord Darcy (1641-1671) and also of Glenfield in Leicestershire (1630-1671), which were over sixty miles apart. Mr Dixon signed the Subscription Book for each parish in July 1662, and was assessed for five hearths in Offord Darcy in 1662.[117] In the 1665 hearth tax return the house was described as 'Empty the own[er] in prison'.[118] The hearth tax debts schedule of 1665 gives slightly more detail with 'the owner Dixon being in prison at Huntingdon'.[119] Although there is no further confirmation of his whereabouts, he was certainly in debt, because the Rectory

[111] TNA E179/122/226; J. Broad ed. *Bishop Wake's summary of visitation returns*, p.525.
[112] TNA E179/122/226.
[113] HA AH4/251/75/3 bundle; Disbursements of the Great Stukeley churchwardens 1669 to 1673.
[114] HA AH4/251/75/3 bundle, Great Stukeley Churchwardens' Accounts 1669.
[115] Ibid.
[116] Broad ed. *Bishop Wake's summary of visitation returns*, p.525, n.69.
[117] LA DIOC/SUB/3, Bishop's Subscription Book 3, 1662-77.
[118] E179/122/226, Huntingdonshire Hearth Tax Assessment 1662/Return 1665.
[119] TNA E179/331/pt. 4, debts Michaelmas 1664 – Michaelmas 1665.

was sequestered in January 1665 'for the debt of John Dixon, rector.'[120] The churchwardens and the Bishop of Lincoln agreed a bond to allow the church-wardens to collect the tithes; thus the 'provision of the cure' could be funded.[121] It seems that John Dixon had previously struggled to collect some of his tithes at Glenfield, and evidence points to there having been similar difficulties in Offord Darcy.[122] John Dixon had partially complied with the 'pluralism requirements' demanded by the Bishop, by appointing a curate, John Michael, and he had cited Edward Fuller of Offord Darcy, for the sub-straction of tithes in 1663.[123] John Michael lived in St Neots rather than in Offord Darcy and perhaps parishioners were concerned over the provision and quality of their own spiritual care, and less willing to offer tithes to a pluralistic rector and an absent curate. By 1670, the parsonage had fallen into disrepair, and John Dixon died in 1671.

Probate inventories and wills of Huntingdonshire clergymen

By occupation, the clergy were one of the most literate groups of society, and approximately thirty-five legible wills and probate inventories, dating between 1663 and 1691, survive for clerics whose names appear in the Hun-tingdonshire Hearth tax documents. Wills may reveal personality traits, such as sentiments, which other documents do not, but do not necessarily present an accurate measure of wealth.[124] Apart from the bequeathing of goods, land and actual money, Huntingdonshire clerics used their will for the settling of their own debts, and also as an indicator of debts owing to them, in the hope that these would be collected by their executors. Amongst the population, will-makers often requested friends or colleagues to witness their will and the clergy were no different. Huntingdonshire clergy often witnessed parish-ioners' wills and were also witnesses or supervisors for the wills of several colleagues. For example, Samuel Backler, who signed exemption certifi-cates as the minister of Somersham in 1673 (he was presumably acting as a curate), witnessed the will of Edmund Rouse, rector of Huntingdon in May

[120] HA AH4/251/54/2, Sequestration, debt of John Dixon, 1665.
[121] Ibid.
[122] F. McCall, *Baal's Priests, The Loyalist Clergy and the English Revolution* Farnham: Ashgate, 2013, p.95.
[123] HA AH/4/251/54/1, John Michael v. Edward Fuller, Offord Darcy, 1662.
[124] For a full discussion of problems associated with wills see for example, T. Arkell, N. Evans, N., and N. Goose eds., *When Death Do Us Part: Understanding and Interpreting the Probate Records of Early Modern England* Oxford: Leopards Head Press, 2000, pp.38-71.

1676.[125] Richard Newman, rector of Hamerton, drew up his will in May of 1663, which was witnessed by James Wildbore, the rector of both Little Gidding and Steeple Gidding.[126] John Wells, rector of Thurning (1627-1664), requested that Samuel Bird, the subsequent incumbent, be one of the supervisors of his will, and he was also one of the witnesses.[127] Huntingdonshire clerics occasionally appraised a will of their colleagues; James Wildbore (above) appraised the goods of John Newcome, rector of Caldecote (1680-1688) in 1688, and William Baker, rector of Wistow (1641-1687) was the appraiser for the probate inventory of John Robins, perpetual curate of Ramsey (1662-1675).

Credit and indebtedness appear to have been a normal function of seventeenth-century life.[128] Debt was an important component of many wills, and it is clear that debts both owing to, and from, clerical testators, were of great concern to Huntingdonshire clerical testators.[129] Thomas Whitehand, rector of Swineshead (1639-1666), desired 'all those debts, dutys as I owe in right or conscience to any manner or person or persons whatsoever, shall bee well and truly contented and payd'.[130]Joseph Hemings, rector of Swineshead (1666-1670) made a short will, effectively leaving 'all my goods and chattels of what nature soever they be' to be sold by his executors to pay his debts, with any residue being given to his son.[131] Mickepher Alphery, rector of Woolley (1618-1668) was very careful with his finances.[132] After 1666 he lived with family members in London, and in his will of 1668 he instructed that his curate should be paid 'so long as I live and no longer', and that his son, also named Mickefer, should collect due payments of rent which

---

[125] TNA E179/331/17; HA, AH16 dated 1677/36, Will of Edmund Rouse.

[126] HA AH16 dated 1663/53, Will of Richard Newman.

[127] TNA Prob/11/315/247, Will of John Wells, 1664.

[128] C. Muldrew, *The Economy of Obligation: The Culture of `Credit and Social relations in early Modern England*, Basingstoke: Palgrave, 1998, pp.96-98. See also K. Sneath, '*Consumption, wealth, indebtedness and social structure in early modern England*', Unpublished PhD, University of Cambridge 2009.

[129] M. Spufford, 'The limitations of the probate inventory' in J. Chartres & D. Hey eds., *English Rural Society 1500-1800: Essays in honour of Joan Thirsk* Cambridge: CUP, 1990, pp.139-74.

[130] HA AH/16/2/6/47, Will of Thomas Whitehand 1666.

[131] TNA Prob/11/334/204, Will of Joseph Hemings, 1670.

[132] Space does not permit a full discussion of this very unusual vicar, but see M. Stephenson's article in the *Journal of the Huntingdonshire Family History Society* no. 91, November 2018, pp.24-27. 'Mr Alphrey, gent,' is listed at the head of the 1663 hearth tax return for Woolley, but the number of his hearths is impossible to read; TNA, E179/122/227, Huntingdonshire Hearth Tax Return Lady Day 1664 (probable date, see TNA website).

had been mounting up for some time.[133] Mr Alphery also referred explicitly to 'the inward doors within the house' at Woolley, instructing that 'if the Incumbent' [curate] 'will give reasonable prise for them then let them stand, otherwise remove them', which indicates his intention to maximise his assets. On the other hand, he assiduously noted his debts owed to his son James, and to his daughter in law 'Stephen's wife', and instructed that they should be paid after his death.

John Bateman, rector of Keyston (1660-1665) made his will in 1665. A number of people were indebted to him, which he seemed anxious to point out, but was prepared to absolve them. He forgave his cousin Thomas Bateman the 'three score pounds' owed to him for an unpaid legacy dating back several years previously.[134] He bequeathed his cousin Joane Eadis three silver spoons 'which she might a had before this tyme, had her husband shewed himself honest'. One bequest to his cousin Ellen Rooding was dependent upon his executor extracting a debt of ten pounds owed to John Bateman by 'my Lord Manchester and Lewis Cannell and Thomas Browning'. He ended by thanking his cousin Bridget for the 'dilligence, attendance, love and care' she gave him in his sickness, and allowed her 'that five pounds which shee lately had of me'. However, there is a sense of balance in that he also gave her the majority of his household goods. Fewer than half the clerics gave money to the poor of their parish, which may seem unusual, but by the late seventeenth-century charitable giving had declined in wills, possibly because testators may have judged the payment of their poor rates to be in lieu of charitable giving.[135] John Bateman gave forty shillings each to be used for the poor of Keyston and Thrapston, which was generous compared to other clerics, as twenty shillings seems to have been the most common amount that was bequeathed to the poor.

Only a small minority of Huntingdonshire clerical testators appeared have been in a strong enough financial position to bequeath land or leases in their wills. The incumbent could not bequeath the clergy house or its land unless he was also the patron, and any other land or property the incumbent possessed in his own right may have been apportioned prior to the drawing up of his will. John Wells, rector of Thurning from 1627 until his death in 1664, did own the patronage, and he conditionally bequeathed the advowson, the right of patronage, and additional lands, to Emmanuel College, Cambridge, subject to Samuel Bird being appointed as the subsequent incumbent, but

---

[133] TNA Prob/11/328/ 267, Will of Mickefer Alphery, 1668.

[134] TNA Prob/11/322/236, Will of Thomas Bateman, 1666.

[135] B. Waddell, *God, Duty and Community in English Economic Life 1660-1720* Woodbridge: Boydell, 2012, p.107.

this example is a rare occurrence in post-restoration Huntingdonshire. [136] Robert Newcome, rector of Alwalton (1656-1679) and of Caldecote (1645-1657 & 1662-1679) had either inherited or bought, through the course of his life, several properties which he bequeathed to his children in his will, including five houses (or farms) with appurtenances and messuages. [137] His probate inventory survives but despite being one of the highest values, at nearly £240, it gives a misleading value of his total assets, because property and land are excluded from probate inventories. [138] This demonstrates that a more accurate picture of wealth might be gained if a testator's will and probate inventory have both survived. [139] Life for Huntingdonshire rectors and vicars, most of whom lived in rural parishes, revolved around agriculture, and the relevance of agriculture for Huntingdonshire rectors is also better demonstrated in their probate inventories, rather than in their wills. Three quarters of the probate inventories of vicars and rectors included references to barns, agricultural implements, grains, or cattle, and the item of at least one horse in over half the inventories indicates the method by which these clerics probably travelled around their parish. The Warwickshire clergyman John Perkins owned a horse 'upon which he almost certainly perambulated the parish' and it can be presumed that many Huntingdonshire clergy did the same. [140]

Huntingdonshire clergy probate inventories hint at some differentiation between rectors and vicars, but the smallness of the number only allows for generalisations to be made. For example, probate inventory values of vicars (£112) and curates (£65) appear to be lower than those of rectors (£180), however, fewer inventories of vicars and curates have survived in comparison to those of rectors. This is not surprising, given that Huntingdonshire had a greater number of rectories, and that inventories survive in greater numbers for rectors, but the highest valued inventory (£385.14.0) was that of William Young (four hearths), vicar of Diddington (1663-1682). [141] The lowest value of all Huntingdonshire clergy probate inventories – nearly £12 - was that of Isaac Johnson, curate of Holme. [142] The terrier for Glatton (Holme's mother church) included the possessions of Holme Chapel but omitted any reference

---

[136] TNA Prob/11/315/247, Will of John Wells, 1664.

[137] HA AH16 dated 1679/63, Will of Robert Newcome.

[138] HA AH/18/14/79, Probate of Robert Newcome, 1679.

[139] Arkell *et al*, *When Death Do Us Part*, p.95; M. Spufford, 'The limitations of the probate inventory' pp.139-74.

[140] Hindle, 'The Sad Fortunes of the Reverend John Perkins', p.75; the horse was valued in his probate inventory at £3 10s.

[141] HA AH18/24/25, dated 1682, Probate inventory of William Young.

[142] HA AH18/10, dated 1666, Probate inventory of Isaac Johnson.

to the provision of a curate's house and the assumption is that Isaac Johnson did not have a benefice house.[143] Curates did not usually possess entitlement to a benefice glebe, and this fact probably decreased Isaac Johnson's financial opportunities; his stipend was likely to have been small.[144] His debts came to nearly £28, approximately seventy per cent of his gross probate valuation.[145] It is not always easy to detect the number of rooms in a household from information on the inventory alone, but the implication of his probate inventory, together with the fact that he only paid tax on one hearth, is that he lived very humbly in just three rooms (table 3).[146] Twelve additional probate inventories survive from which it was also possible to calculate a minimum number of rooms, which were then compared to hearth tax numbers on the hearth tax schedules. It can be seen that a house with one or two hearths had a lower proportion of hearths to rooms, than is the case for a house with four-plus hearths. It is also likely that in a house with a higher number of hearths, some were upstairs, as explained earlier. However, this is a very small sample of probate inventories from which to draw a firm conclusion.

---

[143] HA AH/30/5, Terrier for Glatton, 1709.
[144] Pruett, *Parish Clergy Under the Later Stuarts*, p.84; the stipend was provided by the rector of Glatton, HA AH/30/5, Terrier for Glatton, 1709.
[145] HA AH18/10, dated 1666, Probate inventory of Isaac Johnson.
[146] Ibid.

Table 3: Inferred room numbers in clergy probate inventories compared to hearth numbers[147]

Hearth numbers recorded in hearth tax returns	Number of clergy houses	Implied minimum number of rooms in probate inventory		
1	1	3		
2	1	7		
3	3	8	7	
4	3	8	8	10
5	1	8		
6	3	10	9	
(7)				
8	1	12 plus		

By the late seventeenth-century, Spaeth suggests that the preparation of inventories required appraisers to be cognisant of market values, which was dependent upon the existence of a 'culture of appraisal'.[148] However, clerics formed a very select group of testators, some of whose possessions were occupation specific, such as their books and clerical gowns. Libraries and studies, which are often mentioned in probate inventories of Huntingdonshire clerics, were only normally referred to in connection with the gentry or clerics, and so all appraisers might not have frequently encountered these items in probate valuations.[149] Notwithstanding this, books did feature in most of the clerics' probate inventories and in several wills. The average value given to books in these inventories was around £18, and as books were often the second highest household item valued, it seems that these appraisers were aware of the value of clerics' literature. The highest valuation of a cleric's books was £60, in the probate inventory of John Robins, the perpetual curate of Ramsey (1642-1675), which amounted to just over half the total inventory value (£118 10s).[150] John Robins cannot be found as a householder

---

[147] Data from selected clerics' probate inventories HA AH18, 1666-1691; TNA E179/122/226 and /227, E179/249/1 and /2; Huntingdonshire hearth tax assessment and returns 1662-1674.

[148] D. Spaeth, '"Orderly made': re-appraising household inventories in seventeenth-century England', *Social History*, 2016, 41(4), pp.417-435.

[149] Spufford, *Contrasting Communities*, p.211.

[150] HA AH18/18/101, dated 1675, Probate inventory of John Robins.

or tax-payer in any hearth tax schedule. His inventory is very brief, and offers no suggestion of the number of rooms he lived in. It is possible that he lodged in rooms in the town, rather than being a householder, and is therefore invisible in the hearth tax schedules.

Some valuations of clerics' books in probate inventories were low, but this does not necessarily imply that the testator owned few books. Joan Dils' research into clergy probate inventories earlier in the seventeenth century contains many examples of unrealistically low book valuations.[151] She suggests that appraisers were often unaware of the true value of books.[152] Although this does not seem to be the case for the inventories above, and despite the growth in book ownership and in the 'culture of appraisal' by the late seventeenth century, it does seem questionable that two appraisers who made their marks on the inventory of John Bush, rector of Hartford (1662-1684), could accurately appraise his books. Illiteracy was not synonymous with an inability to read, and it might simply be coincidence, but the appraisers' valuation of John Bush's books at £1 7s was the lowest amongst the Huntingdonshire clergy probate inventories. That being said, different types of books were available and some clergy differentiated between the types of books they owned.[153] Thomas Fowle (five hearths), rector of Everton-cum-Tetworth (c.1662-1663) instructed his executor that all his 'paper notes and bookes be burned', whilst all his 'Books' were to be sold.[154] The nature of the former is unknown, but to Thomas Fowle, they had no worth, whereas he regarded the latter as having worth, and a monetary value.

Conclusion

The Huntingdonshire hearth tax sources demonstrate that the parish clergy lived in a range of differently sized homes, and paid tax on hearth numbers ranging from one to ten. Most rectories were the largest or second largest houses in their parish but most perpetual curates had one or two hearths. The mean number of hearths for rectories and vicarages was four, and eighty-four per cent of clergymen had three or more hearths, compared to twenty per cent of the rest of the county's population. The majority of the clergy therefore inhabited houses of a larger size than most of their parishioners. However, some clergy, particularly those with only one hearth, were not in

---

[151] A. Hughes ed. *Sussex Clergy Inventories 1600-1750* Lewes: Sussex Record Society, 2009, vol. 91, p.xviii, n.21.

[152] Ibid.

[153] Spufford suggests that there was an increased availability of cheap books by this time, which caused them to be omitted from probate inventories; Spufford, 'The limitations of the probate inventory', p.149.

[154] HA AH16, dated 1663/31, Will of Thomas Fowle; Spufford, 'The limitations of the probate inventory', p.149.

a favourable situation. It was normal at this time to operate within a framework of credit and debt, and this is demonstrated in the probate sources. However, other documents demonstrate that not all clergymen were in a position to pay the hearth tax. Isaac Johnson, Bartholomew Mountford and James Seabourne, all of whom had just one hearth, had debts of a large enough nature to impinge dramatically upon their lives. Isaac Johnson's debts amounted to seventy per cent of the gross value of his probate inventory. James Seabourne may have effectively been worthless and unable to pay his hearth tax. Mountford suffered from bouts of drunkenness, which may ultimately have caused him to be deprived of his living. That being said, it appears that financial problems were not confined to clergy in smaller properties. John Dixon paid tax on five hearths and was possibly imprisoned for debt. The sequestering of his living would have increased the challenges he faced in attempting to reduce his debts. A substantial number of Huntingdonshire clergymen proactively sought to protect their income, and to recover tithe debts from parishioners by taking court action against them, with varying degrees of success. John Merriton was one rector who successfully recouped lost tithes, but the Regius Professor of Divinity at Cambridge University, in a case lasting several years, effectively lost the right to £100 of annual tithes. Huntingdonshire clerics used their wills to make their executors aware of debts owed to them, and debts owed by them, and debts featured in many of the probate documents. It is therefore evident from many of the surviving sources that financial concerns impacted enormously on the lives of clerics in post-restoration Huntingdonshire.

9

DISSENT IN POST-RESTORATION HUNTINGDONSHIRE

Simon Clemmow

The Religious Background

During the Commonwealth the Church of England was abolished; local presbyteries were established which paid no attention to parish boundaries and allowed congregations to control their own membership, but the failure to establish a new national church paved the way for what John Spurr describes as 'largely unchecked religious experimentation'.[1] However, with the restoration of the monarchy in 1660 came the re-establishment of the Church of England, underpinned in 1662 by an Act of Uniformity which required all clergy to have episcopal ordination, to subscribe to the doctrine of the Church as encapsulated in the Thirty-Nine Articles, and to abide by every word and ceremony of the revised Book of Common Prayer. Out in the parishes, all members of the community were legally obliged to attend Church of England services - and to pay tithes to their incumbent, church rates for the upkeep of the building, and fees for baptisms, marriages and funerals according to Church of England rites. These commitments to Anglican observance and infrastructure were enforced by both ecclesiastical and secular courts, since there was a natural convergence of interests between the established church and the governing elite. The result was that, for a large majority of the population, conformism was the name of the game, even if it was just an outward display of affiliation to keep out of trouble.

The effect of the Act of Uniformity was to outlaw non-Anglican religious denominations. Protestants who had always worshipped outside the Church of England, such as Baptists and Quakers, now found themselves joined by others in one nonconformist category labelled 'dissenters'. These others were Puritans who could not accept Anglicanism as defined by the Act. Moderate Puritans found themselves in a difficult position: did they attempt

---

[1] J. Spurr, *The Post-Reformation: Religion, Politics and Society in Britain, 1603-1714* Harlow: Pearson, 2006, p.119.

to remain within the established church, or did they accept the label of 'dissenter' as a Presbyterian or Congregationalist or Independent? Some puritan clergy managed to retain their parish livings. An example often cited is that of Ralph Josselin, who was the vicar at Earls Colne in Essex from 1641 to 1683. His diary contains frequent mentions of the 'Society' – a godly group which met under his leadership – and 'illustrates the insecurities of the Restoration for a man on the borderline of nonconformity.'[2] But some two thousand clergy left their livings in the early 1660s - mostly not through choice, but through deprivation: evidence has been found for 1,760 ejections between 1660 and 1662.[3] Just a few miles away from Earls Colne, at Terling, the puritan minister John Stalham was one of those ejected from his living in 1662; he was replaced by a conforming vicar. Stalham lived on in the village and became minister of the Congregational church, taking many of his flock with him – seventy-five villagers were prosecuted for dissent between 1662 and 1685.[4] The situation in Terling illustrates how the Act of Uniformity could backfire in its attempt to establish the Church of England as the sole, comprehensive church of the nation.

This is not to say that there was a clear dividing line between conformity and dissent. The practice of partial conformity, whereby a nonconformist minister might attend the Church of England as a layman, or a parishioner might attend the parish church in the morning and a local conventicle in the afternoon, was widespread. Nevertheless, the Act of Uniformity had cut English Protestantism in two, even if the two halves were unequal and some people kept a foot in each one. And to the category labelled 'dissenters', containing Protestant nonconformists, we must add Roman Catholics. In post-Restoration England, Catholicism was not just a potential threat to the establishment from overseas or from a catholic successor to Charles II, but a real tendency that existed at the heart of court and government. There is evidence of a high church persuasion in the restored Church of England, and many dissenters felt they could not conform because in their view Anglican-

---

[2] A. Macfarlane ed., *The Diary of Ralph Josselin, 1616-1683* Oxford: OUP, 1976, p.xxiv.

[3] A.G. Matthews, *Calamy Revised: being a Revision of Edmund Calamy's Account of the Ministers and Others Ejected and Silenced, 1660-1662* Oxford: OUP, 1934, pp.xii-xiii.

[4] K. Wrightson and D. Levine, *Poverty and Piety in an English Village: Terling, 1525-1700* (second edition), Oxford: OUP,1995, especially pp.160-168.

ism still contained too many relics of popery. Those who identified as Roman Catholics were persecuted as dissenting 'papists' alongside Protestant nonconformists.[5]

Persecution of dissenters took several forms. The Act of Uniformity was only one of a series of laws, collectively known as the Clarendon Code, designed to suppress dissent. For example, the Conventicle Act of 1664 made it unlawful for groups of people to meet in assembly for religious purposes other than those of the Church of England. Prosecution of illegal conventicles was further encouraged by the renewed Conventicle Act of 1670, which rewarded informers and penalised negligent officials. Under such laws, dissenters were spied upon, harassed, reported and punished with fines, imprisonment, transportation or even death. Education opportunities and civil office were denied to those who did not conform. There was a step towards toleration in 1672, when a Declaration of Indulgence allowed Catholics to worship in the privacy of their own homes and Protestant dissenters to procure conventicle licences – around 1,500 were issued for nonconformist ministers and meeting houses. Nevertheless, the fear and experience of persecution suffered by non-Anglican religious groups between the early 1660s and the late 1680s leads one to consider how determined they must have been to worship apart from the Church of England. Against this background, what was the level and pattern of dissent in post-Restoration Huntingdonshire? Where did it take hold in particular? And why?

Primary Sources and Historiographical Debates

There are several types of record that can provide evidence for the persecution of dissenters – they include presentments at assizes, proceedings against dissenters, and calendars of prisoners. Unfortunately, there do not seem to be any surviving examples of these for late seventeenth-century Huntingdonshire. But there are examples from neighbouring Bedfordshire, including documentation of the imprisonment of John Bunyan.[6]

There is also an important study of dissent in neighbouring Cambridgeshire. Margaret Spufford finds that although Presbyterianism was the strongest

[5] The terms 'nonconformist' and 'dissenter' are generally not clearly differentiated, and often used interchangeably; some historians refer to 'Protestant dissent' and 'Catholic dissent', so let us here use 'dissenters' as an umbrella term and 'nonconformists' to describe Protestant dissenters; 'papists', of course, are Catholic dissenters.

[6] W.M. Wigfield, ed., 'Recusancy and Nonconformity in Bedfordshire, illustrated by Select Documents between 1662 and 1842', *Bedfordshire Historical Record Society,* vol. 20 1938, pp. 145-229, especially p.172.

sect in the country by 1669, in Cambridgeshire it was very small with around thirty adherents.[7] She goes on to look in depth at three villages in which different landscapes produced different social structures: Chippenham, Orwell and Willingham. Two of these villages were almost as economically contrasted as it was possible to be: in Orwell, on the corn-growing clay uplands, the disappearance of the small landowner resulted in an economy polarised between larger holdings and landless labourers; in Willingham, on the edge of the fens, stock farming and dairying made small holdings economically viable. Both villages had flourishing Congregational conventicles in the 1670s, but Orwell's Congregationalists were distributed throughout every layer of village society from the poor to the prosperous, whereas Willingham's were almost entirely confined to the substantial middle stratum. Spufford observes that the most likely reason for this surprising result is that it ties in with the very different socio-economic situations in the two villages.[8] But there were also complaints made by parishioners in Orwell about their rector failing both to appoint a vicar and to cover for the lack of one, and this could be a contributing factor to the degree and pattern of dissent that Spufford found.[9] Spufford subsequently broadened her inquiry into 'the world of rural dissenters', from where she and her colleagues report that 'stability, together with the nature of ... post-Restoration dissent, running completely across the social spectrum, is our most important finding.'[10] The conclusion is that there was a kind of 'descent of dissent' through generations of dissenters integrated into their local communities.

A census of religious affiliation undertaken in 1676 - known as the Compton Census, more of which later – indicated the proportion of dissenters in the population to be around 5 percent. Or, to put it another way, it confirmed what was required by the law and presumed by the establishment: that a large majority of the population - 95 percent – was Anglican. It was not until after the rise of 'new dissent' in the eighteenth and nineteenth centuries that the Church of England was confronted with evidence that it no longer commanded the allegiance of most English people. The 1851 Religious Census

---

[7] Spufford's source for these figures is G. Lyon Turner, *Original Records of Early Nonconformity under Persecution and Indulgence* 3 vols., London, 1911-14.

[8] M. Spufford, *Contrasting Communities: English Villagers in the Sixteenth and Seventeenth Centuries* (second edition), Stroud: Sutton, 2000, especially pp.300-306.

[9] G. Hart, ed., *The Cambridgeshire Committee for Scandalous Ministers, 1644-1645* Cambridge: Cambridgeshire Records Society, 2017, pp.96 and 137.

[10] M. Spufford ed., *The World of Rural Dissenters, 1520-1725* Cambridge: CUP 1995, p.37.

took advantage of the machinery of the general census to survey the country's religious institutions and found that more places of worship belonged to dissenting denominations than to the established church. It also found that less than half the total attendances on Census Sunday - 30th March 1851 - were at Anglican churches.[11] There appears to have been a fundamental shift in religious affiliation between the Compton Census and the Religious Census.[12] A comparison of the two censuses is difficult, because they record different things: the Compton Census sought to enumerate the beliefs of parishioners, the Religious Census the behaviour of worshippers. Nevertheless, careful comparison can be instructive, and a major pioneering study of this kind was undertaken at parish level in eight English and four Welsh counties by Alasdair Crockett and K. D. M. Snell. It set out to investigate, quantitatively and statistically, whether the geographical distribution of dissent in 1676 bore any resemblance to the pattern in 1851. It found little evidence of parochial continuity except amongst Catholics, suggesting that Protestant dissent was relatively fluid.[13] Crockett and Snell conclude that nonconformists were more mobile and transient than previously believed, in contrast to Spufford's finding of 'stability' and the historiography of continuity in general. They claim that 'one advantage of a more quantitative approach is that it tends to eschew linear and survivalist kinds of thinking, and thus may throw up alternative perspectives which might be missed by other lines of study.'[14]

Crockett and Snell clearly regard their quantitative approach as having broken the paradigm of qualitative study by arriving at different conclusions rather than propagating accepted perspectives. But their contribution would have been stronger if it had been presented as complementary to rather than contradictory of other lines of study, since the best history finds quantitative and qualitative approaches working together. And Crockett and Snell's findings might have been different again had their inquiry sampled different counties, since patterns of dissent varied markedly across the country, and within counties. Or if they had looked at continuity and discontinuity in the other direction - from the Compton Census back to the Lollards rather than forward to the Religious Census: a comparison between the geography of

---

[11] H. Mann, *Census of Great Britain, 1851: Religious Worship in England and Wales – Abridged from the Official Report* London: Routledge, 1854.
[12] No attempt was made to measure comprehensively the nation's religious affiliation between 1676 and 1851; a third attempt was not made until 2001, when a religious element was introduced to the decennial census.
[13] A. Crockett and K. D. M. Snell, 'From the 1676 Compton Census to the 1851 Census of Religious Worship: Religious Continuity or Discontinuity?', *Rural History*, vol. 8, no. 1 (April 1997), pp.55-89.
[14] Ibid., p.82.

the Lollards and that of the Compton Census might have found that some areas were traditionally prone to dissent. Such considerations indicate the value of attempting to incorporate determinants of dissent into the analysis – asking not just what and where, but why – to produce a rounder and more robust picture.

Possible Determinants of Dissent

It could reasonably be supposed that dissent might flourish in three broad circumstances: where the Church of England was weak; where dissenting influence was strong; or where there was a greater level of receptiveness to dissenting ideas. Alan Everitt suggests that the Church of England was likely to be weak in market towns, in fen and boundary areas, and in large parishes, where manorial control was weak.[15] Market towns were natural meeting places inclined to independence of trade and opinion. In rural areas, dominant landlords could intervene to prevent the spread of nonconformist opinion, but non-resident lordship or manorial subdivision could allow dissenting seeds to take root, especially in large parishes with scattered populations and hamlets or isolated dwellings far from the parish church. The boundary areas of such parishes might be ill-defined, and inter-commoning could lead to squatter communities on the fringes of the parish system. The Church of England might also be weak where its authority was undermined by an incumbent who was unpopular or ineffective. Donald Spaeth identifies problems caused by poverty and pluralism.[16] A vicar whose entitlement to one third of the tithes was not a living wage might be forced into pluralism – taking on more than one parish – to find somewhere to live and make ends meet. Alternatively, a minister might have sought pluralism through financial greed; either way, he would have been open to criticism for non-residence, absenteeism and pastoral neglect – as was the case in Orwell. There might be a certain amount of sympathy amongst fellow parishioners for those with dissenting views. Magistrates might be less than vigilant in their duties on behalf of the establishment.

It might be that rather than the Church of England being weak, dissenting influence was strong. We have seen that in a strongly puritan parish like Terling a popular incumbent could be ejected from his living but retain his congregation as a nonconformist minister. But dissenting influence could

---

[15] A. Everitt, 'Nonconformity in Country Parishes', *Agricultural History Review,* vol. 18, supplement (1970), pp. 178-199; and A. Everitt, *The Pattern of Rural Dissent: the Nineteenth Century* London: Leicester University Press, 1972.

[16] D.A. Spaeth, *The Church in an Age of Danger: Parsons and Parishioners, 1660-1740* Cambridge: CUP, 2000, especially pp.30-58.

come from outside the parish too. Ejected incumbents might become peripatetic ministers, preaching to gatherings of dissenters and founding dissenting churches well beyond the confines of their 'home' parishes. Charismatic figures could stimulate interest in dissent. Such activity would bear most fruit where there was a greater level of receptiveness to dissenting ideas. There might be a dissenting tradition in some areas, perhaps stemming from political and religious views running through the generations of families – Spufford's 'descent of dissent'. Schooling not supervised by the Church of England might be a factor: the membership of dissenting churches tended to be predominantly female, and women were frequently the people who taught children reading. And literacy must be considered as a determinant of religious conviction. A higher level of literacy – perhaps a function of superior economic status – might open minds to alternative opinion. This could lead to dissent in a conformist context – and to conformity in a dissenting one. The reason dissent flourished in some areas and not in others will almost certainly be a combination of partial factors. As Spufford puts it: 'No determinism, economic, social, educational or geographical, will fully account for the existence of religious conviction'.[17] We might add genealogical and pastoral determinants to her list.

The Compton Census

The Compton Census is a good starting point for any analysis of religion in post-Restoration England. It was taken in 1676, four years after the Declaration of Indulgence had allowed dissenting worshippers some degree of toleration. In the intervening period the government's attitude to dissent had hardened: in 1673 the Indulgence was withdrawn, and a Test Act was introduced which required every civil and military office holder to take oaths acknowledging the supremacy of, and confirming personal allegiance to, the Church of England. In 1675 it was proposed that an oath against alteration of church or state government – part of the Clarendon Code - should become a requirement for all public offices. Keen to establish the feasibility and wisdom of such policy in support of the established church, the government sought confirmation that most of the population was Anglican. As we have seen, the Compton Census – named after Henry Compton, Bishop of London, who was heavily involved in the administration – did indeed indicate a very high proportion of conformists in the population, at around 95 percent. But did even such an overwhelming majority give licence for intolerance and persecution of the minority? The Compton Census returns were a source of disagreement amongst politicians at the time, and subsequently have posed problems and challenges as a source for historians.

---

[17] Spufford, *Contrasting Communities,* p.352.

The census asked incumbents for the number of inhabitants in their parishes, for the number of "Popish Recusants" amongst them, and for the number of "other Dissenters … (of what Sect so ever) which either obstinately refuse or wholly absent themselves from the Communion of the Church of England at such times as by Law they are required." The third request was ambiguous: did it mean people were to be counted as dissenters if they attended the parish church but did not receive the sacrament? Or did they have to be absent from church altogether to 'qualify'? Many people attended both the church in the morning and a conventicle later in the day – were such partial conformists to be classified as dissenters, or not? Reception of communion even amongst regular churchgoers was often very infrequent; to report such behaviour as dissent would mean high numbers of nonconformists. On the other hand, to report only total separatists as dissenters – counting partial conformists as conformists – would make dissent look less widespread than it was.

Further problems arise with the numbers of conformists. 'Inhabitants' were variously reported as households or families, men only, men and women over sixteen, or the whole population irrespective of age. Additionally, although presumably the figures for papists and nonconformists were to be subtracted from the figure for inhabitants to give the number of conformists, sometimes the subtraction was not done, so the figures under the heading "Conformists" in the final manuscripts are sometimes figures for 'inhabitants'. The returns made by the parish incumbents were edited locally before being sent to London or York to be written up formally, so there was plenty of scope for inconsistency and inaccuracy.

Fortunately, the ability of historians to identify and respond to inconsistencies, inaccuracies, omissions and accusations of bias in the Compton Census has been considerably advanced by the scholarship of Anne Whiteman, whose critical edition has opened it up as a source.[18] The primary benefit of Whiteman's edition is the transcription, whereby the three key surviving manuscripts in which the returns appear are printed together in full for the first time. But there is much more to Whiteman's achievement than this: in gathering together and transcribing the material, she has assessed its reliability as a source, endeavouring to establish what the figures represent and evaluate them as evidence. She has examined original documentation concerning the initiation and planning of the census; she has supplemented the

---

[18] A. Whiteman ed., *The Compton Census of 1676: a Critical Edition* Oxford: OUP, 1986.

key texts where possible with incumbents' returns and tabulations of the results made at archidiaconal and diocesan level; and she has used comparative material, including the Hearth Tax, to help in the interpretation of the figures. Whiteman's edition therefore provides not only a more accessible and legible version than the original, but also a vital assessment of the data it contains. Whiteman suggests that there is no evidence of bias in the way the survey was launched, and no evidence of any attempt to prevent an honest return. She maintains that generally incumbents did their best to give truthful answers according to their understanding of the questions, and the process of tabulating the returns and transmitting the results was carried out in good faith. And at a practical level, she tells us whether to opt for 'conformists' or 'inhabitants'. She identifies those dioceses in which the figures under the heading "Conformists" are really for 'inhabitants', and those – including Lincoln, which contained the county of Huntingdonshire – in which, because the subtraction was done, the figures are for 'conformists'.

Crockett and Snell made heavy use of Whiteman's edition. Their methodology addressed the problems caused by the different interpretations of 'inhabitants' and the ambiguous definition of 'dissenters' by calculating internal ratios and percentages on a parish-by-parish basis. Their assumptions were that each incumbent would have applied the same interpretation across the three categories he was returning figures for, and that therefore the ratios between each figure, for distinct parishes, are likely to be reliable indicators of the relative levels of conformity or dissent and allow feasible comparisons between parishes. Approached carefully in this way, the Compton Census is a valuable source for the history of dissent - although it tells us nothing, for example, about the different dissenting denominations and their circumstances.[19] Whiteman is adamant that generalisations about the census are dangerous, and that the figures must be analysed locally in conjunction with other available evidence. Using the Compton Census as a starting point, what can we say about dissent in post-Restoration Huntingdonshire?

Dissent in Huntingdonshire

The Compton Census lists 88 parishes in Huntingdonshire: 22 in the deanery of Yaxley, 22 in the deanery of St Ives, 2 in the deanery of Huntingdon, 21 in the deanery of St Neots, and 21 in the deanery of Leightonstone – all within the archdeaconry of Huntingdon and the diocese of Lincoln. There

---

[19] Some information of this kind was given by some incumbents in their returns but edited out of the final manuscripts; no surviving incumbents' returns for Huntingdonshire have been found.

are 6 omissions, all in the Leightonstone deanery, and all peculiars.[20] Overall, the proportion of dissenters in the county is about 5 percent – the same as that across the whole country. The number of "Conformists" recorded ranges from 825 in the parish of St Neots to 16 in Little Gidding, and although we cannot be sure whether these absolute numbers represent individuals or families, we can see that the entire population of Little Gidding was deemed conformist, since no "Papists" or "Nonconformists" were recorded in the parish. The number of "Nonconformists" ranges from 66 in Warboys to none in 32 parishes – so we can see immediately that according to the Compton Census dissent was far from evenly spread across the county.

In Warboys there were 296 "Conformists", no "Papists", and 66 "Nonconformists", so we can calculate the 'strength of dissent' in the parish as 18.2 percent (66 as a percentage of 362 'inhabitants'). Two other parishes with high numbers of dissenters are Godmanchester with 65, and Yaxley with 58.[21] But - as Crockett and Snell argued - ratios are more reliably comparable than absolute numbers, and in percentage terms Godmanchester and Yaxley are not as strongly dissenting as Warboys, due to their larger populations. Yaxley has 413 inhabitants, making its strength of dissent 14.0 percent; Godmanchester has 801 inhabitants, making its strength of dissent 8.1 percent.[22] On the other hand, three parishes are more strongly dissenting than Warboys, due to relatively high numbers of dissenters in smaller populations: these are Grafham (24.1 percent), Hemingford Abbots (26.9 percent), and Ellington (27.3 percent). Table 1 sets out all Huntingdonshire parishes with a 'strength of dissent' of 6 percent or more. These parishes are mapped in Figure 1, which reveals that there are three areas of the county where dissent appears to have taken a particular hold: two apparently 'standalone' areas of Warboys and the neighbouring parishes of Ellington and Grafham, and a

---

[20] Peculiars were exempt from the jurisdiction of the bishop, and were generally omitted from the Compton Census; in Huntingdonshire they were all prebendal (that is, they were assigned by the bishop of Lincoln to a prebendary who was a canon or member of the chapter of the cathedral and who alone exercised ecclesiastical jurisdiction), and were Brampton, Buckden, Easton, Leighton Bromswold, Long Stowe with Little Catworth chapelry, and Spaldwick with Barham chapelry.
[21] Yaxley is interesting in that it contains 11 of the 24 papists recorded by the Compton Census in Huntingdonshire - no other parish in the county has more than 3, and there are no papists at all in 80 of the 88 parishes; there is also a Yaxley in Suffolk, the home of the Yaxley family who were prominent Catholics in the seventeenth century – whether they had any connection with Yaxley in Huntingdonshire is beyond the scope of this inquiry.
[22] The 1674 Hearth Tax records nearly 300 households in Godmanchester; whatever reasonable multiplier is used, this suggests a population higher than the 801 recorded by the Compton Census, and supports Crockett and Snell's argument for using ratios rather than absolute numbers.

string of parishes along the valley of the river Ouse consisting of Godman-chester, the Hemingfords, Fenstanton, Holywell, Bluntisham-cum-Earith, and Colne.

Table 1: Huntingdonshire Parishes with a 'Strength of Dissent' of 6% or more in 1676			
Parish	Number of Conformists	Number of Dissenters	'Strength of Dissent'
	n	n	%
Diddington	63	4	6
Old Weston	136	9	6.2
Fletton	151	11	6.8
Godmanchester	736	65	8.1
Brington	67	6	8.2
Hemingford Grey	191	17	8.2
Holywell	283	28	9
Southoe	137	14	9.3
Kimbolton	394	41	9.4
Fenstanton	286	39	12
Bluntisham	355	49	12.1
Colne	160	24	13
Abbotsley	125	19	13.2
Yaxley	355	58	14
Kings Ripton	71	15	17.4
Warboys	296	66	18.2
Grafham	85	27	24.1
Hemingford Abbots	136	50	26.9
Ellington	80	30	27.3

Source Compton Census 1676

Dissent in Warboys is not in fact isolated but is connected to the Ouse valley string of parishes by a relationship with Fenstanton. In the 1640s, Henry Denne was baptised in London. 'The [Baptist] church of which he was a member sent him forth into Bedfordshire and Cambridgeshire to propagate the long-oppressed truth of the word of God. His labours were effectual, many churches sprang into existence, and amongst them the churches at Warboys and Fenstanton.'[23] Denne embarked on an evangelising tour of the neighbouring districts. He was clearly a charismatic figure who could stimulate active participation in dissent: by the 1650s his Baptist churches were drawing members from no less than thirty surrounding parishes. The Warboys church was continuing to thrive two centuries later: the 1851 Religious Census recorded the size of the general congregation at the morning service at the Baptist church at Warboys to be more than twice that at the parish church.[24] And Horace Hyde notes that 'As the flourishing church entered the last half of the nineteenth century there was no doubt that the Baptist cause was on the crest of a wave'.[25] At Warboys, dissenting influence would appear to have found an enduringly receptive audience.

---

[23] E.B. Underhill, ed., *Records of the Churches of Christ Gathered at Fenstanton, Warboys and Hexham, 1644-1720* London: Hanserd Knollys Society, 1854, pp.vii-viii.

[24] D.M. Thompson, ed., *Religious Life in Mid Nineteenth-Century Cambridgeshire and Huntingdonshire: the Returns for the 1851 Census of Religious Worship* Cambridge: Cambridgeshire Records Society, 2014, p.110.

[25] H.A. Hyde, *The Warboys Baptists* Warboys: Pastor A. Stone, 1963, p.40.

Figure 1 Huntingdonshire Parishes with a 'strength of dissent' of 6% or more in 1676

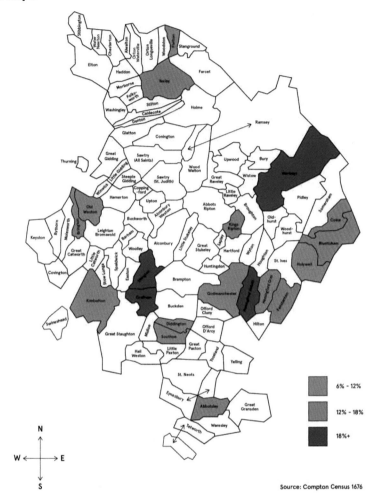

Source: Compton Census 1676

We can begin to identify some of the determinants of this situation with the help of Bishop Wake's visitation returns. These record the results of three unusually systematic and closely-spaced surveys – conducted in 1706, 1709 and 1712 – of the parishes in the diocese of Lincoln. Information on parish size and population, the clergy and the state of their churches, and other aspects of parochial life and social structure, was collected by means of a printed questionnaire; for the historian this provides an extremely valuable comparison with, and extension to, the Compton Census data.[26] The Wake returns for Warboys indicate the kind of parish where Everitt suggests the Church of England might be weak: it is a large parish on the edge of the fen, with an absent landlord - "There is a Mannor house [that] is let to a Tenant."[27] There is also a suggestion of an educational influence on religious belief that fills a vacuum left by the Church of England: "A private Schole is taught by James Stoakly, to write & read. He has about 20 or 30 Scholars: What care is taken of their Religion: N[ot] L[icensed] … No Catechizing: The Rector leaves that, with the Religious Education of the Children to the Schole master."[28] If we calculate 'strength of dissent' from the figures for population and nonconformity given in the Wake returns – as shown in Figure 2 – we can see that it 'holds up' at between 14 and 24 percent in Warboys during the early part of the eighteenth century, at least one generation on from Compton. Such evidence would appear to support the Spuffordian theory of stability of post-Restoration Protestant dissent, rather than Crockett and Snell's finding of discontinuity.

[26] J. Broad ed., *Bishop Wake's Summary of Visitation Returns from the Diocese of Lincoln, 1706-1715: Part 1, Lincolnshire* and *Part 2, Outside Lincolnshire* Oxford: OUP 2012.
[27] Ibid., p.527.
[28] Ibid., pp.527-528.

Figure 2: 'Strength of Dissent' in Warboys and Hemingford Abbots, 1676-1712

	Warboys	Hemingford Abbots
1676	362 inhabitants 66 dissenters 'strength of dissent' = 18.2%	186 inhabitants 50 dissenters 'strength of dissent' = 26.9%
1706	130 families 23 Baptist, 5 Quaker 'strength of dissent' = 21.5%	50-60 families 3 Baptist, 3 Quaker 'strength of dissent' = 10.9%
1709	100 families 20 Baptist, 4 Quaker 'strength of dissent' = 24.0%	250 inhabitants 21 dissenters 'strength of dissent' = 8.4%
1712	135 families 20 Baptist and Quaker 'strength of dissent' = 14.8%	61 families 1 Baptist, 2 Quaker 'strength of dissent' = 4.9%

Source: Compton Census 1676, Wake Returns 1706-1712

The Wake returns for Warboys record between 100 and 135 families in the parish, which is broadly consistent with the Compton figure of 362 inhabitants – giving us confidence in using the two sets of data in conjunction with each other. The Wake returns for Ellington and Grafham, however, contradict rather than support the Compton numbers. Figure 3 shows that the 'strength of dissent' in Ellington and Grafham suggested by Wake – 11.1 percent and 5.9 percent respectively – is significantly lower than the 27.3 percent and 24.1 percent indicated by Compton. The reason for the lower figure in Ellington is that, although the number of dissenters recorded is about the same (30 individuals in Compton, and 8 families in Wake), the population is much higher in the Wake return (72 families – suggesting well over 200 inhabitants – compared with only 110 inhabitants in the Compton Census). The reason for the lower figure in Grafham is different: the population is about the same (112 inhabitants in Compton, and 34 families in Wake), but the number of dissenters is much lower in the Wake return (only

2 dissenting families, compared with 27 dissenting individuals in the Compton Census). There are too many contradictions here to take the analysis of dissent in Ellington and Grafham further within the scope of this inquiry, and we must regard these parishes as outliers from the main areas of dissenting activity in post-Restoration Huntingdonshire, which were Warboys, Fenstanton and other parishes in the Ouse valley.

Figure 3 'Strength of Dissent' in Ellington and Grafham 1676 and 1706

	Ellington	Grafham
1676	110 inhabitants 30 dissenters ① 'strength of dissent' = 27.3%	112 inhabitants 27 dissenters 'strength of dissent' = 24.1%
1706	72 families 6 Baptist, 2 Quaker 'strength of dissent' = 11.1%	② 34 families 2 Independent 'strength of dissent' = 5.9%

Source: Compton Census 1676, Wake Returns 1706

Note the discrepancy between the two surveys in:
① the population of Ellington
② the number of dissenters in Grafham

Dissent in the Ouse Valley

By the 1650s Denne's Baptist church at Fenstanton was exerting a powerful influence on surrounding parishes. Dissenting ministers were ejected at Hemingford Abbots in 1660, and at Bluntisham in 1662. The ejected rector of Bluntisham, James Bedford, was later fined and imprisoned for preaching at a conventicle in London.[29] The Baptist churches at Warboys and Fenstanton, along with Baptist churches at Godmanchester and St Ives, were granted licences under the Declaration of Indulgence of 1672-3.[30] The local market town of St Ives – the largest in the county according to the Compton Census, with 835 inhabitants (compared with Huntingdon's 642) – would have been a natural meeting place, ideal for fermenting and spreading dissenting ideas throughout the region. Manorial control was weak at Bluntisham and Earith, which shared common land and meadows, and were self-governing by feoffees rather than under a resident landlord. And at Colne in the fens there was inter-commoning with Somersham, and 'fen houses' which might have been beyond the reach of a minister in the normal course of his parish

[29] Matthews, *Calamy Revised*, p.44.
[30] W.T. Whitley, ed., *Minutes of the General Assembly of the General Baptist Churches in England: vol. 1, 1654-1728* London: Baptist Historical Society, 1909, p.lix.

duties. Circumstances were ripe for dissent to flourish in the Ouse valley in the late-seventeenth century.

But the expansion of the Fenstanton church then slowed. By the time of the 1851 Religious Census, it is obvious that the General Baptist church at Fenstanton had fallen on hard times – its return states that there was "no settld Minister", and the general congregation averaged only 40 in the morning and afternoon, whereas the parish church recorded 119 attendees in the morning and 172 in the afternoon.[31] The trend at Hemingford Abbots is even more striking: from one of the highest levels of dissent in the county in 1676, to one of the highest indexes of Anglican attendance in 1851.[32] To what can we attribute this decline in the fortunes of the Baptists and resurgence of the Church of England in this corner of Huntingdonshire? One consideration must be the rapid expansion of the Quakers: many Quaker converts were gained from the Baptists. A Quaker meeting-house was built in St Ives in 1691 and extended in 1725.[33] The Wake returns show that by the early eighteenth century, Quakers outnumbered other dissenters in several parishes in the Ouse valley, including Godmanchester. At Bluntisham, 'The Quakers have had a Meeting house ... above 40 years & it is constantly made use of for their Weekly & General Meeting ... the Anabaptists also meet, but seldom, & not regularly.'[34]

A rise in the Quakers at the expense of the Baptists would not, of course, account for a resurgence of the Church of England. But might there also have been a waning appetite for dissent in general in the Ouse valley, and a corresponding trend to conformity - in contrast to the situation in Warboys? It has already been suggested that literacy as a function of superior economic status might be a factor in religious determinism, and we can get an idea of the contrasting socio-economic profiles of Hemingford Abbots and Warboys from the 1674 Hearth Tax – as shown in Figure 4.[35] The Hearth Tax

---

[31] Thompson ed., *Religious Life,* pp.123-124.

[32] Calculating 'indexes of attendance' is a methodology for comparing the attendances at religious institutions in the 1851 Religious Census between parishes; it was used, along with other methodologies, by Crockett and Snell – see Crockett and Snell, 'From the 1676 Compton Census to 1851 Census of Religious Worship', notes 8 and 19, pp.83-84.

[33] C. Stell, *An Inventory of Nonconformist Chapels and Meeting-Houses in Eastern England* Swindon: English Heritage, 2002, p.157.

[34] Broad ed., *Bishop Wake's Summary,* pp.509-510.

[35] Figures for Huntingdonshire from T. Arkell, 'Identifying Regional Variations from the Hearth Tax', *The Local Historian,* vol. 33, no. 3 August 2003, pp.148-174

was a property tax on households, rated according to the number of fire-places – or hearths – they contained. Although there are problems with the data arising from the collection of the tax - including various exemptions, attempts at evasion, and inconsistency of administration – the number of hearths recorded is a possible indicator of the householder's wealth and so-cial standing.[36] Figure 4 shows that Warboys' socio-economic profile is sim-ilar to that of Huntingdonshire overall, with similar proportions of house-holds with one or two hearths (around 80 percent) and with three or more hearths (around 20 percent). Hemingford Abbots' socio-economic profile, however, has a markedly higher proportion of households with three or more hearths (over 40 percent) and conversely fewer households with only one or two hearths (less than 60 percent). This might be indicative of a higher level of literacy in Hemingford Abbots, and consequently a greater tendency to question rather accept the status quo; in a strongly dissenting context, such alternative opinion might have fostered conformity.

Figure 4 Socio-economic profiles of Huntingdonshire Warboys and Hemingford Abbots in 1674

	Huntingdonshire	Warboys	Hemingford Abbots
Total Households	5208	124	68
Non-chargeable	23%	28 (23%)	19 (28%)
5+ Hearths	5%	1 (1%)	3 (5%)
4 Hearths	18%	3 (3%) 23%	6 (12%) 44%
3 Hearths	13%	18 (19%)	13 (27%)
2 Hearths	27%	32 (33%)	13 (27%)
1 Hearth	55% 82%	42 (44%) 77%	14 (29%) 56%
		96 (100%)	49 (100%)

Source: Arkell 2003, Hearth Tax 1674

(see table, p. 156); figures for Warboys and Hemingford Abbots from *Huntingdon-shire Hearth Tax Assessments 1674* transcription of Public Record Office E179/249/2, Huntingdonshire Archives, Huntingdon, 1992.

[36] Such an interpretation can be made only in broad terms, because there are many specific exceptions: for example, the occupier of a one-hearth household could have wealth – in the form of goods, chattels, crops and livestock in a probate in-ventory – comparable with that of a householder with four or five hearths; con-versely, inns could have many hearths, but innkeepers were rarely of high social standing.

A third explanation for a trend towards conformity in the Ouse valley is the possibility of changing attitudes within the Church of England itself, leading to a broadening of its appeal and greater inclusivity. Problems with ineffective incumbents have already been mentioned, and the Church of England did much to address them over the course of the eighteenth and nineteenth centuries. Nigel Yates points to a growing professionalism of a clergy who set an example to their parishioners, paid attention to their flocks and encouraged regular church attendance.[37] The Wake returns for Hemingford Abbots hint at an attentive incumbent - they record that "The Rector resides in his Parsonage House … Catechizing promised to be duly performed."[38] They also suggest that the level of dissent in the parish declined dramatically from the 26.9 percent recorded by the Compton Census in 1676 – to 10.9 percent in 1706, to 8.4 percent in 1709, and to just 4.9 percent in 1712 (see Figure 2). And this was in the period after the Toleration Act of 1689 had put an end to the persecution of dissent and replaced it with a right to worship. In the 1830s the rector of Hemingford Abbots was an evangelical minister who was embraced – or at least tolerated – rather than ejected by the Church of England. He was the only evangelical clergyman in the immediate area, and as such was drawing to the Anglican church many who might otherwise have been 'lost' to dissent.[39] The same rector – Edward Selwyn – was the incumbent at the time of the Religious Census, which recorded the total attendance at the morning service at the parish church to be the equivalent of nearly half the population (43 percent; 232 attendees and a population of 544).[40]

Dissenting Parishes, Different Determinants

The situation in Hemingford Abbots contrasts with that in Warboys in terms of both the continuity or discontinuity of dissent and the local circumstances that may have determined these trends. Both parishes were strongly dissenting in 1676: Warboys through the influence of Denne, because of its geographical characteristics, and with suggestions of weak manorial and educational control; Hemingford Abbots at the centre of a tripartite Baptist influence from Godmanchester, Fenstanton and St Ives. But by 1851 there was a marked contrast in the strength of dissent in the two parishes. At Warboys,

---

[37] N. Yates, *Eighteenth-Century Britain: Religion and Politics, 1714-1815* Abingdon: Routledge, 2014; first published 2008, especially pp.130-142.
[38] Broad ed., *Bishop Wake's Summary*, p.536.
[39] R.W. Dixon, 'Religious Life and Work', in A. Goodman ed., *Potto Brown: the Village Philanthropist* St Ives: Albert Goodman, 1878, pp.109-199, especially pp.117-118.
[40] Thompson, ed., *Religious Life*, p.122.

the Baptists continued to thrive - supporting the Spuffordian thesis of the stability of Protestant dissent. At Hemingford Abbots, on the other hand, Anglican attendance was among the highest in the county - illustrating Crockett and Snell's finding that Protestant dissent was relatively fluid. Here, a superior socio-economic profile indicative of a higher level of literacy, and effective pastoral care, appear to have contributed to a 'conversion' to conformity.

Contrasts such as these show the importance and value of researching individual parishes when dealing with something as fragmented and fluctuant as dissent in post-Restoration England. The situation in Huntingdonshire – or any other county – can be likened to looking at a patchwork quilt. We can establish and articulate its overall colour and texture, but only closer inspection reveals that this is made up of a myriad of small pieces, each with its own shape and size, its own colour and texture.

GLOSSARY

Advowson The right of a patron to present a priest for appointment to an ecclesiastical benefice.

Appropriation Annexing of a benefice, historically by a monastery, usually for the retention and profit of the greater tithes.

Chaldron A measurement of coal which equated to approximately 25cwt.

Compton Census an ecclesiastical census taken in 1676, named after Henry Compton, Bishop of London,

Copyhold A tenancy whereby the person holds their land or other property by copy of the court roll. Sometimes called Customary Tenancy.

Cottager In Anglo-Saxon times a person who held up to 5 acres of land but did not own a plough. He rented a cottage and provided labour services to the lord of the manor. Later the term became synonymous with a person living in a cottage.

Declaration of Indulgence In 1672, Charles II extended religious liberty to Protestant nonconformists and Roman Catholics. Catholics were allowed to worship in the privacy of their own homes and Protestant dissenters could procure conventicle licences.

Demesne The land of a manor reserved for the lords use, to provide food for his table, or for him to sell for profit.

Dole A share. The term is usually applied to a meadow or other pasture which is shared by more than one person.

Freehold Originally, land or property that was rented from, and free from service to the lord of the manor. Later it became land or other property that had been purchased and was wholly owned.

Hearth Tax A tax based on the number of hearths in a property. Introduced in 1662 and abolished after William III's accession in 1689.

Hundred Subdivisions of counties originally probably comprising a hundred hides. Huntingdonshire had four: Norman Cross, Leightonstone, Toseland and Hurstingstone.

Husbandmen Literally a person engaged in husbandry, tending animals and tilling the soil. Husbandmen typically worked smaller plots than yeomen and relied mostly upon family labour.

Imparkment The process of creating a park from land formerly used for arable or animal husbandry.

Lady Day The Feast of the Annunciation of the Blessed Virgin Mary, 25th March.

Lamms/Lammas lands 1st August, originally a harvest festival in England till the early 18th century. Lammas land is meadow or pasture land that was in private ownership until Lammas when it was opened to the animals of those of the townsfolk who held common right over the open fields.

Leasehold A form of tenure in which a fee was paid when the lease was taken out. The lessee paid rent throughout the period of the lease, which was agreed as either being for a term of years or lives. Leases for a term were often very long and example of leases of 80 years or more are not uncommon. Leases for lives were generally for periods of three to five lives and as long as one person remained alive the lease continued.

Michaelmas The feast of St Michael and All Angels, 29th September.

Rectory The original endowment for a benefice, consisting of land and tithes for the rector's income, usually including a house for the Rector. After the dissolution of the monasteries, tithe rights were confiscated and granted or sold.

Recusants Those who refused to attend the Church of England; a crime until 1791. Punishments included fines, confiscation of property and imprisonment.

Sequestration The act of taking legal possession of assets (confiscation)

Severalty An estate held by its owner or a tenant for his use and interest and over which no common rights exist.

Thirty-Nine Articles The Thirty-nine Articles of Religion went through several revisions before being finalised in 1571. They set out the doctrine and practice of the Church of England.

Tithes or tenths of agricultural production. Great tithes of crops and small tithes of livestock, wool and non-cereal crops were payable to the Rector.

Total Factor Productivity A measure of the efficiency of all inputs to a production process. Improving efficiency frequently results from technical change in individual sectors of the economy or structural change.

Township The smallest unit of land possessing a complete and independent field system.

Vicarage Residence of a vicar (Latin vicarious meaning substitute or deputy) who was appointed by the Rector. Where the Rector's tithes were appropriated by monastic or collegiate foundations, lesser tithes were received by the vicar together with a salary.

BIBLIOGRAPHY

PRIMARY SOURCES

College of Arms
Visitation of Huntingdonshire King's copy of the Hearth Tax 5+ houses from the Michaelmas 1683 return.

Huntingdonshire Archives:
21ˢᵗ February & 24ᵗʰ April 1677 HA AH4/251/35/2-3
Account book of John Simpson of Covington 1735-40 HA 52
Alconbury Field Map HA Map 451
Attorney General v Simpson 1898 HA BLC5/5/1
Barham terrier dated 1668. HA AH30/5,
Articles v. Thomas Beadles 1676 HA AH4/251/35/1
Bishop's Subscription Book 3, 1662-77 LA, DIOC/SUB/3
Bluntisham Terrier of land in before enclosure HA HP 5/3/4/19
Bond for Robert Mosse, 1695 2519/117
Citation against John Acton re substraction of tithes, 1682 HA AH4/251/64/9
Citation against Thomas Sutton re substraction of tithes, 1693 HA AH4/251/68/58
Diddington Terrier LA, 16/28
Disbursements of the Great Stukeley churchwardens 1669 to 1673 HA AH4/251/75/3
Enclosure Act HA HCP/6/1907/2
Estate book of the Earl of Sandwich 1775 HA 223/5
Eynesbury Terrier dated 1607 and 1709 HA AH/30/5
Mr Farrar's Accompt, 1663 HA AH4/251/31/1
Fenstanton Churchwardens' Accounts, 1660-1668 HA HP27/5/13-19
Fenstanton Surveyors Accounts HA HP27/8/3/1
Fletton Terrier dated 1607 and 1709 HA AH/30/5
Goddard letter 1810 HP34/13/4/7
Grafham Map of the Lordship c.1750 HA Map 330
Great Gransden Churchwardens' Book, HA HP 36/5/1
Great Gransden Constables' Accounts HA HP 36/9/1
Great Gransden Overseers of the Poor Accounts HA HP 36/5/1
Great Gransden Parish Register, HA HP 36/1/1
Great Paxton Composite Register 1583-1702 HA HP64/1/1/1
Great Staughton Churchwardens Accounts HA HP82/5/1
Great Staughton Terrier of the vicarage with an account of the separate rights of the vicar & parson, HA HP 82/3/1/1
Great Stukeley Bishops' Transcripts, 1604-1673 HA AH28/85/1
Great Stukeley Manorial Court Fines 1662 HA TORK 15/258
Great Stukeley Disbursements of the churchwardens 1669 to 1673 HA AH4/251/75/3
Haddon Terrier dated 1709 HA AH30/6

Hemingford Grey 1664 Citations v. parishioners HA AH4/251/40/2-7
Hemingford Grey 1666 Citations v. parishioners HA AH4/251/45/1-3
Hemingford Grey Terrier 20th March 1668 LA TER12/81.
Hilton terrier, dated July 9th 1709 HA AH30/6
Hilton Churchwardens Accounts HA HP42/8/3/1
Libel cases for subtraction of tithes heard between 1660 and 1670:
HA AH4/251/44/3, AH4/251/45/1-3 and AH4/251/46/4
Huntingdon All Saints, composite register 1678-1783 HP46/1/1/2
Huntingdon All Saints, vestry book 1731-1776 HP46/8/1/2
Huntingdon All Saints with St John vestry minute book 1776-1818 HP46/8/1/3
Huntingdon St John, overseers' account book 1776 HP46/12/2/5
Huntingdon settlement documents 1697-1795 HP46/13/1-3
Huntingdon Plan of Hinchingbrooke House, gardens and estate 1757 HA 223/2
John Robinson v parishioners, 1666 HA AH4/251/10/2
Kimbolton composite register 1647-1748 HP52/1/1/1
Kimbolton overseers' account book 1649-1689 HP52/12/1
Kimbolton overseers' account book 1741-1753 HP52/12/4
Kimbolton overseers' account book 1753-1774 HP52/12/5
Kimbolton bond, John Eaton, 1692 HP52/18/1/5
Little Gidding Map 1596 HA 5806
Little Gidding Terrier, dated 1708 HA AH30/5
Map of the Great Park by Thomas Stirrup 1673 HA Map 83
Articles v. Bartholomew Mountford HA AH4/251/18/1-3, March 1669 - March 1670
Instructions to Bartholomew Mountford HA AH4/251/18/4, March 1670
April 1674, Deprivation of Living, Bartholomew Mountford HA AH4/251/18/6
Offord Darcy John Michael v. Edward Fuller, 1662 HA AH4/251/54/1
Parnell v. Merriton, 1674 HA AH4/251/64/3
Interrogatory questions, Parnell v. Merriton, 1674 HA AH4/251/64/4
Probate Inventories 1660-1750, HA AH 18
Quarter session minute books 1782-1802 HCP/2/1030/1-2, HCP/2/1031/1-2, HCP/2/1179/1-2
Ramsey Parish Baptism Registers 1617-1627, HA HP 67/1/1/1
Raunds overseers uncatalogued, letter HP46/12/1/1
St Ives Parish Baptism Registers 1706-1715, HA HP 72/1/1/2
St Ives settlement certificates ND HP72/13/4/1
Sequestration, debt of John Dixon 1665. HA AH4/251/54/2
Stanground Rate Book HA HP 80/11/2/1-2
Steeple Gidding enclosure maps HA Map 120, Map 121 CON 4/2/5/9.
Sentence of Thomas Sutton, 1694 HA AH4/251/64/63
Upton Map of Lordship 1659 HA CON4/2/21/1
Wills 1663-1679 HA AH 16

Bedfordshire Archives

William Cole certificate, 1760 P50/13/1/11

Oxfordshire Archives

Enclosure Papers Little Gidding E6/12/13D/4-16

Suffolk Archives
William Neave certificate, 1732 FL536/7/3/1/33

The National Archives
College of Arms, Visitation Papers, Huntingdonshire 1683/1684; TNA 179/249/2
Huntingdonshire Hearth Tax 1665 TNA E 179/122/226
Huntingdonshire Hearth Tax Lady Day 1666 TNA, E179/249/1
Huntingdonshire Hearth Tax Assessments 1674 TNA E179/249/2
Huntingdonshire Hearth Tax arrears TNA E 179/331
Huntingdonshire Hearth Tax Debts schedule Michaelmas 1664 – Michaelmas 1665 TNA E179/331/pt. 4
Huntingdonshire Hearth Tax Exemption certificate, Kings Ripton, 1664 TNA E179/331/132/21
Huntingdonshire Hearth Tax Exemption certificate, Great Gransden, 1666 TNA, E179/331/132/121
Huntingdonshire Hearth Tax Exemption certificate Orton Longville, 1664. TNA, E179/331/132/135
Huntingdonshire Hearth Tax Exemption certificate, Hemingford Grey, 1674 TNA E179/122/231/179
Huntingdonshire Hearth Tax Exemption certificates 1662-1674 TNA E179/122/231/192
Poll tax and Sheep Census, Little Gidding TNA E179/122/146 rot. 3
Pre-enclosure map of Great Staughton. TNA MR1/1570
War Office Stabling Returns 1686 TNA WO 30/48
Will of John Wells, 1664.TNA Prob/11/315/247
Will of Thomas Bateman, 1666 TNA Prob/11/322/236
Will of Mickefer Alphery, 1668 TNA Prob/11/328/ 267
Will of Joseph Hemings, 1670 TNA Prob/11/334/204
Will of John Luccock 1787 Prob/11/1151/266
Will of Neville Tomlinson 1809 Prob/11/1501/11

Published primary sources
Bland, A.E. Brown, P.A. and Tawney, R.H. *English Economic History Select Documents*, London: G. Bell & Sons, 1925.
Broad, J. *Bishop Wake's Summary of Visitation Returns for the Diocese of Lincoln 1706-1715,* London: The British Academy Records of Economic and Social History, New Series 50, 2012.
Davies, M. Ferguson, C. Harding, V. Parkinson, E. Wareham. A. eds., *London and Middlesex 1666 Hearth Tax*, London: The British Record Society, 2014.
De Beer, E.S. ed., *The Diary of John Evelyn*, Vol. IV 1673-1689, Oxford: Clarendon Press, 2000.
Evans, N. (ed.) *Cambridgeshire Hearth Tax Returns Michaelmas 1664* London: British Record Society & Cambridgeshire Record Society 2000.
Hart, G. ed., *The Cambridgeshire Committee for Scandalous Ministers, 1644-1645* Cambridge: Cambridgeshire Records Society, 2017.
Hughes, A. ed. *Sussex Clergy Inventories 1600-1750* Lewes: Sussex Record Society, 2009.

Latham R. & Matthews W. eds., *The Diary of Samuel Pepys Vols 1-10*, London: Harper Collins, various.

Lord, E. Sneath, K. & Ford, L. *The Huntingdonshire Hearth Taxes*: London & Cambridge, British Record Society and Cambridgeshire Records Society, forthcoming.

Macfarlane, A. ed., *The Diary of Ralph Josselin, 1616-1683* Oxford: OUP, 1976.

Mann, H. *Census of Great Britain, 1851: Religious Worship in England and Wales – Abridged from the Official Report* London: Routledge, 1854.

Meekings, C. ed., *The Surrey Hearth Tax 1664*, Kingston upon Thames: Surrey Record Society, 1940.

Meekings, C. ed., *Dorset Hearth Tax Assessments 1662-1664*, Dorchester: Friary Press, 1951.

Moore, J. *Mapp of the Great Levell of the Fenns, facsimile edition*, Cambridge: Cambridgeshire Records Society, 2017.

Shaw, M.A. ed., *Calendar of Treasury Books, 1667-1668*, London: HMSO, 1905.

Shaw, M.A. ed., *Calendar of Treasury Books 1660-1666*, London: HMSO, 1907.

Simpson, J.A. & Wheeler, E.S.C. eds., *Oxford English Dictionary*, Oxford: Clarendon Press, 1989.

Vaisey, D., ed. *The Diary of Thomas Turner, 1754-1765*, Oxford: OUP, 1985.

Underhill, E.B. ed., *Records of the Churches of Christ Gathered at Fenstanton, Warboys and Hexham, 1644-1720* London: Hanserd Knollys Society, 1854.

Whiteman, A. ed., *The Compton Census of 1676: a Critical Edition* Oxford: OUP, 1986.

Whitley, W.T. ed., *Minutes of the General Assembly of the General Baptist Churches in England: vol. 1, 1654-1728* London: Baptist Historical Society, 1909.

Contemporary books and articles

Burn, R. *The justice of the peace, and the parish officer*. By Richard Burn, … The eighteenth edition, corrected and considerably enlarged. … To which is added an appendix, … In four volumes. Volume 3 of 4 London: 1797, ECCE reprint, ND.

Carter, M. ed. *Edmund Pettis' Survey of St Ives, 1728* Cambridge: Cambridgeshire Records Society, 2002.

Carruthers, R. *History of Huntingdon*, Huntingdon: A.P Wood, 1824.

Defoe, D. *Tour through the Whole Island of England and Wales*, London: Everyman Edition, n.d.

Fiennes, C. *The Journeys of Celia Fiennes* London: Futura, 1983.

Goldie, M. ed. J. Locke, *Two Treatises of Government* London: Everyman, 1993.

Harrison, W. *Description of England* Washington: Folger Shakespeare Library, 1968.

Jefferys, T. *The County of Huntingdon Surveyed* London: T. Jefferys, 1768.

Ogilby, J. *An Actual Survey of all the Principal Roads of England and Wales. …,* London: M Senex, 1675.

Parry, E.A. ed., *Letters from Dorothy Osborne to Sir William Temple 1652-1664*, revised ed., London: Sherratt and Hughes, 1903

Rimbault, E. ed., *The miscellaneous works in prose and verse of Sir Thomas Overbury* London: J. R. Smith, 1856.

Stone, T. *General View of the Agriculture of the County of Huntingdon* London: J. Nichols, 1793.

SECONDARY SOURCES

Arkell, T. ed. with Alcock, N. *Warwickshire Hearth Tax Returns: Michaelmas 1670 with Coventry Lady Day 1666* Stratford on Avon and London: Dugdale Society and British Record Society, 2010.

Allen, R.C. *Enclosure and the Yeoman* Oxford: Clarendon Press, 1992.

Blackwood, B. G. *The Lancashire gentry and the Great Rebellion* Manchester: Manchester University Press, 1978.

Boyes, J. Russell, John and R. *The Canals of Eastern England*, Newton Abbot: David & Charles, 1977.

Braddick, M. *Parliamentary Taxation in the Seventeenth Century*, London: Royal Historical Society, 1994.

Bradley, J.E. *Religion, revolution and English radicalism* Cambridge: CUP 1990.

Brayshay, M. *Land Travel and Communication in Tudor and Stuart England*, Liverpool: Liverpool University Press, 2014.

Broadberry, S. Campbell, B. Klein, A. Overton, M. and van Leeuwen, B. *British Economic Growth, 1270-1870* Cambridge: CUP, 2015.

Burn-Murdoch, B. *St Ives Bridge and Chapel: A History and Guide,* St Ives: Friends of the Norris Museum, 2nd ed, 2001.

Chandaman, C.D. *The English Public Revenue 1660-1688*, Oxford: Clarendon Press, 1975.

Charlesworth, L. *Welfare's Forgotten Past: A Socio-Legal History of the Poor Law*, Abingdon: Routledge, 2010.

Coleman, S. & Wood, J. *Historic Landscape and Archaeology Glossary of Terms* Bedford: Bedfordshire County Council, 1988 rev.ed.

Collinson, P. '*De Republica Anglorum*' in P. Collinson, *Elizabethan Essays*, Basingstoke: The Hambledon Press, 1994.

Coss, P. *The origins of the English gentry* Cambridge: CUP, 2003.

Crawford, P. *Parents of Poor Children in England*, 1580-1800, Oxford: OUP, 2010.

Doran, S. & Doran, C. *Princes, Pastors and People, the Church and Religion in England 1529-1689* London: Routledge, 1991.

Dyos, H.J. and Aldcroft, D.H. *British Transport: an economic survey from the seventeenth century to the twentieth,* Leicester: Leicester University Press, 1969.

Ellis, P. and Shepherd, D. *A Millennium History of Great Gidding* Great Gidding: Great Gidding and Little Gidding Parish Council, 2001.

Everitt, A. *The Pattern of Rural Dissent: the Nineteenth Century* London: Leicester University Press, 1972.

Everitt, A. *Landscape and Community*, London: Hambledon Press, 1985.

Fideler, P.A. *Social Welfare in Pre-Industrial England*, Basingstoke: Palgrave, 2006.

Fox, A. *A Lost Frontier Revealed*, Hatfield: University of Hertfordshire Press, 2009.

French, H. and Barry J. eds. *Identity and agency in England, 1500-1800* Basingstoke: Palgrave, 2004.

French, H. *The Middle Sort of People in Provincial England 1600-1750* Oxford: OUP, 2007.

Glennie, P. *Distinguishing men's trades: occupational sources and debates for pre-census England* Bristol: Historical Geography Research Group, Series 25: 1990.

Gray, H.L. *The English Field Systems*, London: Merlin Press, 1959.

Halliwell, J.O. *Dictionary of Archaic Words,* London: Bracken Books 1850, facsimile ed., 1989.

Hampson, E.M. *The Treatment of Poverty in Cambridgeshire 1597-1834*, Cambridge: CUP, 1934, revised 2009.

Hart, M.C. *The Making of a Bourgeois State,* Manchester: Manchester University Press, 1993.

Heal, F. and Holmes, C. *The gentry in England and Wales, 1500-1700* Basingstoke: Palgrave, 1994.

Hey, D. *An English rural community. Myddle under the Tudors and Stuarts,* Leicester: Leicester University Press, 1974.

Hunt, M. R. *The middling sort: commerce, gender and the family in England 1680-1780* Los Angeles: University of California Press, 1996.

Hyde, H. A. *The Warboys Baptists* Warboys: Pastor A. Stone, 1963.

Jacob, W. *The Clerical Profession in the Long Eighteenth Century 1680-1840,* Oxford: OUP, 2007.

Jenkins, H.J.K. *Along the Nene,* Wheaton: Cambridgeshire Books, 1991.

Kerridge, E. *The Agricultural Revolution* London: Allen and Unwin, 1967.

King, S. *Poverty and Sickness in Modern Europe: Narratives of the Sick Poor, 1780-1938*, London: Continuum International, 2012.

Kussmaul, A. *A general view of the rural economy*, Cambridge: CUP, 1993.

Kussmaul, A. *Servants in Husbandry in Early Modern England*, Cambridge: CUP, 1981.

Author unknown (?Lambarde, W.) *The Complete Parish Officer*, Devizes: Wiltshire Family History Society, facsimile edition 1999.

Macfarlane, A. *The Origins of English Individualism*, Oxford: Basil Blackwell, 1978.

Marshall, D. *The English Poor in the Eighteenth Century: A Study in Social and Administrative History*, Abingdon: Routledge, reprint, 2007.

Matthew, H.C. & Harrison, B. *Oxford Dictionary of National Biography,* Oxford: OUP, 2004.

Matthews, A.G. *Calamy Revised: being a Revision of Edmund Calamy's Account of the Ministers and Others Ejected and Silenced, 1660-1662* Oxford: OUP, 1934.

McCall, F. *Baal's Priests, The Loyalist Clergy and the English Revolution* Farnham: Ashgate, 2013.

Muldrew, C. *The Economy of Obligation: The Culture of `Credit and Social relations in early Modern England* Basingstoke: Palgrave, 1998.

Muldrew, C. *Food, Energy and the Creation of Industriousness* Cambridge: CUP, 2011.

Nolan, M. *A Treatise on the Laws for the Relief and Settlement of the Poor*, Vol. 2, London, 1814, 3rd edition.

Outram, T.W. *Coaching Days and Coaching Ways,* London: Macmillan, 1931.

Overton, M. *Agricultural revolution in England* Cambridge: CUP, 1996.

Overton, M. Whittle, J. Dean D. and Hann, A. *Production and consumption in English households 1600-1750* Abingdon: Routledge, 2004.

Page, W. Proby, G. & Inskipp Ladds S. eds., *The Victoria History of the Counties of England, Huntingdonshire,* London: Institute of Historical Research, Dawson Reprint, 1974, Vol. 2.

Palmer, W.M. *William Cole of Milton,* Cambridge: Galloway & Porter, 1935.

Parkinson, E. *The Establishment of the Hearth Tax 1662-1666*, London: List and Index Society, Special Series, Vol.43, 2008.

Pooley C. & J. Turnbull, *Migration and mobility in Britain since the 18th century*, London: Routledge, 1998.

Potts, R. *A Calendar of Cornish Glebe Terriers 1673-1735* Torquay: Devon & Cornwall Record Society, 1974.

Pruett, J.H. *Parish Clergy Under the Later Stuarts: The Leicestershire Experience* Chicago: University of Illinois, 1978.

Richardson, C. *Household Servants in Early Modern England,* Manchester: Manchester University Press, 2010.

Shaw, W.A. *A History of the English Church During the Civil Wars and Under the Commonwealth* London: Longmans, 1900.

Sadler, S. L. *A Royal Entertainment? Huntingdon, August 1645* Huntingdon: Cromwell Museum, 1995.

Schurer, K. and Arkell, T. eds., *Surveying the People*, Oxford: The Leopard's Head Press, Local Population Studies Supplement, 1992.

Slack, P. *The English Poor Law, 1531-1782* Basingstoke: Macmillan, 1990.

Smith, A. *An Inquiry into the Nature and Causes of The Wealth of Nations*, Hampshire: Harriman House, reprint, 2007.

Sneath, K. and P. *Godmanchester: A Celebration of 800 Years* Cambridge: EAH Press, 2011.

Snell, K.D.M. *Annals of the Labouring Poor: l Change and Agrarian England, 1660-1900*, Cambridge: CUP, 1985.

Snell, K.D.M. *Parish and Belonging: Community, Identity and Welfare in England and Wales, 1700-1950* Cambridge: CUP, 2006

Spaeth, D. A. *The Church in an Age of Danger: Parsons and Parishioners, 1660-1740* Cambridge: CUP, 2000.

Spufford, M. ed., *The World of Rural Dissenters, 1520-1725* Cambridge: CUP, 1995.

Spufford, M. *Contrasting Communities: English Villagers in the Sixteenth and Seventeenth Centuries* (second edition) Stroud: Sutton, 2000.

Spurr, J. *The Post-Reformation: Religion, Politics and Society in Britain, 1603-1714* Harlow: Pearson, 2006.

Spurr, J. *The Restoration Church of England, 1646-1689* New Haven: Yale University Press 1991.

Stell, C. *An Inventory of Nonconformist Chapels and Meeting-Houses in Eastern England* Swindon: English Heritage, 2002.

Summers, D. *The Great Ouse: The History of a River Navigation*, Newton Abbot: David & Charles, 1973.

Sweet. H, *The Student's Dictionary of Anglo-Saxon*, Oxford: Clarendon Press, 1991.

Taylor, J.S. *Poverty, Migration, and Settlement in the Industrial Revolution, Sojourners' Narratives,* Palo Alto, California: Society for the Promotion of Science and Scholarship, 1989.

Tebbutt, C.F, *St Neots,* Chichester: Phillimore, 1978.

Thirsk, J. *Tudor Enclosures* London: The Historical Association, 1967.

Thirsk, J. *Food in Early Modern England,* London: Hambledon Continuum, 2006

Thompson, D. M. ed., *Religious Life in Mid Nineteenth-Century Cambridgeshire and Huntingdonshire: the Returns for the 1851 Census of Religious Worship* Cambridge: Cambridgeshire Records Society, 2014.

Turner, M. Beckett, J. and Afton, B. *Farm Production in England, 1700-1914* Oxford: OUP, 2001.

Waddell, B. *God, Duty and Community in English Economic Life 1660-1720* Woodbridge: Boydell, 2012.

Wade Martins, S. *Farmers, Landlords and Landscapes* Macclesfield: Windgather Press, 2004.

Webb, S. & B. *English Local Government: English Poor Law History: Part I. The Old Poor Law*, reprint by Read Books Ltd., 2011.

Whyte, I. D. *Migration and Society in Britain 1550-1830*, Basingstoke: Macmillan, 2000.

Wickes, M. *A History of Huntingdonshire* Chichester: Phillimore, 1985.

Willan, T.S. *The Navigation of the Great Ouse between St Ives and Bedford in the Seventeenth Century.* Bedford: Bedfordshire Historical Records Society, 1946.

Williams, S. *Poverty, gender and life-cycle under the English poor law, 1760-1834*, Woodbridge: Boydell, 2011.

Williamson, T. *The Transformation of Rural England: farming and the landscape 1700-1870* Exeter: University of Exeter Press, 2002.

Wood, A. *The Politics of Social Conflict. The Peak Country 1520-1700*, Cambridge: CUP 1999.

Wrightson, K. *English society, 1580-1680* London: Routledge, 2003.

Wrightson, K. *Earthly necessities* New Haven: Yale, 2000.

Wrightson, K. and Levine, D. *Poverty and Piety in an English Village: Terling, 1525-1700* (second edition) Oxford: OUP, 1995.

Wrigley, E. *Energy and the English Industrial Revolution,* Cambridge: CUP, 2010.

Wrigley, E. Davies, R. Oeppen J. and Schofield, R. *English Population History from Family Reconstitution 1580-1837* Cambridge: CUP, 1997.

Yates, N. *Eighteenth-century Britain: religion and politics* Harlow: Pearson, 2008.

Yelling. J.A. *Common Field and Enclosure in England 1450-1850* Hamden: Archon Books, 1977.

Young, R. *St Neots Past* Chichester: Phillimore, 1996.

Book chapters and articles

Arkell, T. 'A Student's Guide to the Hearth Tax: some truths, half-truths and untruths', in N. Alldridge, ed. *The Hearth Tax: Problems and Possibilities* Hull: Humberside College of Education 1983 23-44.

Arkell, T. 'The incidence of poverty in England in the later seventeenth-century', *Social History* 12, 1987 23-47.

Arkell, T and Evans, N. 'Wills as a Historical Source' in T. Arkell, N. Evans, and N. Goose, eds. *When Death Do Us Part: Understanding and Interpreting the Probate Records of Early Modern England* Oxford: Leopards Head Press, 2000 38-71.

Arkell, T. 'Identifying Regional Variations from the Hearth Tax', *The Local Historian,* Vol. 33, no. 3 August 2003, 148-174.

Barnwell, P.S. 'Houses, hearths and historical enquiry', in P.S. Barnwell, and M. Airs, eds. *Houses and the Hearth Tax: the later Stuart house and society* York: CBA Research Report 150, 2006 177-183.

Bedells, J. 'The gentry of Huntingdonshire', in *Local Population Studies,* 44 1990, 30-39.

Burnette, J. 'Agriculture 1700-1870' in R. Floud, J. Humphries and P. Johnson eds. *The Cambridge Economic History of Modern Britain Volume 1* Cambridge: CUP, 2014, 89-117.

Carter, M. 'Town or Urban Society? St Ives in Huntingdonshire 1630-1740 in C. Phythian-Adams ed. *Societies, Cultures and Kinship, 1580-1850* Leicester: Leicester University Press, 1993, 77-130.

Clark, M. 'The gentry, the commons and the politics of common right c 1558-1603' *The Historical Journal,* Vol. 54:3, Sept. 2011, 609-630.

Crockett, A. and Snell, K. D. M. 'From the 1676 Compton Census to the 1851 Census of Religious Worship: Religious Continuity or Discontinuity?', *Rural History,* Vol. 8, no. 1 (April 1997), 55-89.

Darby, H.C. 'The draining of the English clay-lands'. *Geographische Zeitschrift* 52, Jahrg., 3. H. 1964, 190-201.

Dixon, R. W. 'Religious Life and Work', in A. Goodman ed. *Potto Brown: the Village Philanthropist* St. Ives: Albert Goodman, 1878, 109-199.

Dymond, D. 'The Parson's Glebe: Stable, Expanding or Shrinking?' in C. Harper-Bill, C. Rawcliffe, R. Wilson eds. *East Anglia's History,* Woodbridge: Boydell, 2002 73-92.

Everitt, A. 'Nonconformity in Country Parishes', *Agr. Hist. Rev.,* vol. 18, supplement 1970, 178-199.

Everitt, A. 'Farm labourers 1500-1640', in C. Clay ed. *Rural Society: landowners, peasants and labourers 1500-1750* Cambridge: CUP, 1990, 161-245.

Ferguson, C.M. 'The hearth tax and the poor in post-Restoration Woking' in E. Vallance, T. Dean, & G. Parry, G. eds. *Faith, Place and People in Early Modern England* Woodbridge: Boydell, 2018, 111-132.

Franklin, W. 'Drainage and the town plough', *Agr. Hist. Rev.,* Vol. 63, Part II, 2015, 311-320.

Franklin, W. 'The Ferrars and the Enclosure of Little Gidding, *PCAS,* Vol. CVI, 2017, 89-98.

French, H. 'Social status, localism and the middle sort of people in England, 1620-1750' *Past and Present,* 166 2000, 66-99.

Hall, D.N. 'Drainage of Arable Land in Medieval England' in H. Cook and T. Williamson eds. *Water Management in the English Landscape,* Edinburgh: Edinburgh University Press, 1999, 28-40.

Hampson, E.M. 'Settlement and removal in Cambridgeshire, 1662-1834', *Historical Journal,* 2, 1926-28, 273-289.

Hindle, S. 'Persuasion and Protest in the Caddington Common Enclosure Dispute 1635-1639' *P& P* 185, Feb. 1998, 37-78.

Hindle, S. 'The Sad Fortunes of the Reverend John Perkins', in E. Vallance, T. Dean, & G. Parry, G. eds. *Faith, Place and People in Early Modern England* Woodbridge: Boydell, 2018, 70-92.

Humphries, J. 'Enclosures, common rights and women: the proletarianisation of families in the late eighteenth and early nineteenth centuries', *J. Econ. Hist.*, 50, 1990, 17-42.

Husbands, C. 'Hearth tax exemption figures and assessment of poverty in the seventeenth-century economy', in N. Alldridge ed. *The Hearth Tax: Problems and Possibilities* Hull: Humberside Polytechnic, 1974.

Husbands, C. 'Hearths, wealth and occupations: an exploration of the Hearth tax in the later seventeenth century', in K. Schurer and T. Arkell, eds. *Surveying the People: the interpretation and use of document sources for the study of population in the later seventeenth century* Local Population Studies Supplement Oxford: Leopards Head Press, 1992 65-77.

Keibek, S. and Shaw-Taylor, L. 'Early modern rural by-employments: a re-examination of the probate inventory evidence', *Agr. Hist. Rev.*, 61, 2013, 244-281.

Kent, D. 'Gone for a soldier': Family breakdown and the demography of desertion in a London parish, 1750-91', *Local Population Studies*, 45, 1990, 27-42.

Landau, N. 'The laws of settlement and the surveillance of immigration in eighteenth-century Kent', *Continuity and Change*, 1988, 391-420.

Landau, N. 'The regulation of immigration, economic structures and definitions of the poor in eighteenth-century England', *The Historical Journal* 33:3, 1990, 541-571.

Landau, N. 'The eighteenth-century context of the laws of settlement', *Continuity and Change*, 6:3, 1991, 417-439.

Levene, A., 'Poor Families, removals and 'nurture' in late Old Poor Law London', *Continuity and Change*, 25:2, 2010, 233-262.

Lindert, P.H. and Williamson, J.G. 'Revising England's social tables 1688-1913' *Explorations in Economic History*, 19, 1982, 385-408.

Long, M. 'A study of occupations in Yorkshire parish registers in the eighteenth and early nineteenth centuries', *Local Population Studies*, Vol.71, 2003, 14-39.

Lord, E. 'Samuel Pepys and Huntingdonshire', *Huntingdonshire Hearth Tax*, London: British Record Society and Cambridgeshire Records Society, forthcoming.

Marshall, L. 'Levying the Hearth Tax, 1662-1668', *EHR*, Oct. 1936, 628-648.

Mitson, A. 'The Significance of Kinship Networks in the Seventeenth Century: South West Nottinghamshire' in C.V. Phythian-Adams ed. *Societies, Culture and kingship 1580-1850,* Leicester: Leicester University Press, 1993, 24-76.

Noble, W.M. 'Incumbents of the County of Huntingdon', in *Transactions of the Cambridgeshire and Huntingdonshire Archaeological Society*, vol. 2 part 3, York, 1909 271-286.

Overton, M. 'Prices from inventories' in T. Arkell, N. Evans and N. Goose eds. *When Death Us Do Part* Oxford: Leopard's Head Press, 2000, 120-141.

Porter, S. 'The Livestock Trade in Huntingdonshire, 1600-1750' in *Records of Huntingdonshire* 1982, Vol.2, 13-17.

Porter, S. 'Farm Transport in Huntingdonshire, 1610–1749', *Journal of Transport History,* 3 Ser, Vol. III, 1 1982, 35-45.

Ryan, P. with Stenning D. and Andrews D. 'The Houses of Essex in the Late

Seventeenth Century' in C. Ferguson, C. Thornton & A. Wareham, *Essex Hearth Tax Returns, Michaelmas 1670* London: British Record Society, Essex Society for Archaeology and History, 2012 69-106.

Shaw Taylor, L. 'The Rise of Agrarian Capitalism' *Ec.HR*, 65(1) 2012, 26-60.

Shaw-Taylor, L. and Wrigley, E.A. 'Occupational Structure and Population Change', in R. Floud, J. Humphries and P. Johnson eds. *The Cambridge Economic History of Modern Britain* Cambridge: CUP, 2014, 53-88.

Snell, K.D.M. 'Pauper settlement and the right to poor relief in England and Wales', *Continuity and Change* vol.6, 1991, 375-415.

Song, B. K. 'Agrarian policies on pauper settlement and migration, Oxfordshire 1750-1834', *Continuity and Change*, vol.13, issue 3, December 1998,363-389.

Spaeth, D. "Orderly made': re-appraising household inventories in seventeenth-century England', *Social History*, 2016, 41(4), 417-435

Spufford, M. 'The Significance of the Cambridgeshire Hearth Tax', *Proceedings of the Cambridgeshire Antiquarian Society,* 55, 1962 53-64.

Spufford, M. 'The limitations of the probate inventory' in J. Chartres & D. Hey eds. *English Rural Society 1500-1800: Essays in honour of Joan Thirsk* Cambridge: CUP, 1990, 139-74.

Styles, P. 'The Evolution of the Law of Settlement', reprinted in *Studies in Seventeenth Century West Midlands History*, Kinetin: The Roundwood Press, 1978, 175-204.

Taylor, J.S. 'Voices in the Crowd: The Kirkby Lonsdale Township Letters, 1809-36', in T. Hitchcock, P. King, & P. Sharpe (eds.), *Chronicling Poverty: The Voices and Strategies of the English Poor 1640-1840*, Basingstoke: Macmillan, 1997, 109-126.

Thirsk, J. 'The Fantastical Folly of Fashion: the English stocking knitting industry, 1500-1700'. in J. Thirsk, ed. *The Rural Economy of England: Collected Essays* London: Hambledon, 2003, 235-258.

Tomkins, A. "Labouring on a bed of sickness': The material and rhetorical deployment of ill-health in male pauper letters', in A. Gestrich, E. Hurren, and S. King, *Poverty and Sickness in Modern Europe: Narratives of the Sick Poor, 1780-1938,* Continuum International: London, 2012 51-68.

Wareham, A. 'The hearth tax and empty properties in London on the eve of the Great Fire', *The Local Historian*, Vol.41, No. 4, November 2014, 278-292.

Wells, R. 'Migration, the law, and parochial policy in eighteenth- and nineteenth-century southern England', *Southern History*, 15, 1993, 87–139.

Wigfield, W. ed., 'Recusancy and Nonconformity in Bedfordshire, illustrated by Select Documents between 1662 and 1842', *Bedfordshire Historical Record Society,* vol. 20 1938, 145-229.

Winter, A. 'Migration, Poor Relief and Local Autonomy: Settlement Policies in England and the Low Countries in the Eighteenth-Century', *Past and Present,* 2013, 218:1, 91-126.

Woledge, H. and Smale, M.A., 'Migration in East Yorkshire in the Eighteenth Century', *Local Population Studies,* 70, 2003, 29-48.

Wood, A. 'Plebian, Languages and Defiance in England c 1520-1640' in T. Harris ed. *The Politics of the Excluded*, London: Palgrave, 2001, 67-98.

Wordie, J. R. The Chronology of English Enclosure 1500-1914 *Ec.HR* 2nd Series Vol. XXXVI No. 4 1983, 483-505.

Wrigley, E. 'English County Populations in the later eighteenth century', *Ec.HR* Vol.60, 1, Feb 2007, 35-69.

Unpublished papers, theses and dissertations

Brodsky Elliott, V. *Mobility and marriage in pre-industrial England* unpublished Ph.D. thesis, University of Cambridge, 1979.

Carter, M. *'An urban society and its hinterland: St Ives in the seventeenth and early eighteenth centuries',* unpublished Ph.D. thesis, University of Leicester 1988.

Porter, S. *An Agricultural Geography of Huntingdonshire, 1610-1749*, M. Litt. Cantab. 1973.

Shaw-Taylor, L. *The Nature and Scale of the Cottage Economy*, unpublished paper, University of Cambridge.

Shaw-Taylor, L. *The occupational structure of England and Wales, 1600-1911* Economic History Society Conference, University of London, 2017.

Sneath, K. *Consumption, Wealth, Indebtedness and Social Structure in Early Modern England* unpublished Ph.D. thesis, University of Cambridge, 2008.

Sugden, K. *The Occupational and Organizational Structures of the Northamptonshire Worsted and Shoemaking Trades, circa 1750-1821* MSt in Local and Regional History, Cambridge 2011.

Vialls, C. *The Laws of Settlement: their impact on the poor inhabitants of the Daventry area of Northamptonshire, 1750-1834*, unpublished Ph.D. thesis, University of Leicester, 1998.

Internet sources

Bell Inn, Stilton, www.thebellstilton.co.uk/bell-inn-history

British History online, History of Somersham parish, pp. 223-230, *Hist. MSS. Com. Rep.* xiii (v), 467. https://www.british-history.ac.uk/vch/hunts/vol2/pp223-230

Cambridge University Alumni; http://venn.lib.cam.ac.uk/Documents/acad/2018/search-2018.html

The clergy database; http://theclergydatabase.org.uk

Geological Survey of Great Britain, (Sixth Edition), Ordnance Survey https://www.bgs.ac.uk/data/maps/home.html

Journal of the House of Commons Vol.21, pp. 126, 133, 135. *British History Online.* http://www.british-history.ac.uk/catalogue

Journal of the House of Lords, Vol.23, pp. 220-231. 27 March 1727. *British History Online.* http://www.british-history.ac.uk/lords-jnrl/vol23/pp220-231

London Lives 1690-1800 Crime poverty and social policy https://www.londonlives.org/

National Bell Registry, www.georgedawson.homestead.com/nbr/html

Pepys, Samuel, *Diary,* www.pepysdiary.com

Statutes of the Realm https://www.british-history.ac.uk/statutes-realm/vol5

Taylor, J. *The Carriers Cosmographie,* London, 1632. http://ota.ox.ac.uk/tcp/headers/A13/A13431.html

The Workhouse http://www.workhouses.org.uk

INDEX